Fayette County Alabama

Index

to

Wills *and* Estates

- 1850-1970 -

Compiled by:
Herbert M. & Jeanie P. Newell

Southern Historical Press, Inc.
Greenville, South Carolina

This volume was reproduced
from a personal copy located in
the Publishers private library

Please direct all correspondence and book orders to:
SOUTHERN HISTORICAL PRESS, Inc.
PO Box 1267
Greenville, SC   29602-1267

Originally printed: Fayette, AL   1970
Reprinted By: Southern Historical Press, Inc.
ISBN #978-1-63914-058-9
Printed in the United Sattes of America

INDEX TO PROBATE COURT MINUTES
RECORDS and WILLS

FAYETTE COUNTY, ALABAMA
1851 - 1974 -

PCM = PROBATE COURT MINUTES
PCR = PROBATE COURT RECORDS
WR = WILL RECORDS

PCM 1	= Probate Court Minutes =	Vol. 1 New Series	1= 23 Sept. 1851 to 12 Sept. 1855
PCM 2	= " " "	= Vol. New Series 3	- 4 June 1859 to 13 Dec. 1861
PCM 3	= " " "	= Vol. New Series 2	- 14 July 1866 to 10 Mar. 1873
PCM 4	= " " "	= Vol. 1	- 1 Oct. 1866 to 2 Sept. 1875
PCM 5	= " " "	= Vol. 2	- 6 Feb. 1872 to 20 Oct. 1877
PCM 6	= " " "	= Vol. 3	- 14 Nov. 1877 to 22 Dec. 1883
PCM 7	= " " "	= Vol. 4	- 5 Jan. 1884 to 2 July 1889
PCM 8	= " " "	= Vol. 5	- 6 July 1889 to 31 Jan. 1903
PCM 9	= " " "	= Vol. 6	- 15 Aug. 1894 to 9 July 1906
PCM 10	= " " "	= Vol. 7	- 22 Mar. 1905 to 23 Dec. 1913
PCM 11	= " " "	= Vol. 8	- 6 Jan. 1914 to 12 Aug. 1921
PCM 12	= " " "	= Vol. 9	- 15 Aug. 1921 to 16 Mar.1931
PCM 13	= " " "	= Vol. 10	- 28 Mar. 1931 to 20 Feb. 1941

PCR 1	= Probate Court Record =	Vol. 1A	- 30 Jan. 1857 to 24 Nov. 1858
PCR 2	= " " "	= Vol. 11	- 30 Oct. 1861 to 4 Jan. 1863
PCR 3	= " " "	= Vol. 12	- 5 Aug. 1863 to 15 Nov. 1867
PCR 4	= " " "	= Vol. 2	- 13 Aug. 1875 to 23 Dec. 1875
PCR 5	= " " "	= Vol. 3 New Series 4	- 3 Sept. 1879 to 30 Aug. 1887
PCR 6	= " " "	= Vol. 4	- 17 Aug. 1883 to 2 Sept. 1887
PCR 7	= " " "	= Vol. 5	- 9 Dec. 1886 to 2 April 1892
PCR 8	= " " "	= Vol. 6B	- 24 Dec. 1890 to 6 Jan. 1909
PCR 9	= " " "	= Vol. 7	- 12Dec. 1907 to 8 Sept. 1916
PCR 10	= " " "	= Vol. 8	- 1 June 1915 to 22 May 1920
PCR 11	= " " "	= Vol. 9	- 26 July 1920 to 1 May 1926
PCR 12	= " " "	= Vol. 10	- 30 Mar. 1926 to 29 Dec. 1931
PCR 13	= " " "	= Vol. 11	- 15 Mar. 1930 to 10 Aug. 1937
PCR 14	= " " "	= Vol. 13	- 29 Oct. 1943 to 17 May 1948
PCR 15	= " " "	= Vol. 14	- 28 Oct. 1942 to 8 Oct. 1951
PCR 16	= " " "	= Vol. 15	- 26 April 1951 to 20 Oct. 1954
PCR 17	= " " "	= Vol. 16	- 17 Sept. 1954 to 17 Dec. 1957
PCR 18	= " " "	= Vol. 17	- 3 Dec. 1959 to 7 Jan. 1960
PCR 19	= " " "	= Vol. 18	- 3 Oct. 1959 to 16 Nov. 1960
PCR 20	= " " "	= Vol. 19	- 21 Oct. 1960 to 8 Jan. 1962
PCR 21	= " " "	= Vol. 20	- 5 July 1961 to 3 Mar. 1964
PCR 22	= " " "	= Vol. 21	- 21 June 1963 to 23 April 1965
PCR 23	= " " "	= Vol. 22	- 4 Aug. 1965 to 4 Oct. 1965
PCR 24	= " " "	= Vol. 23	- 19 July 1955 to 26 Oct. 1967
PCR 25	= " " "	= Vol. 24	- 6 Jan. 1965 to 28 April 1969
PCR 26	= " " "	= Vol. 25	- 28 Mar. 1969 to 8 Mar. 1971
PCR 27	= " " "	= Vol. 26	- 18 Feb. 1971 to 11 Feb. 1972
PCR 28	= " " "	= Vol. 27	- 28 April 1969 to 15 May 1973
PCR 29	= " " "	= Vol. 28	- 17 May, 1975 to 18 June 1974
PCR 30	= " " "	= Vol. 29	- 7 May 1974 to

WR 1	= Will Records =	Vol. 1-A	= 1869 to 1873
WR 2	= " "	= Vol. 1	= 1888 to 1934
WR 3	= " "	= Vol. 2	= 1934 to 1958
WR 4	= " "	= Vol. 3	= 1962 to 1975

R11a   Abbott, Mary - 11 to 16, 137, 144

R25   Abernathy, Clayton Miles, Dec'd, - 25, 37-40

R15   Abernathy, Curtis Joseph, Jr. - decd. - 582, 89

R27   Abernathy, D. H. - 27, 140-146

M(3)   Abernathy, Jane M., Estate of - 439 to 448

R11a   Abernathy, Jane M. - 145-146

R1A   Abernathy, Jane M., Estate - 247 to 250

R27   Abernathy, Leatha - 27, 133-139

R21   Aldridge, Delmas - Inc. - 21, 135-147

R22   Adams, Charles Ray, Dec'd. - 22, 597 - 600

R23   Adams, James Edward, Dec'd. - 23, 729-732

R23   Adams, Marion A. - Dec'd. - 23, 652-655

M9   Adams, W. R. - dec'd Estate - 210, 211

W1   Adams, W. (or M.) R. - Will Proof - 241 - 242

R9   Adams, W. R. - decd. Estate - 43, 433-434

M9   Adoption of 2 children by Bayer & Bessie Wilson - 407

M1(2)   Adkins, Morton, - Estate - 108, 109

R8   Adkins, Sam - decd. Estate - W. A. Aldridge, guardian - 278

W1   Agnew, H. W. - Will - Pg. 71-72

M1(1)   Agnew, James - Estate of - 428

R6B   Agnew, A. W. - Decd. - 316 to 320

M10   Akin, Dora - decd. Estate - 293

R11   Akin, Dora - 532 - Decd. Estate

M9   Alabama Power Co. - 447

R10   Alabama Power Co. - 301 to 337

R14   Alabama Power Co. vs. Charles Worth Cannon, Jr. - et al - 592, 597

R27   Alabama Power Co. vs. Howard Pendley - etal - 27, 803-815

R27   Alabama Power Co. vs. Ruby Cannon - et al - 274,320,342,361,364,397,421

R28   Alabama Power Co. vs. Tezzie Lou Daerowich - 28, 461, 494

M9   Alabama Power Co. vs. W. M. Cannon - etal - 227

R9   Alabama Power Co. vs. W. M. Cannon, etal - 467, 470

M9   Alabama Power Co. vs. Esther Rutherford - etal - 195, 196, 197

R9   Alabama Power Co. vs. _____ Rutherford - etal application - 404,409,412

M8   Alexander, A. H. - declaration adopting Charles Jones & changing name to
                Chester Alexander - 464

M10   Alexander, Mrs. Amanda - decd. Estate - 164, 315

R11   Alexander, Amanda - decd. Estate - 364,365,366, 563, 564

M6   Alexander, Bertice, - Minor - G. S. Alexander, guardian - 573

R6B   Alexander, Bertrice - Minor - G. S. Alexander - guardian - 480, 481

R21   Alexander, Luther Jesse, Inc. - 21, 250,262

M1(1) Aldridge, Isham, Estate of 8,13,56,203,221,222

W2   Aldridge, J. F. - deceased, Will & Proof - 412, 413

R19   Aldridge, J. P. - Unsound Mind - 19-36,49

R20   Aldridge, J. F. - Decd. __ - 20 - 576,582

M9   Aldridge, Lou Ellen & Others joint owners - 73

R9   Aldridge, Lou, Ellen & Others - Joint owners - 212

M8   Aldridge, W. A. - guardian - 270

W2   Allen, Alice - Will & Proof - 580

R24   Allen, Alice - Decd. - 24 - 909, 915

W1A   Allen, N. F. - 568,569,570,571,572,587,588,589, 590, 591

R12A   Allen, N. F. - decd. Estate - 119, 120

M1(2) Allen, W. F. - 536, 537,550,552,568

M1(1) Alloy, Nicholas - Estate of - 444

R8   Allred, J. M. - etal - joint owner - 368

M9   Allred, J. M. - Estate - 501

M9   Allred, James M. - decd. Estate - 403, 411

R10   Allred, James M. - decd. Estat - 254,255,285,286,287 481

M10   Allred, Mrs. Rachel - decd. Estate - 391, 392

W2   Allred, Mrs. Rachel - 22, 23

M8   Allred, M.J. M. - etal. joint owner - 324,336,346

M8   Amerson, E. W. - declaration adopting Frances Jones - Amerson - 466

M1(2)   Amerson, Hugh, - Justice Bond - 119

W2   Anders, Ortice Clyde - Will & Proof - 530, 532

R24   Anders, Ortice Clyde - Decd. - 24 - 324, 330

M9   Anderson, David M. - etal - from Doughty, T. W. - 45

M9   Anderson, J. C. - guardian - 266

R10   Anderson, J. C. - guardian - 5, 6

R16   Andrew, George - decd. - 366-67, 484, 484

R17   Andrews, George - decd. - 461-62

R13   Andrews, J. B. - Estate - 360 through 364

M-1   Angel, Richard - Compounding fellony - 341

R23   Anthony, Robert - Decd. - 23 - 741 - 744

M6   Appling, Francis B. - Decd. Estate - 299

R6B   Appling, Frances B. - 381, 382

R1A   Appling, Lervicy, Estate - 221 to 223 - 394 to 400

M(3)   Appling, Rebecca - Estate of - 119 to 120, 121

R11A   Appling, Samuel - 147, 150

M1   April Term, - 1882 - 176

M1   April Term, - 1883 - 209

M1(2)   Archer, Mary L., - Decd. Estate - 71,97,98,162,435, 448, 449

W1A   Archer, Many L. - 350, 357

R12A   Archer, Mary L. - decd. Estate - 374 to 376

R22   Armstrong, Robert Lee - Henry Lee, Minor - 22 - 350 - 368

M6   Arnold, J. D. - guardian for Ola A. & Mattie J. Erwin - 459,460,461,462

R6B   Arnold, J. D. - guardian of Ola & Martha Ervin - Minors - 366 to 374

R16   Ary, Charles D. - deceased - 15 - 19

W2   Ashcraft, James Harvey - 192

R15   Ashcraft, James Harvey - decd. - 551,556,556A

M1(1)   Ashcraft, & Shepherd vs. Richard Gray - Will Adquadalunnum to raise William
                  P-104

M2   Ashcraft, Thomas & others - lein note to F. W. Stoke - 243

M1(1)   Atkins, Mary - Estate of - 295,319,341,342,383,425,474

R2A   Atkins, Morton - decd. Estate - 781, 782

R14   Atkinson, Charles - et al, vs. Fayette County - 17 through 25

R17   Atkinson, Clinton - Minor - 212, 213

W2   Atkinson, Samuel Benson - 55

M1   August 1st, 1881 - 155

M1   August Term - 1883 - 228

M1   August Term - 1884 - 255,256,257

M1   August Term - 559,560

R11A   Austin, Mrs. - 784, 785

W2   Avery, Louella - Will & Proof -465

R21   Avery, Louella - Est of - 21 - 718- 730

R7   Awtry, Elizabeth - Estate - 444

M10   Aycock, G. T. - decd. Estate - 29,30,33,114

W1   Aycock, G. T. - Estate - 331

R11   Aycock, G. T. - decd. Estate - 17,18,19,20,21,27,28,253,254,255

W2   Ayres, Ed - deceased - Will - 382, 383

R20(24?)   Ayres, Ed - Estate of - 20 - 16-28

W2   Ayres, John A. - Will & Proof - 499,500

R23   Ayres, John A. - decd. - 23 - 776, 782

-4-

R16	Bagwell, Ecter A. - decd. - 120-24	
R17	Bagwell, Ecter A. - Estate - 484	
R19	Bagwell, Ector Lane - Estate of - 19 - 187-197	
W2	Bagwell, Ector A. - 240-242	
W2	Bagwell, Ector L. - Will & Proof - 351-352	
R15	Bagwell, H. B. - Estate - 193, 209	
R14	Bagwell, Howard - Decd. Estate - Guardianship - 282 through 305	
R14	Bagwell, Howard - decd. Estate - Administration - 306 through 308,314,315	
M7	Bagwell, J. W. & R. C. - decd. Estate - 107,117,124,128,129,160,197, 244,314,367,376	
R6B	Bagwell, J. W. & R. C. - Estate - 518,519,524 to 537,574	
R14	Bagwell, Sarah Evelyn - Petition (Guardian for Howard & Barbara Bagwell-562,561	
R15	Bagwell, Sarah Evelyn - gdn. sale of two parcels of land - 221,235,398,408	
M(3)	Baird, John - Estate of - 350,349,201,200,199,198,197,196	
M2	Baird, Henry - Estate - 110,241	
W1A	Baird, A. W. L. - 329, 330	
M3	Baker, Annetta - Apprentice - P- 291,292	
R3	Baker, Avanetta - Estate - 305, 301	
M7	Baker, Clara Belle - a minor - Estate of T.F.Shepherd - guardian - 446	
R7	Baker, Clara Belle - minor - T. F. Shepherd - guardian - 314	
M2	Baker, C. C. - apprenticeship - 691	
R3	Baker, C. C. - Mort. - 162,163	
R1A	Baker, G. W. - Estate - 668	
M1(1)	Baker, Gilbert W. - Estate of - 192,199,208,239,290,306,317,318	
R11A	Baker, Gilbert - Estate - 172	
R17	Baker, Icie - Incompetent - 162-63	
R15	Baker, Jimmie Louise - a Minor - 379 - 80	
M1(1)	Baker, Joel - Estate of - 407,410,416,448,475,476,506	
R1A	Baker, Joel - Estate, Final Settlement - 752 to 754	
R7	Baker, Lee - Minor - Estate - S. P. Baker, guardian - 360	

R20   Baker, Loyal - Inc. - 20 - 691, 705

M7   Baker, M. J. - decd. Estate - W.D.Newman, admr. - 194,195,201,231,316,332,333

M2   Baker, Obadiah - Estate - 671,672,673,707,708,735

M3   Baker, Obediah - Estate - P-436,437,625

M4   Baker, Obediah - decd. Estate - 11,20,21022,23,24,25

R2   Baker, Obadiah - Estate - 258 to 265, 272 to 275

R3   Baker, Obediah - Estate - 485

R4   Baker, Obediah - Estate - 37,44 to 57

M7   Baker, S. P. - guardian - Lee Baker - 476

M7   Baker, W. F. - decd. Estate - Z. A. Graham, admr. - 352

R7   Baker, W. F. - decd. Estate - J. F. Graham, adm. - 204,205

M5   Baker, William G. - Guardian for Viola A. & Nancy E.A.Henderson - 72, 94

W2   Balke, William S. (Misc. Rec. 11 Page 537) (Balfe)

R13   Ballad, John Lock - Estate - 285 thru 288

M5   Ballard, Lewis J. - Decd. Estate - J.W.Ballard, Admr. - 126,136,137,146,147,
                                                              188,323,330,328

R5   Ballard, Lewis J. - decd. Estate - 390, 396

R22   Banister, James Ralph & Barbara Jean, Minors - 22 -1-11

R13   Bankhead, A. J. - Estate - 413,414,415

W2   Bankhead, A. J. - 80

R20   Barnes, Clarice - 20 - 53,63

W2   Barnes, Clarice - Will & Proof - 377, 378

R14   Barnes, Habbison F. - Incompetent - 443

R15   Barnes, Hobbson - 290

R16   Barnes, Hobbison F. - Incompetent - 13 - 146,495

R17   Barnes, Hobbison - Incompetent - Gdn. Bond - 341

R18   Barnes, Hobbison F. - Incpt. - 12 - 367,405

R19   Barnes, Hobbison F. - Inc. - 323,326

R19   Barnes, Hobbison F. - Incpt.   19 - 793,805

R23   Barnes, Hobbison F. - Inc.   - 304. 384

M1   Barnes, James B. - Order for removal to jail of Tuscaloosa - 418

M5   Barnes, James B. - Guardian for minor heirs of Henry Etta Barnes, decd. - 231   (431)

M10   Barnes, J. H. - decd. Estate - 368-369

M1(1)   Barnes, Jesse, Estate of - 197,206,220,261,498,533 to 536.

M1(2)   Barnes, Jestin - 406,408

M(3)   Barnes, Jethro, Estate of - 401 to 417

W1A   Barnes, Jethro - 263 thru 275

M6   Barnes, John - decd. Estate - 401,402,403,411,412,495

M7   Barnes, John - decd. Estate - J. H. Barnes, admr. - 230,235,289,294,295,

R6B   Barnes, John - Estate - 442 etal

R7   Barnes, John - decd. Estate - J. H. Barnes - Admr. - 178

W2   Barnes, R. H. - 20, 21

R26   Barnes, Mary Frances - R 26 - Pages 617,623

R26   Barnes, Mavis - 26 - 422, 426

R28   Barnes, Wm. Velter - R 28 - 400

W3   Barnes, William Velter - 385

R27   Barnes, Wm. Austin - R 27 - 337,347

R17   Barnes, William Randall - Estate of Deceased - 42,44

M4   Barnett, Elishu - Estate - 438,440,441,463,498,502,579,607,615,618

M5   Barnett, Elihu - decd. Estate - A.C.Barnett,Admr. - Final Settlement - 178,184

R5   Barnett, Elihu - decd. Estate - 228,340,346

W2   Barnett, John Mitchell (Prob.Ct.Rec.Vol.12,pg.587)

M10   Barnett, Reuben Mitchell - 568,569,570,571,572

M8   Barnett, Vester - Minor adopted of W. M. Crump - 72

R4   Barnette, Mrs. E. J.,etal, - Power of Atty. to Robert Black - 422

R13   Barley, John D. - Estate - 322 thru 330

M1(2)   Barnmer, Paul, decd. Estate - 273,274,275,276,277,278,302,442,443,454,455

R15   Barton, Charles, Bobbie, Carlton & Carolyn - Minors - 93,94

M7   Baskett, Lee & Tom - joint owners - 261,268,269,270,278,279

R7   Basket, Lee & Tom - joint owner - partition & division - 140,141 to 145.

R1A   Bass, Liles - Estate -   143,144,558,to 568, 595 to 691

R13   Beard, James - To change Name - 532

M9   Beard, Mitchell - decd. Estate - 11,130

R9   Beard, Mitchell - decd. Estate of-G.L.Smith,Admr. - 109,306,308

R23   Beard, Stella Samiella, Esekiel & Dinaine - Minors - 23 - 409,414

R11A   Beard, W. J. L. - 179, 184

W2   Beasley, Cecil R., Sr. - Will - 360

R11A   Beasley, Galriel D. - 160,167, 185, 186

R25   Beasley, James - Decd. - 25 - 41,44

M2   Beasley, Jesse C., - Estate - 627

R1A   Beasley, Jesse C. - Estate - 214 to 217, 368 to 372, 511 to 516, 740 to 742

R2   Beasley, Jesse C. - Estate - 192 to 194

R18   Beasley, Warren B. - Inc. - 779,881

R20   Beasley, Warren D. - K Inc. - 20 - 107,110,470,427

R15   Beasley, Warren D. - Incompetent - 502,504

R16   Beasley, Warren D. - Incompetent - 518

R21   Beasley, Warren D. - Incompetent - 21 - 553,604

R23   Beasley, Warren D. - Inc. - 23 - 415,474

R26   Beasley, Warren D. - R26 - 964,1026

R27   Beasley, Warren D. - R27 - 156,160

R29   Beasley, Warren D. - R29 - 128,225, - Bond - 253

R27   Beaty,   - R27 - 286,292

M1(2)   Beggers, Malinda T., Estate - 609

R16   Belk, C. O. - decd. - 147,152

W2   Belk, C. O. - 249, 250

M8   Belk, D. J. - Petition for bond belonging to his 4 minor children - 428

R16   Belk, Elijah B. - deceased - 109,114

W2   Belk, Elijah B. - 234, 235

R20	Belk, G. R. - Est. of - 20 - 1,15
W2	Belk, G. R. - Will & Proof - 368,369
M9	Belk, G. W., Sr. - decd. Estate - 381,382
R10	Belk, G. W., Sr. - decd. Estate - 220,221,222
W1	Belk, G. W., Sr. - 252
'R25	Belk, Harold Kieth - Minor - 25, - 33,36
W3	Belk, James O. - 414 A
R28	Belk, James O. - R28 - 585, 617
R21	Belk, Mary W. - Decd. Est. of - 21 - 222, 231
	Belk, O - Reducing Boundaries - r27 - 610,626
W1	Belk, Wilburn M. (c.c.) - 90
M6	Bell, A. F. - decd. Estate - 483 to 492 494
R6B	Bell, A. F. M. - decd. Estate - 172
M3	Bell, A. M. L. - Deceased Estate - P-434,439,441,442
M5	Bell, A. L. M. - Estate of W. W. Jones - guardian - Final Settlement - 404
R3	Bell, A. M. L. - Estate - 490
R11A	Bell, James - 60,64,136,137
M1(2)	Bell, Stephen E., Decd. Estate - 3,6,7,9,10,132,500,521,522,569,570
M3	Bell, Stephen E. - Estate - P-99
R11A	Bell, Steven E. - 151, 160
R12A	Bell, Stephen E. - decd. Estate - 194, to 204, 294, 295
R3	Bell, Stephen E. - Estate - 276 to 278
W1A	Bell, S. E. - 530,531,570,598,607
M1(2)	Bell, S.E., W.W.Jones, - guardian of A.M.Bell - 630,635,636,626,782,783,785
M2	Bell, S. E. - Estate - 377,378
R13	Benton, Earlene - Gdn. for Evelyn, Earline, Henry W. & Shirley Ann (Henry Benton, decd. - 75,76.
R15	Benton, Floyd - decd. 95,96
M7	Berden, W. M. - Minor - A. M. Kitchens - guardian - 406,494,495
	Berman, Paul - decd. Estate - 460 to 481

M5	Best, James S. - Estate - T.E.Goodwin,Admr - 132,137,165,168,174,211,219, 267,342,343,406
R5	Best, James S. - decd. Estate - 536 to 543
R6B	Best, James S. - decd. Estate 412,225
M9	Best, W.W. & Mrs. Sis Williamson, joint owners - 24,28,29
M10	Best, W. W. - Estate - 1,2
R9	Best, W. W. - etal joint owners - 129,159,226
R10	Best, W. W. - decd. Estate - 540,539
M5	Best, William W. - Report as to insanity - 6
M8	Berry, Arlie - adopted Henry T. Berry - 354
R27	Berry, Arlton Y. - Decd. - R27 - 783,798

W3 - Berry, Arlton Y. - 318,320

M7	Berry, Mrs. Birt to John, Amy & Wm. Thomas Berry - 507
M1	Berry, Brad - 554
M8	Berry, Dan W. - decd. Estate - 400
M10	Berry, Dan W. - Estate - 112
R8	Berry, Dan W. - decd. Estate - 460
R11	Berry, Dan W. - decd. Estate - 243, 244,245
M3	Berry, David - Deceased Estate - P-572,612,613,614,617,625,644,646,651,671 to 673
M4	Berry, David - decd. Estate - 144,227,246,253,291,297,302,330,331,554
M5	Berry, David - Estate - A.W-Berry,Admr. - 10,11,16 to 19
R3	Berry David - Estate - 718
R4	Berry, David - decd. Estate - 60 to 68, 374, 387,525
R5	Berry, David - decd. Estate - 376, 381
W2	Berry, E. B. - Will & Appointment of Executor - 398
M1(1)	Berry, George - Estate of - 1,2,3,48,98,511,545,561,562
M10	Berry, George W. - decd. Estate - 543
W2	Berry, Geo. W. - 38
M6	Berry, Harry B. - Estate - 48

R6B	Berry, Henry B. - Estate M.R.Seay & Malissa J.Berry, Daur. - 360
R5	Berry, J. - decd. Estate - 405
M5	Berry, J. A. - Guardian of Bessie, Mack D. & Virgie Berry - 140
M2	Berry, John N. - 778, 779, 782, 800
M3	Berry, John N. - Estate - P-159 to 162;160,170,180 to 183,198,199,254 to 257, 189,290
.R2	Berry, John N. - Estate - 420 to 427
R3	Berry, John N. - Estate - 36 to 43, 233 to 238, 274, 275.
R20	Berry, L. B. - 20 - 89,98
W2	Berry, L. B. - decd. - Will & Proof - 413,414
R13	Berry, Mack D. - Estate - 471,472,473,474,475,476,477,478,479,480
W2	Berry, Mack D. - 6
W2	Berry, Mack D. & wife (cancellation) - 47
W2	Berry, Mack D. - 83
M7	Berry, Robert Lee - decd. - 8
R6B	Berry, Robert Lee - Estate - 490 to 492
R5	Berry, Sidney - decd. Estate - 474
M1 (1)	Berry, Susan, Estate of - 37-48-75-84-85-86-213-241-481-511-544-559-560
R3	Berry, S. V. & Sarah - Power of Atty to Robert Berry - 459, 460
M1 (2)	Berry, Thompson - Estate - 694
M2	Berry, Thompson - Estate - 250
W1A	Berry, Thompson S. - 45
M3	Berry, Town of - Incorporation of Town - P-712
M4	Berry, Town of - 86 - 87
M4	Berry, Ala., Town of - extending boundary - 87
M9	Berry, Walter - decd. Estate - 87-145-146
R9	Berry, Walter - Estate - 244,245,246,247,248,328
M5	Berry, W. C. - Estate of M. A. Berry, Admr. - 322, 324
R4	Berry, Wm. C. - decd. Estate - 20,21,226 to 230, 231 to 233
M3	Berry, William C. - Decd. Estate - P-674

M4	Berry, William C. - decd. Estate - 115,129,149,375,401
M3	Berry, William - Robert Berry, Admr. - P-393,473,474,483,501,718
M4	Berry, William - Estate - 267,365,369
R3	Berry, William - Estate - 561 to 574, 689
M2	Berry, William S., - Adoption of child - 586
R11	Berryhill, J. E. - decd. Estate - 121
M3	Berryhill, William - Estate - P-3 to 8,32,243,286,333,338,342,354 to 359, 397,427,470,488 to 493
R2	Berryhill, William - Estate - 359 to 372
R3	Berryhill, William - Estate - 272,273,366,401 to 406, 417, 418
R3	Berryhill, Wm. - Estate - 553 to 560
W1	Bhan, Wm. J. 9Cert. copy of W. from M. D.) - 266
R3	Bigger, Malinda - Estate - 278
W1A	Bigger, Malinda T. - 1
M9	Bircheat, J. A. - decd. Estate - 470, 471
M10	Birhceat, J. A. - de-d. Estate - 23
R11	Bircheat, J. A. - decd. Estate - 1,2,3,4
W1	Bircheat, J. A. - 299,300
M9	Bishop, Harman Webb, P - decd. Estate - 397
M10	Bishop, Harman Webb P & Mrs. N. E. - decd. Estate - 40,41
R10	Bishop, Harman Webb P. - decd. Estate - 246, 247
R11	Bishop, H. W. P. & N. E. - decd. Estate - 51,52,53,54,88
M9	Bishop, Mrs. N. E. - decd. Estate - 396
R10	Bishop, Mrs. N. E. - decd. Estate - 244, 245
M2	Black, Jacob, Estate - 616,617,621,622,623,643.654
M3	Black, Jacob - Estate - P-52,53,54,55,267 to 271
R2	Black, Jacob - Estate - 126 to 134,311 to 313,469 to 474
R3	Black, Jacob - Estate - 247 to 251, 288,377.
R5	Black, J. N. - decd. Estate - 324 & 382
M2	Black, John N. - Prohib: ion - 558,559,561

M3   Black, John N. - Contest of Election vs. Davis - p.303,304,305,340,341

M4   Black, John N. - Estate - 448

M5   Black, John N. - 87,91,106,287,303,332,336

R11A   Black, John - 186

R5   Black, John N. - decd. Estate - 240

R6B   Black, J. N. - decd. Estate - 146,147

R4   Black, Robert - Power of Atty. from Mrs. E.J.Barnette etal - 422

R10   Blackburn, Carl B. - decd. Estate - 576,577,578

M8   Blackburn, Gideon - Estate - 277,285,291

R8   Blackburn, Gideon - decd. Estate - Lindsey M. Blackburn, admr. - 307

M5   Blackburn, James M. - Guardian - 109

M8   Blackburn, James M. - Estate - 276,285,290

R8   Blackburn, James M. - decd. Estate - Lindsey M.Blackburn, adm. - 304

M9   Blackburn, John - decd. Estate - 118,119

W1   Blackburn, John H. (A. or W.) - 147

R9   Blackburn, John W. - Estate - 288,289,291,292

M10   Blackburn, John W. - decd. Estate - 58,93,96

R11   Blackburn, John W. - decd. Estate - 102,103,187,188,189,190,196

M10   Blackburn, Lenag - decd. Estate - 47,48,58,158,159

R11   Blackburn, Lena - decd. Estate - 77,78,79,80.81,82,103,105,105,119,120,
                                        358,359,360,351

W1   Blackburn, Lena - 334,335

M8   Blackburn, Mary - adotped by John W. Blackburn - 433

R5   Blackburn, Martha - decd. Estate - 402

M7   Blackburn, W. A. - Other joint owners of real estate - 251,265,266,274 to 277

R7   Blackburn, W. A. - etal. Joint Owner - 100 to 105

R11   Blackburn, W. D. - decd. Estate - 301,302

R1A   Blair, Amanitha & Alabama, Estate - 146

W2   Blaffer, Leonora Hassinger - 44,46

R15   Blalokc, John M. - Incompetent - 247,253,520

R16   Blalock, John M. - Incompetent - 211,219,393,400

Blankerbaker, Cornelius - Estate of - 7,36

R11A   Blankenbaker, Cornelius - 8 to 11

M3   Blankenship, S. D. - Estate - P-212,213,235,236,238,242,258,259,326,383,
                             460,475,476,498

M4   Blankenship, S. D. - Estate - 364,445,458,497

R3   Blankenship, S. D. - Estate - 196 to 206,263,440

R3   Blankenship, S. D. - Estate - 599 to 605

R5   Blankenship, S. D. - Decd. Estate - 156

M7   Blankenship. W. H. - guardian - 115, 120,121

R6B   Blankenship, W. H. - guardian for Neville Heirs - 538

R18   Blakeney, A. L. - 38,47,455,456

M4   Blakney, James, - Estate of - 264 to 266

R1A   Blaneney, James - Estate - 623

R11 A   Blakeney, James - 67,68

W2   Blakney, J. L. - Will & Proof - Testimonie & Proof - 316,17,18,326

M6   Blakneny, Thomas - Estate - 68, 70

R6B   Blakney, Thomas - decd. Estate - 205

W1   Blakney, Thomas - 38,39,40

M1(2)   Blakeney, Thomas Morton, Apprentice - 69

W1A   Blakeney, Thomas Master - 255,256

M8   Blakeney, Vera - guardian for Zimmie, Acy, John Hollis & Ila Blakeney - 580,
                                                            581

R9   Blakney, Vera - guardian Estate of Icy,John Hollis & Ila Blakney, minors - 70

R25   Bly, John Leon - Decd. - 25 - 194,197

R25   Bly, Mary Virginia (for Homestead) - 25 - 503,520

M(3)   Bobbett, Wm. - Estate of - 75 to 77 - 344,589,590

R1A   Bobbitt, William, Estate - 166 to 185, 646

R15   Bobo, Arlington Henry - Decd. - 436,438

R16, Bobo,   Arlington Henry - Decd. - 62

W2   Bobo, Arlington Henry - 200

M9   Bobo, C. H. - guardian for Terry /. Bobo, minor -

R10   Bobo, C. H. - Guardian 262

M10	Bobo, C. H. - guardian for Terry W. Bobo - 300
R11	Bobo, C. H. - guardian of Terry W. - 444, 545
W3	Bobo, Charles W. - Recorded for Record, H. M. Patterson - 277,282
M2	Bobo, Edward - guardian for Stacy Yarbrough - 259
M6	Bobo, Foster - Estate - 4
R27	Bobo, Lewis W. - 627,632
M9	Bobo, Lottie - guardian - 151,152,153
R9	Bobo, Lottie - guardian - 333-334-335-336
M1	Bobo, S. A. - 16 & 17
M8	Bobo, Susan E. - decd. Estate - 533, 534,535
R18	Bobo, Ted Arthur & Jerry Max - Minors - 190-194
R25	Bobo, Tessie - Incompetent - 25 - 610-620
R25	Bobo, Tessie - Incompetent - 625,628
R28	Bobo, Tessie - Incompetent - 273,431,436
M6	Bobo, W. L. - decd. Estate - 222, 223
R6B	Bobo, W. L. - decd. Estate - 363,364,365 (L. A. Bobo,L.P.Bobo,Mack Hindman, Nancy Elizabetn Nichols,A.Nichols,Martha J.Collins,Frank Colbin.
W1	Bobo, W. L. - decd. Estate - 59
M2	Bobo, William L. - adoption of child - 715, 716
R20	Bogard, B. J., Sr. - Unsound Mind - 536, 568
R20	Bogard, B. J., Sr. - Decd. Estate - 569, 575
R25	Bohannon, A. E. - Decd. - 734, 740
R11A	Bond, James - 80, 81
R18	Bonner, Lester, - Estate of - 33, 37
R25	Bonner, Mrs. Lester - Decd. - 912, 923
W3	Bonner, Mrs. Lester - 70, 71
W2	Bonner, Odessa - (for Mrs. Reed?) Vol. 2 - 579, 580
M7	Boone, William E. - decd. - W.P.Boone, Admr. - 66, 67,68
M9	Boone, W. P. - Decd. Estate - 241,336,338,339,340
R9	Boone, W. P. - decd. Estate - 511,512,513
R10	Boone, W. P. - decd. Estate - 130,135,136,137,139

M2	Bowen, Z. A. - Deed in Trust to G.W.Gravlee - 245,246 (marked through)
M1(1)	Bowles, James, - Estate of - 135
M10	Bowles, J. L. - decd. Estate - 64
R11	Bowles, J. L. - decd. Estate - 117,118
M1(1)	Bowles, William - Estate of - 47,65,72,82,212,238,283
R27	Bowling, Floyd Neal - 27, 348,349 - Legitemation
W1A	Bowman, P. - 262 - 371 thru 383
R22	Box, Bobby Joe - Decd. - 22, 44,47
R27	Box, Belton E. - 28 - 577,584
W3	Box, Belton E. - 414
M1(1)	Box, Liles, - Estate of - 235,256,257,268,269,326,405,423
M(3)	Box, Lyles - Estate of - 522,524,525,526
R26	Boyce, Johnny Elwood - Minor - 26 - 505,508
W3	Bozeman, Barbara Bagwell - 469 - Original on File Clerk C.
R11A	Bradley, - Jeptha Bradley, adm. - 273,274
M9	Bradley, J. J. - Ellen (wife) adoption of child (Lennie Lee) - 44,63
M1(2)	Braid, W.J.R. - decd. Estate - 331,332,441
M1(1)	Brandon, N. D. - Estate of - 294,307,308,326,330,350,401
M4	Brandon, Nathaniel D. - Estate - 525,528,538
R5	Brandon, Nathaniel D. - decd. Estate - 200
R14	Branyon, C. A. - Deceased Estate of - 368,369
R16	Branyon, Arthur Curtis - decd. - 201
R15	Branyon, Alpha - decd. 146, 147
R20	Branyon, Annie Lee - Decd. Estate of - 20 - 588,594
W2	Branyon, Annie Lee - 425
R28	Branyon, Bernice - 28 - 544,547
M6	Branyon, H. N. - Estate - 470 to 476 to 478 to 537 to 539,566,562,568,569,530
R6B	Branyon, H. N. - decd. Estate - 454,472,473,474,475
W1	Branyon, H. W. - decd. Estate - 181
M3	Branyon, J. A. - Deceased Estate - - 668,672,685

M4   Branyon, James A. - Decd. Estate - 27,549,550,551,552,557,558,572

M5   Branyon, James A. - Estate of - 285,292 to 295

R4   Branyon, J. A. - Decd. Estate - 1 to 10, 11 to 12, 601

M2   Branyon, J. J. - guardian for minor heirs of S. Branyon - 232

R20   Branyon, Max H. - Estate of - 20 - 45,52

W2   Branyon, Max H. - Will - 308

W3   Branyon, Mrs. Otis - 536

R29   Branyon, Otis Ware - 29 - 62,76

R3   Branyon, Sarah - Estate - 415,416

M3   Branyon, Sarah - Minors Estate - P-343,363,364

R24   Branyon, Sallie Era - Decd. - 24 - 948,955

W2   Branyon, Sallie Era - 572,73

R25   Branyon, T. Aaron - Decd. - 25 - 699,705

W3   Branyon, T. Aaron - Deceased Will & Proof - 32,34

M1(2)   Brasher, Aquilla - decd. Estate - 3,4,25,26,53,333,334,350,351,446,460,461

R11A   Brasher, Aquilla - 168,172

R12A   Brasher, Aquilla - decd. Estate - 422 to 428,777,778

R4   Brasher, David H. - guardian for Estate of James Garrison - 320

W1A   Brasher, A. - 368,370

M8   Brasher, Louisa, - Mother of Benny Brasher - a minor - 275

R16   Brasher, Thomas Simeon - Decd. - 48,53,125,26

W2   Brasher, Thos. Simeon - 227,228

R14   Braswell, Billy J. - Guardianship - 318,319

M10   Brazwell, Mrs. Levada Logan - etal (Combination of lands) 508,509,510,511,
        512,513,514,515,516,517

M1(2)   Brazil, John H., Master - 245

R12A   Brazil, John H. - Master - 757

M7   Brazile, Wilson - Decd. Estate - Ira L. Brazil, Admr. - 490

R7   Brazile, Wilson - Decd. Estate - Ira L. Brazile, Admr. - 390

M1(1)   Brewer, John W. - Estate of - 325,337,338,361,380,408,508

M(3)   Brewer, John W. - Estate of - 192 to 195,328,329,327,326,325,324,323

M8	Brewer, Latson - adopting child & changing name from Dan Turner to Dan Brewer 464	
R1A	Brewer, John W. - Estate - 316 to 335, 492, to 495, 496	
M8	Brewer, Leather - Declaration adopting child & changing name - 332	
M1(1)	Brewer, William - Estate of - 249,270,274,323,324,336	
M(3)	Brewer, William, - Estate of 587,588	
R1A	Brewer, William - Estate - 352 to 359, 649 to 650,675, to 677	
M1(1)	Bright, Page R. - Esatate - 575,577,612,619	
R1A	Bright, Page R. - Estate - 126 to 133	
M8	Brock, Dellis - declaration adopting child & changing name - 332,525	
M2	Brock, James - 382 to 385, 631	
R3	Brack, James - Estate - 180, 181	
M6	Brock, Lucile - Minor - Estate - 221	
R6B	Brock, Lucile - Minor - Estate - 323	
M9	Brock, M. M - decd. Estate - 467,468,469,470	
R10	Brock, M. M. - Estate, Will - 351,352,353,354	
W1	Brock, M. M. - 291	
R13	Brock, Mrs. T. W. - Estate - 345,346	
M8	Brotherton, DeRoy - guardian for Frank Anderson - 548	
M9	Brotherton, De Roy - guardian - 129	
R9	Brotherton, DeRoy - guardian for Estate of Frank Anderson - minor -76,304,305	
R15	Brotherton, Frank DeWitt - decd. - 1 thru 6	
W2	Brotherton, Frank DeWitt - 149,150	
R19	Brotherton, Sue Bell - Estate of - 19 - 327,333	
W2	Brotherton, Sue Bell - Will - 372,73	
M10	Brown, Carlton - guardian - 383,384,385	
M1(2)	Brown, Elias - Estate - 413,414	
R11A	Brown, Elias - 174,178	
W1A	Brown, Elias - 276,279	
M1	Brown, George W. - Cound over to circuit court - 550	
M1	Brown, George - 554	

M1(2)	Brown, George D., - Decd. Estate - 160,161,162	
M1(2)	Brown, George - Estate - 681,683,684,693,704,705	
M4	Brown, George - Estate - 86,95,96,97	
R11A	Brown, George - 277,278	
M2	Brown, George - Estate - 92,594,612,632,642,655,688,689,714,729,738,761,762	
M3	Brown, George - Estate - P- 156,374,380,383,394,408,666	
R2	Brown, George - Estate - 217 to 225	
R3	Brown, George - Estate - 132 to 134, 350	
R3	Brown, Goerge - Estate - 543 to 549	
R4	Brown, George - decd. Estate - 58,59,131, to 134	
W1A	Brown, George - 33,36,42,44,51,173	
M1(1)	Brown, George D. - Estate of - 616	
M3(3)	Brown - George D. - Estate of - 280, to 287,534,535	
R1A	Brown, George D. - Estate - 25 to 31, 339 to 342, 704 to 706	
R12A	Brown, George D. - decd. Estate - 700 to 703	
R11A	Brown, George P. - 125, 126	
R14	Brown, Gwendolyn - Minor - 436, 437	
M8	Brown, J. N. - adopting Clepter Jones - 458	
R22	Brown, Jimmy Auston - 22 - 568,571	
R18	Brown, Lem A. - 133,142	
W2	Brown, Lema - Will & Proof - 319,320	
M9	Brown, Luther W. - guardian - 38	
M7	Brown, Mary Etta & Eula - Minor children Mrs. T.L.Wade - 361	

232

M8	Brown, - Declaration adopting Mae Cliford & changing name to Lena May Brown	
M9		
M9	Brown, R. J. - decd. Estate - 423,445,446	
R10	Brown, R. J. - Est. of D____ - 263,264	
M1(1)	Brown, Sarah, - Estate of - 263,276,296	
M10	Brown, W. C. - decd. Estate - 174	
R7	Brown, W. C. C. - guardian for Mary Mae & Anna Pearl Kellen - 386	
M8	Brown, W. P. & Son Levr C____ P.P.Mayfield & Willie Jane Mayfield - 577,591	

M9	Brown, W. P. & Sons, Lumber Co. vs. P.P.Mayfield & wife -5,6,7,8,9,10	
W1A	Bryon, Jacuth H. - 639 or 689	
M1(2)	Bryan, Jacerth H., Wm. J. Brazel - Adm. - 730, 786	
M1 (2)	Bryan, Mary - 342	
M1(2)	Bryan, Thomas H., - Decd. Estate - 127,128,129,130,137,164,165,222,340,352, 380,381,456,510,571,490,491,682,683	
W1A	Bryan, Thomas H. - 383, 388,607	
M2	Bryant, Stephen - Estate Arminda Shackelford, guardian - 296,438,439	
W1A	Bryant, Stephen - Amanda Bryant - Guardian - 658,660	
M1(2)	Bryant, S. U. - Estate, Armenda Bryant, guardian - 599	
M1(1)	Bryon, Willis - Estate of - 541,570,615	
R12A	Bryson, Thomas H. - decd. Estate - 218 to 229, 785 to 789	
M7	Brown, W.C.C. - Guardian for Mary, May & Anna Pearl Killen - 451,477,487	
R9	Brown, W. P. & Sons Lumber Co. vs. P.P. & Willie Jane Mayfield - 110	
R11	Brown, W. C. C. - decd. Estate - 383	
M1(2)	Bullington, Laura - appointment of guardian P. Bishop - 699	
R-3	Bullington, Laura - Estate - 165,166	
M2	Bullington, Lemuel - Estate - 709,706,717,178 718	
M1(2)	Burk, E. C. - decd. Estate - 131	
M1(2)	Burk, E. B. - Decd. Estate - 281,282,283,284	
R12A	Burk, E. B. - decd Estate - 482 to 488	
M1(2)	Burke, Asbury - Decd. Estate - 38,135,167,345,366,367,391,392,395,394,395	
M1(2)	Burke, Asbury - Decd. Estate - 240,241,292,293,294	
R12A	Burkes, Asbury - decd. Estate - 300 to 327, 744 to 747	
W1A	Burkes, Asbury - 208,209,210,211 thru 219	
R23	Burkett, L. B. - Decd. - 23 - 599,607	
W2	Burkett, L. B. - Will & Proof - 489	
R11A	Burks, Asbury - 764,773	
R11A	Burks, Newbern B. - 270, 272	
R15	Burleson, Eva S. - Insane - 71,75,276 ,77,315	

R16   Burleson, Eva S. - Insane - 95,96, - deceased - 504,06, 514-17

R14   Burly, Daniel - Incompetent (Guardianship) - 109,110,111

R13   Burns, John Randolph - Estate - 236,237

M8   Burris - Caroline - decd. Estate - Sanford Burris - Admr. - 45

R7   Burris, Caroline - decd. Estate - 552

R11A   Burris, John M. - 99,118,274,276

R12A   Burris, John M. - 106 to 107

R13   Burris, Sanford - Estate - 34, 59

W1   Bush, George E. (c.c.) - 202

R28   Burson, J. D. - 28 - 234

R15   Busby, Daniel George - Incompetent - 268,269

R18   Busby, Daniel George - Inc. - 268,334

R19   Busby, Daniel George - Inc. - 19 - 319,322

R19   Busby, Daniel George - Inc. - 19 - 513,529

R29   Butler, A. B. - 29 - page 37

W3   Butler, A. B. - 533

M8   Butler, C. L. - guardian - 274

R8   Butler, James Faris & Eva Francis - Estate - C. L. Butler - guardian - 283

R15   Butler, Joe Neal - decd. - 515 - 19

W2   Butler, Joe Neal, Sr. - 212, 213

R28   Butt, Barbara - 28 - 149,150

R17, Byers, Elizabeth Jane Smith - Name Change - 470

R8   Byars, Hollie - guardian - 463

M8   Byars, Hollis - guardianship - 399

R15   Byars, J. C. - decd. - 576,578 (78)

R16   Byers, J. C. - decd. - 158, 159

W2   Byars, J. C. - 220

M4   Byrd, William M. - Estate - 193, 214

R4   Byrd, Wm. M. - decd. Estate - 298,299, Will 300 to 303

W2   Cain, Richard A. (c.c.) - 166

W2   Cain, Samuel Wilson (c.c.) - 167,168

M7   Cain, William C. - Estate - 97

R14   Caine, Robert Edward - decd. Estate - 145,146

M6   Caine, S. V. - Estate - 195

M6   Caine, Wm. E. - decd. Estate - 157 to 161

W1   Caine, W. E. - 65

R16   Cameron, L. G. - decd. - 42-47, 156-57

W2   Cameron, L. G. - 225, 226

R9   Campbell,   - etal joint owners - 427,428,429,430,431

      Campbell, Alfred Olen (Misc. Record) - 215

M2   Campbell, A., - Estate of Isaac B.Johnson, guardian for minor heirs - 262

M10   Campbell, Andrew, Jr., - Estate - 246,247

R11   Campbell, Andrew, Jr. - (Andrew Jackson Campbell, gdn.) - 462

W2   Campbell, Irving Edward - 254,255,256

M7   Campbell, Joseph M. - decd. - 222,227,228

R7   Campbell, Joseph M. - Estate - 70

W1   Campbell, Joseph M. - 106, 107

W2   Campbell, Marguerite Sapp - 243,247,248

      Campbell, Odie - 161, 164

R26   Campbell, F. Odia - 26 - 197, 104

R17   Campbell, Pearl - Incompetent - 221, 228

M9   Campbell, Susan - etal joint owners - 179,206,207,208,209

M9   Campbell, W. A. - guardian - 140,141

M9   Campbell, W. R. & J. H. - guardian for Milton & Billie Sue Little - 395

R10   Campbell, W. R. & J.H. - Guardian for Milton & Billie Sue Little - 243,244

R25   Cannon, Alma S. - Incompetent - 25 - 255,261

R28   Cannon, Alma S. - Vol. 28 - 820, 832

R25   Cannon, Claude C. - Decd. - 25 - 883,890

      Cannon, Claude C. - 61, 63

W2	Cain, Richard A. (c.c.) - 166	
W2	Cain, Samuel Wilson (c.c.) - 167,168	
M7	Cain, William C. - Estate - 97	
R14	Caine, Robert Edward - decd. Estate - 145,146	
M6	Caine, S. V. - Estate - 195	
M6	Caine, Wm. E. - decd. Estate - 157 to 161	
W1	Caine, W. E. - 65	
R16	Cameron, L. G. - decd. - 42-47, 156-57	
W2	Cameron, L. G. - 225, 226	
R9	Campbell, - etal joint owners - 427,428,429,430,431	
	Campbell, Alfred Olen (Misc. Record) - 215	
M2	Campbell, A., - Estate of Isaac B.Johnson, guardian for minor heirs - 262	
M10	Campbell, Andrew, Jr., - Estate - 246,247	
R11	Campbell, Andrew, Jr. - (Andrew Jackson Campbell, gdn.) - 462	
W2	Campbell, Irving Edward - 254,255,256	
M7	Campbell, Joseph M. - decd. - 222,227,228	
R7	Campbell, Joseph M. - Estate - 70	
W1	Campbell, Joseph M. - 106, 107	
W2	Campbell, Marguerite Sapp - 243,247,248	
	Campbell, Odie - 161, 164	
R26	Campbell, F. Odia - 26 - 197, 104	
R17	Campbell, Pearl - Incompetent - 221, 228	
M9	Campbell, Susan - etal joint owners - 179,206,207,208,209	
M9	Campbell, W. A. - guardian - 140,141	
M9	Campbell, W. R. & J. H. - guardian for Milton & Billie Sue Little - 395	
R10	Campbell, W. R. & J.H. - Guardian for Milton & Billie Sue Little - 243,244	
R25	Cannon, Alma S. - Incompetent - 25 - 255,261	
R28	Cannon, Alma S. - Vol. 28 - 820, 832	
R25	Cannon, Claude C. - Decd. - 25 - 883,890	
	Cannon, Claude C. - 61, 63	

M7	Cannon, W. A. - decd. Estate - Bascom Cannon, Admr. - 281,252,286
R7	Cannon, W. A. - decd. Estate - 160
R15	Cannon, W. L. - decd. 373,379
W2	Cannon, W. L. - 196, 197
R11	Cannon, William M. - decd. Estate - 174, 175
R14	Cannon, W. M., Sr. - Estate - 450, 452
R15	Cannon, William Arthur & James Franklin - Minors - 167, 177
R14	Cannon, Weightman M. & Lewis, vs. City of Fayette - 86 thru 98
M10	Cannon, William M. - decd. Estate - 86, 87
W1	Cannon, Wm. M. - 343
M10	Cannon, Wiley M. - decd. Estate - 106
M10	Cannon, Wiley M. - decd. Estate - 128
R11	Cannon, Wiley M. - decd. Estate - 221,222,281,282,283,284
M6	Canten, Aberdeen & Nashville R.R. c in Oklahoma, vs. Elizabeth Erwin - 250
M6	Canten, Aberdeen & Nashville R.R.Co. in Oklahoma, vs. Ormity Kuykendall - 264
R26	Canterberry, Dennis Wayne - (Dodson) - 650-5 Declaration legitimation
M4	Caraway, Andres H. - guardian for - 526
M5	Caraway, A. H. - Guardian - 288, 299
R6B	Caraway, A. H. - guardian for minors - 98,99,100,248
R15	Caraway, Cullen B. - Insane - 299, 303
R17	Caraway, Cullen B. - Incompetent - 113,122
R24	Caraway, H. N. - decd. - 24 - 916,923
W2	Caraway, H. N. - Will & Proof - 570,571
R28	Caraway, P. W. - Vol. 28 - 689, 695
	Caraway, P. W. - 444,447
R14	Caraway, William A. - decd. Estate of - 130,133
W2	Caraway, William A. - 87
R24	Cargile, Clyde C. - Decd. - 24 - 245,248
M5	Cargel, George - Insane - 183
R14	Cargile, George Stacy decd. Es : of - 421 thru 424

W2	Cargile, Stacy - 135	
R24	Cargile, Margie - Decd. - 24 - 253,254	
M8	Cargile, T. R. - etal Joint owners - 49,53,62,64	
R7	Cargile, William - Estate - 560	
R19	Carr, Harriet - Decd. Estate of - - 19 - 63, 78	
W2	Carr, Harriet - Will & Proof - 353,354	
R14	Carr, Ike - De-d. Estate of - 126, 127	
R18	Carr, Ike, Jr. - Decd. Estate of - 18 - 461, 464	
R26	Carr, Lucille - 26 - 481,496	
	Carr, Lucile - 158,160	
R25	Carter, Douglas C. - 25 - 171, 175 - Vol. 27 - 162, 195	
R27	Carter, Douglas C. - 27 - 162, 196	
R27	Carter, Douglas C. - Inc. - Vol. 27 - 818, Vol. R28 - pg. 896,900	
M3	Carter, E. M. - Estate, E. W.Carter, Admr. - 138,139,140,145,146,163,164	
R2	Carter, E. M. - Estate - 547 to 562	
R3	Carter, E. M. - Estate - 278	
M8	Carter, Maude - guardian for Estate of Carleton Carter, Minor - 505	
R8	Carter, Maude - guardian - 578	
M7	Carter, Timothy E.- name changed & adopted J.J.Cawthens - 330, 331	
R14	Carver, Alice Jane - a Minor - 441, 442	
R16	Carver, Alice Jane - Minor-12	
R18	Carver, Alice Jane - Minor - 18 - 553, 643, 427,440	
M10	Casey, Robert S. - Decd. Estate - 36, 83, 84	
R11	Casey, Robert S. - Decd. Estate - 37,38,167,168,169,170,171	
M6	Castleberry, Soloman - Estate - 151,179,193,194	
R6B	Castleberry, Solomon - W.H.McCollum Bond - 262,334,355,356,375,377,388	
M7	Cawthen, John - adopted & name John Cawthen given - 3,14,10,330,331	
W1	Ceaggett, Frederick Dorsey (c.c. from D.C.) 340,341,342	
R23	Cecil, Millard F. - Inc. - 23 - 757,764	

R27   Chaffin, Floyd Gilford - Vol. 27 - 558, 570

             Chaffin, Floyd Gilford - 293, 297

M10   Chambless, Bruce - guardian - 11,14,45

R10   Chambless, Bruce - guardian for Clister Chambless - 565,566

R11   Chambless, Clister - Estate exp. - 66,67,68,69

M10   Chambless, D. I. - decd. Estate - 9, 10

M4   Chapin, Mrs. M. A., - widow of Wm.Chapin, decd, esmeption - 461

M5   Chappell, Miles - Estate - 23,24,39,67,347 to 352

R5   Chappell, Miles - decd. Estate - 362, 363

R21   Christenberry, Johnie H. - Decd. Estate of - 21 - 731, 738

W2   Christenberry, Johnnie H. Jrs. - Will & Proof - 461

M9   Christian, John Malichi - adopted by W.W. & Martha A.Christian - 417

R15   Christian, Mary Neice - decd. - 439, 445

W2   Ghristian, Mary Neice - 201

M10   City of Fayette, Condemnation of lands, vs. T.H.Cannon, etal - 218,219,220,
             221,222,223,224,225,226,240,241,239,238,233

M10   City of Fayette, Condemnations of lands - 121,122,123,124,125

M10   City of Fayette, condemnation of lands, vs. Mrs.Dora Hinson, etal - 227,228,
             229,230,232,232,236,237
                                           453,454
R11   City of Fayette, condemnation Proceedings vs. T.H.Cannon et al - 435,438,333,
                                         452,453
R11   City of Fayette, Condemn.proceedings vs. Mrs.Dora Hinson etal -439,440,450,451,

R11   City of Fayette, Condemn.proceedings vs. J.L.Sumerall et al - 264,275

R14   City of Fayette, vs. Artie Lee Corbett , et al - 531,553

R14   City of Fayette, vs. Weightman M.Cannon, et al - 86 thru 88 (98)

R12   City of Fayette, vs. Aaron Blackburn, et al - 425, 444

R16   City of Fayette, vs. B.J.Bogard, et al - 449-67

R16   City of Fayette, vs. S.W.Lucas (Mrs.) - 304,317

R16   City of Fayette, vs. Molly Jo Patterson Myers - 327,336

R21   City of Fayette, vs. Raymond Gordon, et al. - 271, 326

R22   City of Fayette, vs. Dr.' G. & Naomi Hodo - 22 - 12,27

R22   City of Fayette, vs. J D. & Estelle Parks - 22 - 5 ,535

R28   City of Fayette, vs. James F. Cannon - Vol. 28 - 495,526,541,543

M10   Claggett, Frederick Dorsey - decd. Estate - 88

R6B   Clar, Caroline - a person of unusual mind - Thomas Tucker guardian - 412 to417

M1   Clarke, J. E. - 556

                                                                              232
M8   Cleford, Lena May - name changed to Lena May Brown & adppted by Nancy Brown -

M1(2) Cline, J. H. - guardian for J.E.Gwynn - 636

W1A   Cline, J. H. - (Guardian for Joanna Elyzanna) - 17

R11A   Cobb, Kelcy M. - 189, 200

M1(1) Cobb, Wilson, Estate of - 214,273,285,to 289,351,363,385,409,412,433,483

R18   Cochran, George - Estate of - 18 - 28, 32

M9   Cochran, James - a minor insurance collection - 367

M1(1) Cochran, John - Estate of - 45,54

M9   Cochran, Hassie - guardian - 271,412,413

R10   Cockran, Hassie - Guardian - 12, 13

M1(1) Cokerham, Elijah - Estate of - 237,255,256,260,274,370,540,549 to 551

M1(2) Cockerham, Elijah - decd. Estate - 115,127,156,242,243

R1A   Cockerham, Elijah - Estate - 161 to 164, 484,664,681 to 685

R11A   Cockerham, Elijah - 204, 209

R12A   Cockerham, Elijah - decd. Estate - 623 to 634

R15   Cockran, H. G. - decd. 19, 23

M10   Cockrell, Frances & John - Minors Estate - 151

R11   Cockrell - Frances & John - Minors Estate - 344,345

M10   Cockrell, J. H. - condemnation of lands - 500,501,502,503,504,505,506,507

M1(1) Coggins, Daniel - Estate of - 122,125,136,164,202,227,230,243,257,258,259,260,
            273,279,280,281,477,512,514 to 525,541 to 543,553,554,564 to 567,580,
                                                                              587
M(3)   Coggin, Daniel - Estate of - 204,203,202,201

R27   Coggins, George Atwell - Vol. 27 - 216,225

W2   Coggin, Carrie - 93

       Coggins, Goerge Atwell - 242, 245

R25   Colburn, Guy Milton - Legitimation - 25 - 324

R25   Colburn, Joe Neal - 25 - 324

R21	Colburn, Wanda - Minor - 21 - 106,109
R13	Cole, Andrew J. - Estate - 331,332
R27	Cole, Anthony Genea - Vol. 27 - 652 - Legitimation
R13	Cole, C. N. - Estate - 251,252,253,254
W2	Cole, E. D. - 56
R17	Cole, Ernest L. - Incompetent - 337,339
R22	Cole, Ernest L. - Inc. - 22 - 901,996
R23	Cole, Ernest L. - Inc. - 23 - 117, 228
R25	Cole, Ernest L. - Inc. - 25 - 45,107, Vol. R27 page 860,874
R26	Cole, Ernest L. - Inc. - 26 - 149,152 - C. W. Gross - Gdn.
R26	Cole, Ernest L. - Inc. - 26 - 101,148 - David Enslen - Gdn.
M2	Cole, John B. - Estate of J.F.Jackson, admr. - 530 to 532,547 to 549, 560
M1(1)	Cole, John B. - Estate of - 53,56,219,291,303,573
R1A	Cole, John B. - Estate - 224,226,645
M3	Cole, John B. - Estate - P-341,367,684,694,697 to 700
R2	Cole, John B. - Estate - 31 to 36, 119 to 125
R3	Cole, John B. - Estate - 620,428,429,430
R4	Cole, John B. - Decd. Estate - 69 to 72
M1(2)	Cole, John R. Decd. Estate - 63,64
R12±	Cole, John R. - decd. Estate - 773,774
M1(2)	Cole, Littleton - Estate - 729, 769
M2	Cole, Littleton - Estate - 64,102,554,428, to 430, 407 to 418,554,749,781
M3	Cole, Littleton - Estate - P-248 to 251
R2	Cole, Littleton - 47,48,274 to 276,305 to 308
R3	Cole, Littleton - 238 to 247, 282
W1A	Cole, Littleton - 61,62,774
R13	Cole, Thomas D., A. J. & James A. - Minors - 411, 412
R15	Cole, Thomas D., A. J. & James A. - Minors - 216,218
M(3)	_ole, Wm. B. - Estate of - 337,336
R1A	Cole, Wm. B. - Estate - 6 to 392 02 to 609, 665 to 666

M1(2)	Cole, William D. - decd. Estate - 86
M3	Cole, William D. - Estate - P-30, 31
R3	Cole, W. D. - Estate - 74
R12A	Cole, W. D. - Decd. Estate - 796 to 798
W1A	Cole, W. D. - 59, 91
R11A	Cole, Wm. K. - 85, 86
R11A	Cole, W. R. - 85, 86
R1A	Coleman, John - Estate - 83 to 87, 518 to 519
R14(16)	Collins, Mrs. Allie Al___ - decd. - 368
M2	Collins, Benjamin - Estate - 452 to 459,497 to 499, 524,653
M3	Collins, Benjamin - Estate - P-31,32,35,36,47,48,378,385
R2	Collins, Benjamin - Estate - 23
R3	Collins, Benjamin - Estate - 144,175,176,454,455,456
R6B	Collins, B. F. - Estate - 258
R25	Collins, Emilie - Inc. - 25 - 26,32
R24	Collins, Emma - Decd. - 24 - 419,427
W2	Collins, Emma - Will & Proof - 547
M10	Collins, Frances M. - guardian, Wilma Ayres - 135
R11A	Collins, F. M. - 218, 222
R10	Collins, Frances M. - 541,542,564
R11	Collins, Francis M. - Gdn., Wilma Ayres - Minor - 300
R20	Collins, H. D. - 20 - 487,528
W2	Collins, H. D. - Will & Proof - 401
R9	Collins, J. B. - Decd. Estate - 34
W1	Collins, J. B. - 216
M8	Collins, James B. - Decd. Estate - 529,537,538,540
R16	Collins, John Newton - Dedd. - 39, 41
R17	Collins, John N. - Estate Decd. - 328,330B
R7	Collins, J. W. - Decd. Estate - 460
M8	Collins, J. W. - Decd. Estate - 3,7,73,77,318

R20   Collins, Lonnie, Decd. Estate of - 20 - 478,485

M7   Collins, M. L. - other joint owners - 245,262,263,297

R7   Collins, M. L. - etal joint owners, partition & division - 130 to 135

M6   Collins, R. N. - decd. Estate - 522, 523

M1(2) Collins, W. F. - 551,560,561

M(3) Collins, William F. - Estate of - 288,292,291,290,289,288

W1A   Collins, W. F. - 592

M10   Collins, Wilma Agnes - Minor, Estate - 5,11,12

M9   Collins, W. O. - guardian of Estate of Rhoda Miller - non corpus mentes - 81

M9   Collins, W. O. - guardian for Rhoda Miller -95,96

M10   Collins, W. O. - decd. Estate - 127 (Marked through)

M10   Collins, W. O. - Estate - 5,127

R9   Collins, W. O. - guardian Rhoda Miller - 258

R10   Collins, W. O. - decd. Estate - 544, 543

R11A Collins, William F. - 209,213

R11   Collins, Wm. O. - decd. Estate - 278,279,280

                                                                    370
R13   Commercial Union Ins. of N.Y., est. of Sam J.Stanley, - In Assumption Certificat

M10   Company, M. E. - decd. Estate 184

R14   Cook, George Clyde - decd. Estate of - 413,414

R14   Cook, Icie - et al - vs. Fayette County - 7 through 14

W2   Cook, John B. - Will & Proof - 578,579

M1(2) Cook, Lemiel - Estate - 527,528,549,562

M(3) Cook. Lemuel - Estate of - 566 to 573

R11A Cook, Lemuel - 213,216

M5   Cook, Lula E. - Estate of only granting letters - 338

R24   Cook (or Coleman), Mary Elizabeth - Minor - 24 - 428

M10   Cook, Mary Louise - decd. Estate 381

R21   -Cook, William V. - Decd. Estate of - 21 - 120,128

W2   Cook, William V. - Deceased - 449, 450

M4   Cooper, Edney - changed to Edney Sudduth - 453 (or 493)

M10   Cooper, Hayes - decd. Estate - 72

R11   Cooper, Hayes - decd. Estate - 144, 145

M9   Cooper, Hosea - declaration adopting Minie & Rufus Stewart - 407

M9   Cooper, Mrs. J. C. - guardian for Ila (Blakeney) Shelnutt - 331

M2   Cooper, J. H. - guardian for Malinda & S. J. Harris - 168 to -

M4   Cooper, Joseph & Anthony - 121

M1(2) Cooper, Morten - decd. Estate - 559,576,290,304,353,379

M2   Cooper, Martin - Estate - 130

R12A   Cooper, Martin - decd. Estate -   456, to 459

W1A   Cooper, Martin - 118-19

W1A   Cooper, Martin - 258,259,593

M(3)   Cooper, Nancey - Estate of 60 to 74

M(3)   Cooper, Nancy - Estate of - 339

R1A   Cooper, Nancy - Estate - 425 to 429

R10   Cooper, Mrs. Vera Blakney (Mrs. J. C.) - Guardian - 118,119

M7   Copeland, Mrs. J. E. - guardian - Estate of - Raburn Whitson, minor - 542

R7   Copeland, Mrs. J. E. - guardian Raburn Whitson, minor heir of J.L.Whitson - 482

R13   Corbett, A. B. - Estate - 528 thru 531

W2   Corbett, A. B. - 95

M4   Corbett, Andrew J. - decd. Estate - 390,393,465

M7   Corbett, A. J. - Estate - R.H.Corbett,admr. - 176,177,182,183,237,244,247,248

R5   Corbett, Andrew J. - decd. Estate - 52

R7   Corbett, A. J. - Estate - 1, 2

R16   Corbett, Andrew J. - decd. - 520,523

W2   Corbett, Andrew J. - 276,277

R11A   Corbett, Jesse - 222

M7   Corbett, Melissa, Clennie & Minnie - minor heirs Burt Corbett, decd. - 209

Corbett R7   Corbett, Melissa,Clemmie & Minnie - minor heirs of Burt Corbett, decd. - 30

M8   Corbett, Walter Lee - guardian - 348

R8   Corbett, Walter Lee - guardian - 396

M2   Corbett, William - Estate - 449 to 452

R1A   Corder, Wlias - 187 to 197, 677 to 680

M8   Connelieus, John P. - decd. Estate - 206

R8   Cornelieus, John P. - decd. Estate - W.B.Cornelieus, admr. - 214

M4   Corona, Special Robert - Connerly - 178

M1(1) CORPORATION, Petition - 116,129

M7   Corporation Town of Fayette - exl ____ - 401

R6B   Cothren, B. B. - decd. - 378, 379, 380

M1(1) COUNTY, Admr. McConnell, Thomas P. - 120

R11A County, Administrator Bond - 217

R17   County, Fayette - condemnation proceedings - 217, 220

M10   County of Fayette, condemnation of lands vs. W.C.McCaleb & J.H.Hallmark - 351,352,353,354,355

R19   Cotten, Augusta R., - et al vs. John C. Robertson, et al - 19 - 530,532

R25   Cotten, Augusta Robertson, Decd. - 25 - 597, 605

W2   Cotton, George B. - Deceased Will - 453, 454

      Cotten, Augusta R. - Will - 28, 31

R21   Cotton, George B. - Decd. Estate of - 21 - 232, 238

M6   Cotton, G. H. - Estate - 196, 199

M7   Cotton, Isaac - Minor - Estate of - 396

R7   Cotton, Isaac - Minor - J.H.Oswalt, sheriff, guardian - 84,85,86

R8   Cotton, J. D. - Minor, J.B.Deavours, guardian - 26

R15   Couch, G. W. - decd. - 316, 320

W2   Couch, G. W. - 188

M10   Couch, John M. - Malinda C. Weeks - joint owners - 356

M8   Couch, J. P. - decd. Estate - 541, 542,544

R9   Couch, J. P. - decd. Estate - 52

R25   Couch, Roy D. - Decd. - 25 - 900, 911

      Couch, Roy D. - 67, 69

R8   Corbett, Walter Lee - guardian - 396

M2   Corbett, William - Estate - 449 to 452

R1A   Corder, Wlias - 187 to 197, 677 to 680

M8   Connelieus, John P. - decd. Estate - 206

R8   Cornelieus, John P. - decd. Estate - W.B.Cornelieus, admr. - 214

M4   Corona, Spetial Robert - Connerly - 178

M1(1) CORPORATION, Petition - 116,129

M7   Corporation Town of Fayette - exl _____ - 401

R6B   Cothren, B. B. - decd. - 378, 379, 380

M1(1) COUNTY, Admr. McConnell, Thomas P. - 120

R11A County, Administrator Bond - 217

R17   County, Fayette - condemnation proceedings - 217, 220

M10   County of Fayette, condemnation of lands vs. W.C.McCaleb & J.H.Hallmark -
                351,352,353,354,355

R19   Cotten, Augusta R., - et al vs. John C. Robertson, et al - 19 - 530,532

R25   Cotten, Augusta Robertson, Decd. - 25 - 597, 605

W2   Cotton, George B. - Deceased Will - 453, 454

       Cotten, Augusta R. - Will - 28, 31

R21   Cotton, George B. - Decd. Estate of - 21 - 232, 238

M6   Cotton, G. H. - Estate - 196, 199

M7   Cotton, Isaac - Minor - Estate of - 396

R7   Cotton, Isaac - Minor - J.H.Oswalt, sheriff, guardian - 84,85,86

R8   Cotton, J. D. - Minor, J.B.Deavours, guardian - 26

R15   Couch, G. W. - decd. - 316, 320

W2   Couch, G. W. - 188

M10   Couch, John M. - Malinda C. Weeks - joint owners - 356

M8   Couch, J. P. - decd. Estate - 541, 542,544

R9   Couch, J. P. - decd. Estate - 52

R25   Couch, Roy D. - Decd. - 25 - 900, 911

       Couch, Roy D. - 67, 69

M8   Crump, W. M. - declaration adopting Vester Barnett for educating maintenance-72

M1(1) Crump, Simeon V. - Estate of - 453,493,494

R21   Crutcher, Ida Frances - Minor - 21 - 267,270

R19   Crutcher, J. P., Jr. -   19 - 369, 378

W2   Crutcher, John Parker Jr. - Will & Proof - 357

R11A Cunningham, Iredel - 1 to 8, 93, 201, 204

R20   Cunningham, Robert B. - Inc. - 20 - 677, 683

R25   Cunningham, Robert B. - Decd. - 25 - 949, 652

W1A   Cuny, I. B. - 228, 229

W2   Curington, J. C. - Will & Proof - 576, 577

R14   Curington, William Allen - Estate - 128, 129

M4   Curl, Martha J. - widow, et al - 164, 161

M9   Curl, W. C. & other joint owners - 112, 120

R9   Curl, W. C. & Others - Joint owners - 277,278,279,281,292

M9   Curl, W. H. - decd. Estate - 109

R9   Curl, W. H. - decd. Estate - 276, 277

M4   Curry, E. S. - Decd. Estate - 226,228,229,230,235,236,243,403,451,466

R4   Curry, E. S. - decd. Estate - 361 to 369, 622

M1(2) Curry, John B. - decd. Estate - 109,155,160,163

M2   Curry, John B. - Deed. Estate of Samuel Curry, guardian - 370,371,372

M93 M(3) Curry, John B. - Estate of - 493,494,495,496,497

R12A Curry, John B. - decd. Estate - 372,373

R1A   Curry, John B. - Estate - 716 to 719

R24   Daffron, Parrie Lee - Decd. - 24 - 184,189,816,835

R11   Dailey, Eula Mae vs. Sam Daily - 473

M4   Darden, Sampson H. - decd. Estate - 248,249,250,251,263,287,305,359,363,377

M5   Darden, S. H. - decd. Estate - 167,285,298

R4   Darden, Sampson H. - decd. Estate - 400

R6B   Darden, S. H. - decd. Estate - 60 to 64

M1   Darmer, Nick - 282

R13   Darnell, Lillian - Gdn. for Hilda Darnell - 194,195,219,447,450

R1A   Darr, David P. - Estate - 384, 385

M1(1) Davis, Alfred - Estate of - 612

R1A   Davis, Alfred - Estate - 641, 703

R20   Davis, Annie Nancy Cotton Randolph - Estate of - 20 - 99, 102

R28   Davis, K C. K. - Vol. 28 - 835,846

       Davis, C. K., Sr. - 508, 511

M10   Davis, Edwyna - Minor - 154

R12A   Davis, Emily J. - 101

R24   Davis, Eugene C. - Decd. - 24 - 890, 895

W2   Davis, Eugene C. - Will & Proof - 562, 563

M10   Davis, G. G. - guardian for Robert & Herbert Davis - Minors - 24

R10   Davis, G. G. - Guardian for Robert & Herbert Davis - 590

M1(1) Davis, James - Estate of - 234

R11A   Davis, John F. - 258, 262

M8   Davis, John L. - decd. Estate of widows proceedings - 518, 528

R12A   Davis, John L. - 104 to 106

R8   Davis, John L. - decd. Estate - 580

M7   Davis, J. M. - Estate of - proceedings to set grant to widow Sallie Davis
                   Exemption - 70 to 76,78,79

W1   Davis, John M. - 388

R20   Davis, Julia Bell - Decd. Estate of - 20 - 261,264,531,535

M10   Davis, Lester - et al, condemnation of land - 508,509,510,511,512,513,514,515, 516,517

M5   Davis, M. C. - guardian of Charles Price - 252,269,283

M2   Davis, Matthew - Estate - 181 to

M7   Davis, Matthew, - Decd. Petition - M.A.Lambert to sell lands - 1 to 14

W1A   Davis, Matthew - 165

M2   Davis, Nancy - Estate - 133

W1A   Davis, Nancy - 115

W2   Davis, Mrs . Narcissa A. - 37

R11A   Davis, Oliver P. - 267,270,794,799

R20   Davis, _____ Lee, - Estate of - 20 - 64, 75

R26   Davis, Wanda Faye - Inc. - 26 - 511, 515

W2   Davis, Roy Lee - Will & Proof - 373, 374

R1A   Davis, Susanna C., - Estate - 134, 385

R21   Davidson, Tessie Love - Decd. - 21 - 535,552

M1(2)   Davis, Thomas - Estate, James M.Davis, Admr. - 745 to 749

M(3)   Davis, Thomas - Estate of - 306,305,304,303,302,559,560

R1A   Davis, Thomas - Estate - 373 to 376,692 to 700 (Irena H. Davis, wife, Wm.T.Davi son)

W1A   Davis, Thomas - 75

M10   Davis, Thorald P. - Minor - 588

M7   Davis, Wiley - decd. Estate dower proceeding - 105, 106

R12A   Davis, William - 101 to 104

R11A   Davis, William T. - 263,267

M6   Dayher, Peter - Estate - 94,95

M(3)   Deavours, Abraham - Estate of - 141,142,143,144,145,146

M3   Deavours, Abraham - Deceased Estate - P.542,547,562,563

M4   Deavours, Abraham - Estate - 365,378,379

R1A   Deavours, Abraham - Estate - 252 to 257

R3   Deavours, Abraham - Decd. Estate - 725 to 735

R5   Deavours, Abraham - Decd. state - 67

R28   Deavours, H. V. - 28 - 696, 715

       Deavours, Hershel V. - 448, 451

M5   Deavours, Isaac - Guardian of J.C.Deavours - 424

M8   Deavours, Isaac - guardian for Estate of I.D.Cotton, Minor - 93,104,116

M5   Deavours, James - Non Corpus Mentes - Estate - 251, 269

M4   Deavours, James -   - 271,272,273

R5   Deavours, James - Non Corpus Mentes - Estate - 87

R8   Deavours, J. B. - guardian for Estate of J.D.Cotton, Minor - 26

M6   Deavours, J. J. - decd. Estate - 280

M8   Deavours, J. J. - decd. Estate - 67, 68, 74

R8   Deavours, J. J. - decd. Estate - Widow Exemption - 34 - Martha Hamner,adm.- 436

M8   Deavours, John T. - decd. Estate Martha Hamner, Admx. - 389

R24   DeBardeleben, James, Jr., - Decd. - 24 - 204,208

W2   DeBardeleben, James, Jr., - Will & Proof - 523,24

M1   December Term, 1882 -

M1   December Term, 1885 - 296

W2   Del Bondio, Leonora Clara - 48, 50

R9   Denver, Anna E. - Decd. Estate - 403

R20   DePoister, Mrs. J. B. - Inc.- 20 - 627, 640

R22   de Wilton, Edward Linsmore, - Decd. - 22 - 636, 650

W2   de Wilton, Edward Linsmore - Will & Proof - 471, 472

R3   Dickinson, John F. (J) - Estate - 231,232,289,404,622

M3   Dickinson, J. J. - Estate - P. 217,218,348

R27   Dillard, J. W. C. - Inc. - 24 - 978,984

R28   Dillard, Mary Ann - Final Settlement - 28 - 5, 14

R24   Dillard, Sallie - Inc. - 24 - 985, 991

M9   Dillard, Sant - Decd. Estate - 127

R9   Dillard, Sant - Decd. Estate - 302, 303

R21   Dillard, Terry Wm., Jerry Wayne & Mary Ann, Minors - 21 - 379,384

R22   Dillard, Terry Wm., Jerry Wayne & Mary Ann, Minors - 22 - 816,900

R24   Dillard, Terry Wm., & Jerry Wayne - Final Settlement - 24 - 541,552

M8   Dillard, Troy - name changed to Troy Sims - 432

M8   Dillard, W. C. - Decd. Estate - 521, 530

R8   Dillard, W. C. - Decd. Estate - 537

W1   Dillard, W. C. - 214

W1   Divvers, Anna E. - 238

M1(2)   Dobbins, Joseph C., - Decd. Estate - 24,25,61,62,63,85,167,440,451,452

R12B   Dobbins, Joseph C. - Decd. Estate - 291 to 294, 393 to 399

W1A   Dobbins,   - 347,348,354, thru 362

W1A   Dobbins, Nimrod - 351 thru 354

R11A   Dobbs, Barzilla S. - 238, 240

W1   Dobbs, Elizabeth E. - Thos. J. & Morrlov Dobbs - 170

M9   Dobbs, Henry & Jamia Perkins - Minors over 18 point owners in sale of land - 321

M8   Dobbs, Ida - guardian - 523

R8   Dobbs, Ida - guardian - 579

R23   Dobbs, James H. - Decd. - 24 - 656,662

W2   Dobbs, James H. - Will & Proof - 497, 498

R4   Dobbs, J. T. - Bastard Bond - 236

R17   Dobbs, M. C., Sr. - Bond, McNees - 326

M10   Dobbs, Thomas N. - Decd. Estate - 70, 155, 156

R11   Dobbs, Thomas N. - Decd. Estate - 137,138,139,352,379,380

M8   Dobbs, W. S. - guardian of Estate of Eddie & Linton Dobbs, Minors - 495

M8   Dobbs, Wilson - et al joint owners to sell lands for division - 460,470,476,480

M8   Dobson, F. M. - father of Mary Lou, Francis Marion & Zora Ella Dobson - Minors -
                                                                                  13

M10   Dodd, Oletha - Minor Estate - 469,470,471,472

R16   Dodds, Leon M. - decd. - 115,19

W2   Dodds, Leon M. - 236, 239

R27   Dodds, Susie Sanford - 27 - 85' 59, Vol. 28, page 107,1'

M1(2) Dodson, Abner - Estate - 114,115

M3   Dodson, Abner - Estate - P.301,302,303,309,310,495,502,503

R11A   Dodson, Abner - 241,248,251

R12A   Dodson, Abner - Decd. Estate - 368 to 370

R3   Dodson, Abner - Estate - 301 to 304, 321 to 326, 441 to 444, 647 to 650

M10   Dodson, Charlie N. - Decd. Estate - 301,302,454

R11   Dodson, Charlie N. - Decd. Estate - 546,547,548,549,550,551

R26   Dodson, Dennis Wayne or Donnis Wayne Canterberry - 650 - (Declaration of legitim

M10   Dodson, E. L. - et al. condemnation of lands - 519,520,521,522,523,524,525,526,
                                                                                   527

M9   Dodson, E. W. - Decd, Estate - 437,455

W1   Dodson, E. W. - 283

M6   Dodson, Horace - Estate - 57, 58

R6B   Dodson, Horace - Decd. Estate 219,220

W1   Dodson, Horace - 42

M10   Dodson, J. Henry - Decd. Estate - 484

M2   Dodson, J. T. - Estate - W.C.Webster, guardian - 245,475 to 478,515,522,523,573

M3   Dodson, J. T. - Estate - P.216,217,223,317,629,633

M4   Dodson, J. T. - Decd. D.S.Harris - guardian - 163, 180

M4   Dodson, J. T. - Decd. W.C.Wilson - guardian - 167

R2   Dodson, John T. - 17 to 22, 156, 157

R3   Dodson, J. T. - Estate - 262 to 264, 367

R4   Dodson, J. T. - Decd. Estate - 423

R15B115 Dodson, J. T. - Decd. Estate - guardianship of W.C.Webster - 110,115

M3   Dodson, Mary - Estate - P.62,63,92,171,177 to 180

R2   Dodson, Mary - Estate - 498 to 507

R3   Dodson, Mary - Estate - 138 to 141, 289,629

M1(2) Dodson, Nimrod - Estate - 54,55,76,120,148,438,449,450,451,452

R12A   Dodson, Nimrod - Decd. Estate - 212 to 218,443 to 450,589 to 596

M9   Dodson, Mrs. Virginia H. - Decd. Estate - 455, 456

W1   Dodson, Virginia - 285

R26   Dorrough, A. V. - 26 - 59, 66

R28   Dorrough, Ana Verna - 28 - 752,759

        Dorrough, A. V. - 85, 86

        Dorrough, Ana Verna - 477, 481

M6   Dorsey, Maria to R. B. Turner - 408,409,410

M9   Doty, Lee - Decd. Estate - 472, 473

M10   Dotey, Lee - Decd. Estate - 76

R11   Doty, Lee - Decd. Estate - 153,154,155

M8   Doughty, George A. - Decd. Estate - 522

R9   Doughty, George A. - Decd. Estate - 30

R23   Doughty, Hazel - Inc _ 23 - 545,551

M6   Doughty, J. - Decd. guardian - Bond Addie West - 311

M5   Doughty, Joseph F. - Decd. L.C.Shirley, Admr. - 5,7,8,14,15,35,43,250,254

R5   Doughty, Joseph F. - Decd. Estate - 356

R23   Doughty, M. F. - Decd. - 23 - 875,885

W2   Doughty, M. F. - Will & Proof - 510,512

M9   Doughty, T. B. - from David M.Anderson - Estate - 45

R9   Doughty, = to David Anderson - et al - 164,165

R16   Doughty, Thomas Earl - Decd. - 173,175

R14   Doughty, Z. J. - Estate - 316,317,374 to 380

R15   Doughty, Z. J. - Decd. - 38, 43

R16   Doughty, Z. J. - Decd. - 534,542

M1(1) Doughti, N.J.F., - Estate of - 417,431,432,468,551

R13   Dowd, James S. - Estate - 311 thru 313

M9   Dowdle, J. E. - guardian for Verdal Lee - 263,362

R9   Dowdle, J. E. - guardian Verdell Loe - 546,547

R10   Dowdle, J. E. - Guardian for Verdell Loe - 177

       R11A Dowdle, James T. - 225,231

R20   Dozier, Lacy Franklin - Inc. - 20 - 583,587-9

R13   Dralet, George - Letters Testamentary, etc. - 234, 235

W2   Dralet, George - 68

M9   Driver, Anna E. - Decd. Estate - 193,194

R13   Driver, Wiley (Col) Estate - 463,464,465,466,467,468,469,470

M8   Duck, Graden Lee - Minor, O.F.Taylor - guardian - 60

R7   Duck, Grandeo Lee - Minor, O.L.Taylor, guardian - 580

M8   Duck, Timothy - Decd. Estate - 498,500,506

R8   Duck, Timothy - Decd. Estate - 524, 535

M10   Duckworth, Daniel D. - Decd. Estate - 589

M1(1)   Duke, Nancy - Estate of - 4

M1(1)   Dumas, E.B.M.- Estate of - 395,405,406,434,& 588,551

M(3)   Dumas, E. W. - Estate of - 139,140,141

R11A   Dumas, E. W. - 89, 91

R11A   Duncan, Daniel - 28,31,249

M1(2)   Duncan, David - Estate - 647,659

M4   Duncan, David - Decd. Estate - 332,340,343,356,367,612,621,620

R4   Duncan, David - decd. Estate - Thos.E.Goodwin, admr. - 514

M10   Duncan, Jessie, Pauline & Coleman - condemnation of land - 508,509,510,511,512, 513,514,515,516,517

M9   Dunmore, Nan - Decd. Estate - 138,167,168,169,170,217

R9   Dunmore,,Nan - Decd. Eatate - 443,444,320,355,356,357,358,359,360,361,362,363,3(

M5   Dunn, John A. - Decd. Estate - 107,112,(612)

R11A   Dunn, John L. - 231, 238

M1(2)   Dunn, John S. - Estate - 191,192,235,236,237,250,251,416,545,544,556,660,641

M(3)   Dunn, J. S. - Estate of - 167 to 170

R11A   Dunn, John S. - 64,67,231,238

R12A   Dunn, John S. - Decd. Estate - 677 to 679

W1A   Dunn, John S. - 289,290,579,582

R25   Dunn, Melvin - Inc. - 25 - 529, 535

R11A Durr, P. David - 82, 83

R11A Durr, Susan C. - 92

R21   Dyer, Earline Johnson - Decd. Estate - 21 - 110, 119

W2   Dyer, Earline Johnson - Will - 438-39

R11A Dyer, Gilbert M. - 252, 257

R20   Dyer, Virgie - Decd. Estate of - 20 - 232,242

W2   Dyer, Virgie - Will & Proof - 403,404

M4   Eads, Tollie - adopted by Jno. W. Jones - 591

R20   Earnest, Ervin - Estate Of - 20 - 159,166

M1(2) Earnest, James - 443,444,571,(511)

W1A   Earnest, James - Estate of - 507 thru 513

R21   Earnest, John - Decd. - 21 - 215, 221

W2   Earnest, John - Will & Proof - 451

R20   Earnest, Martha Ellen - Estate of - 20 -103, 106

M10   Earnest, M. F. - Decd. Estate - 15, 16

M9   Earnest, Salina - Decd. Estate - 110,113,114

W1   Earnest, Salina - 142

R9   Earnest, Salina - Decd. Estate - 282,283,284

R10   Earnest, W. F. - Estate - 570,571,572

M5   Eason, Harrison - Decd. Estate - 37,45,46,47,60,40,65,74,210

R6B   Eason, Harrison - Decd. Estate - 252

R11A   Eaton, George W. - 278, 280

R25   Echelle, Jean, - name changed from Nans Ectman - 25 - 731

R25   Eichman, Hans -change of name - 25 - 731

R21   Edgeworth, Dorothy, - Decd. - 21 - 244, 249

R13   Edmonds, S. Ike - Decd. - 128, 129

M6   Edney, John N. - Estate - 90

R13   Egan, Stella Maria, Mrs. Pienina Egan - Gdn. for final settlement,etc.- 255,56

W2   Eitsen, Susan Victoria - Will - 305

R17   Eitsen, Susan Victoria - decd. - 265, 266

M7   Election for Prohibition - 173

M9   Elliott, Mattie E. - Guardian - 497 to 499

R10   Elliott, Mattie E. - Guardian - 478,479,480

M9   Elliott, Ray - Estate - 522

M10   Elliott, Roy - Decd. Estate - 79,80,81

R10   Elliott, Roy - Estate - 516,517

R11   Elliott, Ray - Decd. Estate - 54,158,159,160,161,612,163

M(3)   Ellis, James - Estate of - 257,258,259,345,259,258,257

R1A   Elis, James - Estate - 237,238,540 to 544

M1(1) Ellis, William - Estate of - 74,136,299,312,313

W2   Ellis, W. L. - 285

R17   Ellis, W. L. - Decd. - 14, 17

R19   England, Mary Fletcher R., et al. vs. John C. Robertson - 19 - 530,532

M1(2) Enis, Thomas D. - Claim - 97

M8   Erwin, John - Decd. Estate - Roland J. Hagood, Admr. - 79

R8   Erwin, John - 241

M8   Erwin, Nancy J. - Decd. Estate - Roland J.Hagood, Admr. - 80,89,94,109,120,142,
        146,198,199,201,210,215,216,224,234,247,264,272,273

R8   Erwin, Nancy J. - Decd. Estate - 70, 84,85,228

M9   Espey, Thomas - Decd. Estate - 72,76

W1   Espy, Thos. - 140

R9   Espy, Thomas - Decd. Estate - 220

R25   Essary, Sara Lee - Minor - 25 - 469,473

R27   Estes, H. W. - Decd. - 27 - 113,123 - Vol. R. 27 - 226

R27   Estes, H. W. - Decd. - 27 - 434

M2   Evans, Isham W. - Estate - 322

W1A   Evans, Isham - 31

M5   Evans, Salina E. - Insane - 164

R17   Everett, Ella B. - Incompetent - 206-07

M9   Everette, J. H. - Decd. Estate - 472

M10   Everett, J. H. - Decd. Estate - 18

R10   Everett, J. H. - Decd. Estate - 583,584

R23   Faley, Wanda - Minor - 23 - 937,940

M(3)   Fallop, Jesse - Estate of - 147,148,149,150,151,152

R24   Falls, Dwight L. - Decd. - 24 - 331,339

W2   Falls, Dwight L. - Will & Proof - 535,536

M9   Falls, Victor Calvin - Decd. Estate - 363,364

R10   Falls, Victor Calvin - Decd. Estate - 180,181,182,183 to 185,186

M10   Farquhar, Ewell C. - Decd. Estate - 444,445

W2   Farquhar, Ewell C. - 26, 27

M1(2)   Farquhar, James - Estate - 676

M(3)   Farquhar, James - Estate of - 340,349,580,581

R1A   Farquhar, James, Sr. - Estate - 768 to 771

R16   Farquhar, W. W. - Decd. - 163,168

W2   Farquhar, W. W. - 261,262

M2   Farquhar, William - Estate - 696,699,774 to 776,784,785,786,787,788,790,791

M3   Farquhar, William - Estate - P-300,408,508

M4   Farquhar, William - Decd. Estate - J.Henry, admr. - 408,418,420,421,423,532,
                                                              540,543,552

R2   Farquhar, William - Estate - 317 to 329

R-3   Farquhar, William - Estate - 315 to 321

R5   Farquhar, William - Decd. Estate - 208

R14   Fayette County, vs. Charles Atkinson - et al - 17 through 25

R16   Fayette County, vs. Lonzo Baccus - et al. - 261,266

R18   Fayette County, vs. Katherine B. Bruex, etc. - 18 - 213,228

R14   Fayette County, vs. W. M. Cannon, Sr. - et al - 450,452

R14   Fayette County, vs. W. M. Cannon, - et al - 478 through 509

R17   Fayette County, Condemnation - 346,355,366,377

M10   Fayette Co., Ala. - Condemnation of lands, vs. - 519,520,521,522,523,524,525,
                                                          526,527
M10   Fayette Co., Ala. - condemnation of lands, vs. R.H.Harkins - etal - 532,533,534,
                                                          535,536,537,538,540
M10   Fayette Co., Ala. - Condemnation of lands, vs. W.C.McCaleb & J.H.Hallmark - 351,
                                                          352,353,354,355
M10   Fayette Co., Ala. - Condemnation of lands, vs. W.C.McCaleb - 356,357,358,359

M10   Fayette Co., Ala. - Condemnation of lands, vs. W.T.Pate, etals - 410 to 415,
                                               431 to 437, 438 to 442

M10   Fayette Co., Ala. - Condemnation of lands, vs. Tom Spiller,H.G. & C.Y.Taylor -
                             360,361,362,363,364,365

R14   Fayette County, vs. Icia Cook, - et. al - 7 thru 14

R21   Fayette County, vs. Roy D.Couch - et al - 21 - 605, 706

R19   Fayette County, vs. Ezra Cunningham - et al. - 19 - 1 - 17

R16   Fayette County, vs. Delta Farm & Timber Co. - 20,22

R22   Fayette County, vs. Billy Ray & Ethelene Frost - 22 - 618, 634

R24   Fayette County, vs. Dot Austin Fowler - et al - 24 - 613, 636

R21   Fayette County, vs. Lonie Freeman, et al - 21 - 175,210

R18   Fayette County, vs. Macon W. Gravlee - 18 - 413,434

R27   Fayette County, vs. A. M. Grimsley, Jr. - et al - 27 - 61, 104

R16   Fayette County, vs. Felix Grimsley - et al - 31,33

R16   Fayette County, vs. Jack Harris - et al - 222-26,231,232

R18   Fayette County, vs. Thos. W. Hollingsworth - 18 - 199, 212

R23   Fayette County, vs. Hollis - et al - 23 - 941,966

R16   Fayette County, vs. Lotta W. Hollis - et al - 525,532

R14   Fayette County, vs. A. J. Huffman - et al - 399 through 409

R16   Fayette County, vs. Frank Johnson - et al - 227,230,230-247

R27   Fayette County, vs. Frank Johnson - 27 - 261

R15   Fayette County, vs. R.T.McCartney & W.H.A.Killingsworth & W.Ruth Thredkeld &
                                    Minor Heirs-468,479

R16   Fayette County, vs. William O. McCluskey - et al - 507, 513

M7   Fayette County, vs. D. O. McConnell - 515 to 520

R14   Fayette County, vs. Jeff McDonald & W. - 350 thru 357

R16   Fayette County, vs. Clyde Mullinax - et al - 251, 260

R16   Fayette County, vs. Belton Nelson - et al - 268-276

R27   Fayette County, vs. Alton Perry - et al - 27 - 497, 533

R23   Fayette County, vs. Wilma Roberts - etal - 23 - 853, 869

R15   Fayette County, vs. Jack Shepherd - et al - 97, 112

R16   Fayette County, vs. Joyce Garrison Smith - et al - 286, 303

R19   Fayette County Hospital Board - Agreement with State of Ala. - 199, 200

R24   Fayette County, vs. Art Stewart & W. - 24 - 190, 198

R17   Fayette County, vs. Earl Stoker & W. & Purleen Stoker & W. - 214

R25   Fayette County, vs. Jean Wilton Swanson - et al - 25 - 777, 819

R14   Fayette County, vs. John Trimm - et al - defendants - 430 thru 435

R13   Fayette County, vs. John Albert Ward - et al - 508 thru 513

R18   Fayette County, vs. Harris Welburn - et al - 18 - 60, 79

R20   Fayette County, vs. Sam Welburn, et - & Weyerhouser Co. - 20 - 111,143

R19   Fayette County, vs. Weyerhouser Co. - 19 - 543, 560

R21   Fayette County, vs. Weyerhouser Co. - 21 - 28, 43

R22   Fayette County, Vs. Travis Whitehead - et al - 22 - 48, 90

R22   Fayette County, vs. Travis & Dovie Whitehead - 22 - 91, 105

R13   Fayette County, vs. W.C.Williams, G.Lee & Ollie Thompson,   J.V. & Ida
       Tarwater, Vera Millan, Sarah Nall, Ellen Dean & Brenda Gail McCarthy &
       Eloise McCarthy -

R19   Fayette County, vs. James B. Wommack - et al - 19 - 561,590

M7   Fayette, Town of, extension of Corporate Limits - 401

M3   Fayetteville, Town of, Incorporation of Town - P-371

M4   Fears, Mollie Josephine, change of name & adoption by Wilson Fears - 569

M1   February 6th, 1882 - 169

M1   February 5, 1883 - 198

M1   February Term, 1895 - 586

M1(1) Ferguson, James - 5,6,22,23

M9   Ferguson, Mrs. Rebecca - Decd. Estate - 400, 401

W1   Ferguson, Rebecca - 270,271,272

M2   Ferguson, Samuel J. - J.B.Ferguson, Admr. - 516, to 518, 527 to 528, 532

M3   Ferguson, Samuel J. - Decd. Estate - P.560,561,578,579,580

R2   Ferguson, Samuel J. - Estate - 1 to 6, 26 to 29, 42,

R3   Ferguson, S. J. - Estate - 432, 642 to 646

R11A   Flemings, Alexander - 294, 298

R13   Flemming, Alice Hall - 232

W2   Fleming, Alice Hall - 67

R11A   Flemings, William M. - 299, 301

M8   Fields, Dock - 36,40,42,43,223,229

        .R7 Field, Dock - Decd. Estate - Zoning Fields, Admr. - 514,515,540 to 543 to 547

R26   Fields, Essie - 26 - 470,476

M6   Fields, Samuel M. - dec. Petition for Letters Administration - 432

M6   Fields, Samuel M. - Dec. Administration Bond - 433

R20   Files, Denease - Minor - 20 - 209,222

M4   Finch, Willa - Ex. - 114

R26   Flippo, Joe - 26 - 958, 963

M1(2)   Floyd, John - 628,688,689,690,691,47,48,68,69,172,566

R12 A   Floyd, John - Decd. Estate - 451 to 455

W1A   Floyd, Johns - 596, 743,4

R11A   Fondren, Joseph J. - 289,294

M1   Forsyth, Edward N. L. - Decd. Estate - 94,149,153,260

R11   Forsyth, Edward M. - Decd. Estate - 192,193,339,340,341,346,347,474

M9   Fortenberry, P. N. - guardian - 36,37,147,148

R9   Fortenberry, P. N. - guardian - 155,156,157,329,330

R14   Ford, Bertha P. - Estate of - 1 thru 6

M1(2)   Ford, Daniel, Estate - 155

M(3)   Ford, Daniel - Estate of - 153 to 167

R11A   Ford, Daniel - 281,282,288

W1A   Ford, David - 260

M5   Ford, James - Decd. Estate - 280

M8   Ford, N. J. - Decd. Estate - H. P. Roberts, Admr. - 413,489,493

R8   Ford, N. J. - decd. Estate - H.P.Roberts, Admr. - 472

R28   Fortner, Deborah Jane - 28 - 4.

M1   Foster, Abner - order of removal & C., - 325

M 3)   Foster, Andrew J., - Estate of - 546,547,548,549

R23   Foster, Connie - Inc. - 23 - 691,697

M1(1) Foster, Thomas L. - Estate of-3 -

R23   Foster, W. M. - Inc. - 23 - 698,704

R26   Fowler, Billie - 26 - 729, 769

       Fowler, Billie C. & Carrie Elizabeth - Will - 220 - 222

R10   Fowler, C. W. - et al, joint owners to sell land - 227,228,229,230,241,242

R10   Fowler, C. W. & A. W. Cannon - et al, joint owners - 409,410,411,412

M9   Bowler, C. W. & J. B. - et al, Joint owners - 386,387,394,404,463,465

R25   Fowler, Comet Leland - Decd. - 25 - 621,624

R24   Fowler, Delia - Decd. - 24 - 215, 218

M8   Fowler, Dexter Wardlow - Decd. Estate - H.T.Fowler, Admr. - 418,420

R8   Fowler, Dexter (Woodlin) - decd. Estate - 476

M1   Fowler, Felix - 555

M8   Fowler, Fester - et al, joint owners - 398,406,416

R14   Fowler, F. M. - Deceased - 453,454,455

R15   Fowler, F. M. - Estate - 113,297,298

R8   Fowler, Foster, Lizzie Moore - et al, joint owners - 450

R23   Fowler, Howard Thomas - Decd. - 23 - 893,897

M1(1) Fowler, James - Estate of - 11,17,61,174,181,182,183,184,186,188,445,448

M(3)   Fowler, James - Estate of - 175 to 181,593,594,595,596,597,598 to 603

R1A   Fowler, James - Estate - 535 to 539,614,730

R17   Fowler, James A. - 185,198

W2   Fowler, James A. - Deceased - 301

R11A   Fowler, James D. - 302, 304

M9   Fowler, James T. - decd. Estate - 406,478

R10   Fowler, James T. - decd. Estate - 258,275,431, etc.

Fowler, John - Decd. Estate of - Wm. Foster, Admr. - 343,344,345,431,396,397,346,347

M3   Fowler, John - Deceased Estate - P.499

R3   *Fowler, John - decd. Estate - 616

R3   Fowler, John - Estate - 616 710

R11A   Fowler, John - 304, 307

M9   Fowler, J. L. - et al, joint owners - 161

M9   Fowler, J. L. - decd. Estate - 319,320,351,352

R10   Fowler, J. L. - decd. Estate - 96,98,99,100,101,102,103,104,159,160,161,162

M6   Fowler, John W. - Estate - 82,83,84

R6B   Fowler, John W. - Decd. Estate - 213

M5   Fowler, Julia C. - Estate (et al) Heirs - 13, 30

W2   Fowler, Leroy M. - Will - 359

M4   Fowler, Lovina - Decd. Minor Heir of P.M.Newton - Guardian - 156

R4   Fowler, Lavina - Minor heirs of P.M.Newton - guardian - 476

M8   Fowler, M. R. - guardian for Jessie Dobbs, Minor - 489

R8   Fowler, M. R. -guardian - 536

R22   Fowler, N. P. - Decd. - 22 - 585,596

W2   Fowler, N. P. - Will & Proof - 482-83

M7   Fowler, Orceni S. - Decd. Estate - 100

R6B   Fowler, Orion S. - decd. Estate - 456

R24   Fowler, Olen - Decd. - 24 - 209,212

R17   Fowler, Perry M. - decd. - 476,81-82-83

R19   Fowler, Perry (Pervey)M. - Estate of - 19 - 421,425

R16   Fowler, Robert W. & James A. - Minors - 181,186

M3   Fowler, Stephen - Deceased - Minor Heirs, Mary Ann Fowler - Gdn. - P.513

R14   Fowler, Thomas L. - Decd. Estate - 154 thru 169

R8   Fowler, U. E. - guardian - 570

M8   Fowler, V. E. - guardian for Ethel & Lecil Dobbs, Minors - 490

R13   Franklin, James E. - To change name - 532

M1(1)   Franks, Gabriel - Estate of - 236,272,416,419,497

R13   Franks, Mrs. Ida - Estate - 274 thru 283

W2	Franks, Mrs. Ida - 70, 71
M9	Franks, J. W. - Decd. Estate - 528
M1	Franks, J. W. - Decd. Estate - 194,195
R11	Franks, J. W. - Decd. Estate - 406,401,(407)
R21	Franks, Morgan Jerry - Decd. - 21 - 707,709
R21	Franks, Morgan Jerry - Decd. - 21 - 710,717
M10	Franks, Will H. - Decd. Estate - 548,549,555 to 559
R28	Frazier, Sallie Robertson - 28 - 449,452,505,515
	Frazier, Sally Robertson - 392,394,406,410
R24	Frederick, Cenie - Inc. - 24 - 645,650
R13	Freeman, Mrs. Agnes - Gdn. Jimmie Lou, Freda Mae & J.H.Freeman,Jr.,Minors - 353 thru 359
M8	Freeman, A.H. & M.E. - Decd. Estate W.L.Freeman, Admr. - 164,172,173,174,179, 185,190,251,258
R8	Freeman, A.H. & M.E. - Decd. Estate - W.L.Freeman, Admr. - 130,156
M6	Freeman, B. Frank - 168, 212
R6B	Freeman, B. F. - Decd. - 272 to 285
M9	Freeman, G. W. - Decd. Estate - 166
R9	Freeman, G. W. - Decd. Estate - 373,374
M9	Freeman, J. F. - et al, joint owners - 15
R9	Freeman, J. F. - et al, joint owners - 124,135
M10	Freeman, J. H. - Decd. Estate - 584,585
M10	Freeman, J. N. - Decd. Estate - 574, 575
W2	Freeman, J. N. - 41,42
M9	Freeman, Julia - Decd. Estate - 478,479
R11	Freeman, Lela - Decd. Estate - 31,32
M10	Freeman, Lole - Decd. Estate - 34,458
M6	Freeman, Mrs. Lou - Estate - 170,212
R6B	Freeman, Lou - Decd. Estate - 262,288 to 309
M8	Freema-, Malissa - widow of George W. Owens - 570, 575
M2	Freeman, Martha - Estate - 7

M9   Freeman, Martha (col.) - Estate - 512

W1A   Freeman, Martha - 84

R10   Freeman, Math - 509

W1   Freeman, Math - 315,316,317,318

M8   Freeman, M.L., - as Mother of Florence, F.R., Mattie L.,Eula & John Freeman,
                                                  Minors - 275

R14   Freeman, W. D. - Deceased - 574, 577

M1(2) Freeman, William - Decd. Estate - 77,78,79,80,81,523,538,539,551,552,643

M1(2) Freeman, William - Estate, North River - 428,429,436,437,444,460,463

M1(2) Freeman, Wm., - Estate, L.N.Cole, informed settlement - 762

M2   Freeman, William - Estate - 15,420,400,401,398,399

W1A   Freeman, Wm. - 318 to 322,331,332,337,384,537,539,550,554,556,585,586

M1(1) Freeman, William B. - Estate of - 193,198,200,208,239

R12A   Freeman, William - Deceased - 166 to 172, 272 to 275

M9   Fulford, Edward Cleveland - Decd. Estate - 435

M10   Fulford, Joe Arnold - Minor - 172,173

R11   Fulford, Joe Arnold - Minor - 382,383,387

R10   Fulford, Roma - guardian - 394

R13   Fullerton, J. H. - Estate - 267 thru 273

M8   Fulmer, Rhoda - Frank & Howard Fulmer - Minors - 32,33

R20   Gaddis, Effie R. - Inc. - 20 - 623,626

W2   Gale, Hester Sinclair - Will, Letter of Testamentory, etc. - 394,397

M1(1) Gallop, Jesse - Estate of - 360,376,377,396,397,468

M1(2) Gallop, M. W. - Estate - 357,382,383,409,637,638

R11A   Gallop, Murpy W. - 338,342

W1A   Gallop, M. W. - 281 thru 283

R28   Galloway, Bonnie Jane - 28 - 408

R23   Galloway, C. L. - Decd. - 23 - 733, 740

M1(1) Galloway, Thmmas - Estate of - 55, 59,60,61,62

M8   Galloway, W. P. - guardian - 134

R8   Galloway, W. P. - guardian - 100

R9   Gammon, J. L. - Decd. Estate - 167,168,257,258,256,293

M9   Gammon, J. T. - Decd. Estate - 47,110,111

M7   Gammon, L. F. - Decd. Estate - 111, 123

R6B   Gammons, L. F. - Decd. Estate - J.L.Gammon, Admr. 494 to 497

R27   Gardner, B. B. - 27 - 942,952

       Gardner, B. B. - 326,329

M10   Garrison, Edgar Lee - Decd. Estate - 544

W1A   Garrison,   - Estate - 332 thru 336,348 thru 350,19,20

R27   Garrison, J.'E. - Decd. - 27 - 105,112, Will Vol. 3, 198,200,263,264

       Garrison, J. E. - 198,200

R4   Garrison, James - Minor, David H.Baker, guardian - 320 to 322

R16   Garrison, John T. - Deceased - 178,180,248,249

W2   Garrison, John T. - 264, 265

R6B   Garrison, S. C. - application on order charging minor - 260

R21   Garrison, Stephen E. - Decd. Estate of - 21 - 129,134

W2   Garrison, Stephen E. - Will & Proof - 452

M1(2) Garrison, Thomas G. - Estate - 426,427,430,448,631

R3   Garrison, Thomas G. - decd. Estate - 711 to 717, 770 to 775

R4   Garrison, Thomas G. - Estate - 528

M⌣   Garrison. Thomas G. - Deceased Estate - P.596.597.610.611.616.667

M4   Garrison, Thomas P. - Decd. Estate - 122,134 to 137,146,299,342,248,352 to 255

M1(2) Gartmen, Daniel - Decd. Estate - 75

R12 A.Gartman, Daniel - Decd. Estate - 371,372

M1(2) Gartman, John W. - Estate - 22,150,219,220,221,222,223,470,471,492,707,710,711,
                                                                  712,224,225
R12A   Gartman, John W. - Decd. Estate - 331 to 338, 729 to 735

M10   Gartman, Modell & Lottie - Minor Estate - 37

R11   Gartman, Modell & Lottie - Estate - 38,39

R15   Gary, J. C. - Minor - 369,71

R1A   Gault, James, - Estate - 642

W1A   Gautman, John - 452 thru 455, 754,755

R23   Gay, L. K. - Deceased - 23 - 769,775

W2   Gay, L. K. - Will & Proof - 500, 501

R23   Gay, Sam & - Deceased - 23 - 299,303

M1(1) Geartman, Frederick - Estate of - 480,547

M1(1) Gee, Jeremiah - Estate of - 114

M(3)   Gee, Samuel D., - Estate of 182 to 184

R1A   Gee, Samuel D. - Estate - 381 to 383

M10   Geer, W. P. - Decd. Estate - 41, 42

R11   Geer, W. P. - Decd. Estate - 55, 56

R19   Gentry, Pearl - 19 - 385,388

M4   Georgia Pacific R.R.C. - 54,53,56,57,59,70,71,72,75

M3   Georgie Pacific R.R.C. - R/O/W David Berry;, Deceased - p. 536

M3   Georgie Pacific R.R.C. - R/O/W Thomas Gray, Deceased - P. 551

M3   Georgia Pacific R.R.C - R/O/W Jonas B. McClung - P.545

.M3   Georgia Pacific R.R.C - R/O/W J.H.Willigham, Estate - P.553,580,592,561 .

R27   Gibson, Annie Winn - See Vol. 27 - P. 295,301, Vol. 27,Proof of Will - 302,304

        Gibson, Annie Winn - (see Vol.27,p.295,301 - Est. P. 302, Proof, 304)

R23   Gibson, Archie J. - Decd. - 23 - 475,483

M2   Gibson, Benjamin - 718,719,727,278,729

M3   Gibson, Benjamin - Estate - P.22,49,264,318,-15

M4   Gibson, Benjamin - Estate - 31,32,33

R2   Gibson, Benjamin - Estate - 330 to 338

R3   Gibson, Benjamin - Estate - 170,171,365

M8   Gibson, D. C. - Decd. Estate - Mrs. Pearl I. Gibson - Admx. - 238,331,341

R8   Gibson, D. C. - Decd. Estate - 266

R10   Gibson, F. C. - guardian - 299,300,400,401

M2   Gibson, Joel E. - Guardian - 179 to

W1A   Gibson, Joel Elvander - for Minor heirs of M.J.Gibson - 136

M9   Gibson, Mary - A Minor, F.C.Gibson, guardian - 425,418,419

M1(2) Gibson, Nancy - Substitution record Marriage Licenses - 118 (John Gibson &Nancy)
                      Mobley - by Wm. P.Harvey, J.P. - 13 July 1858 MGCharly Grayham
                      15 July 1857 - (580 - (59)   J of Peace

M1(2) Gibson, Tilmon - 400

M(3)   Gibson, Tilmon - Estate of - 392,393 to 401

R11A   Gibson, Tilmon - 336,338

R18   Gibson, Victor F. - Estate of - 18 - 337,366

W2   Gibson, Victor F. - Deceased - Will & Proof - 344-45

R14   Gibson, Virgil B. - Decd. Estate of 381, 386

W2   Gibson, Virgil B. - 124, 125

R11   Gibson, W. F. - Decd. Estate - 395,396,397,443,444,445

M10   Gibson, W. F. - Decd. Estate - 187,188,234,235

M4   Gilbreath, Miles M. - Guardian - 481

R16   Gilliam, Flora Mae & A.D., Nadine - Minor - Sale of Land - 196,200

R13   Gilliam, Mrs. Mary - Gdn. for Mary Bell Gilliam - 246,247,248,249,250

M1(2) Gilliam, Peter, - Decd. Estate - 151, 154

R11A   Gilliam, Peter - Estate - 342, 345

R12A   Gilliam, Peter - Decd. Estate - 404 to 408

R2   Gilpin, Alexander - Estate - 148 to 151

Gilpin, Fay & Ina Mirian - Ida Gilpin, Gdn. - 292 thru 296

M2   Gilpin, Alex - Estate - 557,558

Minors - 148

R13   Gladden, John Martin - Gdn. for Annie Joyce, Thos. Belton & Bobbie Caroll Gray,

R21   Gladden, Roscoe - Decd. Estate of - 21 - 99, 105

W2   Gladden, Roscoe - 445, 446

R17   Glen Allen - Town of - Inc. - 331,36

M4   Glover, J. N. - Decd. Estate - 489,500

R5   Glover, J. N. - Decd. Estate - 130

R25   Godsey, Neal Fred - Decd. - 25 - 241,244

M1   Going, Bob - 556

M(3)   Goodwin, A. P. - Estate of - 270,274,273,272,274,555,556

R1A   Goodwin, A. P. - Estate - 734

R11A   Goodwin, A. P. - 122, 124

R17   Goddwin, Mrs. Bessie B. - Guardian - 262,64

M10   Goodwin, E. P. - Decd. Estate - 126,177,178

R11   Goodwin, E. P. - Decd. Estate - 276,277

R15   Goodwin, Gaines Lee - Decd. - 389,97

R20   Goodwin, Mary - Decd. Estate of - 20 - 607,616

W2   Goodwin, Mary - Will & Proof - 434,35

R15   Goodwin, Michael Lee & Shirley Deanne - Minors - 505, 507

M4   Goodwin, Thomas E. - Guardian, Admr. - 555

M7   Goodwin, Thos. E. - Decd. Estate of - E.P.Goodwin - Admr. - 210,211

R7   Goodwin, Thomas E. - Decd. Estate - E.P.Goodwin, Admr. - 50,51,52

M9   Goolsby, C. D. - Decd. Estate - 214,215

W1   Goolsby, C. D. - 243,244

R9   Goolsby, E. C. - Decd. Estate - 439,440,441

W2   Gordon, Raymond C. - Will & Proof - Will & Proof - 559, 560

R14 Gorman, Donald A. - Minor - 415,578

R17   Gorman, Donald D. - 233, 235

M9   Grace, Missouri J. - Decd. Estate - 476

M10	Grace, Missouri J. - Decd. Estate - 46, 47
R11	Grace, Missouri J. - Decd. Estate - 71, 77
R10	Grace, Missouri J. - Decd. Estate - 417,418,419
R4	Graham, Clay - Decd. Estate - 38,39,40
M8	Graham, Mrs. Dora - guardian for 4 Minors - 377,549,565,574,582
R8	Graham, Mrs. Dora - guardian - 424
R9	Graham, Dora - guardian - 104
R1A	Grand Jury - Report of - 768
R28	Gravlee, Bradley H. - 28 - 182, 186
M9	Gravlee, C. M. - Decd. Estate - 525,526
R10	Gravlee, C. M. - Decd. Estate - 528
W1	Gravlee, C. M. - 322,323,324,325
M9	Gravlee, G. W. - Decd. Estate - 476, 477
R10	Gravlee, G. W. - Decd. Estate - 373
R19	Gravlee, G. W. - Estate of - 19 - 183,186
R20	Gravlee, G. W. - Estate of - 20 - 195,201
W1	Gravlee, G. W. - 295
R19	Gravlee, Macon W. - Estate of - Vol. 19 - 18,28,440,441
W2	Gravlee, Macon W. - Will - 338
M8	Gravlee, Mary Bridges - Decd. Estate - Wiley W. Gravlee, Admr. - 185
R8	Gravlee, Mary Bridges - Decd. Estate - 186
R19	Gravlee, Nell Branyon - Minor - 19 - 29, 35
R22	Gravlee, Nell Branyon - Minor - 22 - 805,809
M9	Gravlee, Wiley - Admr. - 156
R13	Gravlee, Wiley W. - Estate - 82,90
R23 -	Gray, Annie Joyce - Minor - 23 - 65, 114
R13	Gray, Bobbie Carroll - Minor - 23 - 115, 176
R20	Gray, Edward Lee - Minor - 20 - 179,182
R18	Gray, Elmer Ruth - Inc. - 18 - 48, 59

M4   Gray, Mrs. Fanny - Proceeding for Dower - 269,289,296 to 298,300,303

M5   Gray, Mrs. Francis - guardian - 348, 362

M6   Gray, George W. - Decd. Estate - 430

R6B   Gray, George W. - Decd. Estate - John Y. Taylor - 383,384

R25   Gray, Glenda Sue - Inc. - 25 - 849,855

M3   Gray, James - Estate Minor Heirs of Thomas Gray - Deceased - P. 594

M5   Gray, James T. - Estate - 332

R6B   Gray, James T. - Decd. Estate - 108

M1   Gray, James W. - 14, 15

M8   Gray, Mary Frances - adopted & name changed - J.W.Reggs - 198

R19   Gray, Ralph O'Neal - Estate of - 19 - 413,420

M1(1)   Gray, Richard, vs. Ashcraft & Shppherd - Writ of Adquardennum - 92,104

R20   Gray, Richard O'Neal - Minor - 20 - 183,186

R3   Gray, Thomas - Decd. Estate - Mrs. Gray, guardian forheirs - 708,709

R4   Gray, Thomas - Decd. Estate - 470

R23   Gray, Thomas Belton - Minor - 23 - 1 - 63

M2   Grayham, Clay - -72,773,792,793

M3   Grayham, Clay - Estate - P.46,236,694,705

R2   Grayham, Clay - Estate - 393 to 400

R3   Grayham, Clay - Estate - 269,270

R3   Green, Henry - Estate - 288 (278)

R14   Green, Mattie A. - Deceased - 79,80,456,457

M1(1)   Freer, Henry - Estāte of - 33,34,349,451,452,491,492

M1(2)   Greer, Henry - Estate - 254,302,303,326,327,328,330,331,387

R1A   Greer, Henry - Estate - 145,245,246

R11A   Greer, Henry - 16 to 18

R12A   Greer, Henry - Decd. Estate - 561 to 565

W1A   Greer, Henry - 254, 255

R1A   Greer, Henry M. - Estate - 629

M10   Greer, Peter - Incompeter - 483,546,547,580

R13   Greer, Peter - Incompetent - 60,63,229,230,231,350,351,352

R14   Greer, Peter - Incompetent - 61

R16   Greer, Peter - Incompetent - 11

R17   Greer, Peter - Incompetent - 261

R19   Greer, Peter - Incompetent - 19 - 457,512

R22   Greer, Peter - Incompetent - 22 - 572,584

R21   Greer, Peter - Incompetent - 21 - 385,404

M2   Greeg, Jesse B. - Estate - 679,699,758,777,778

M3   Griggs, Jesse R. - Estate - P.25,45,272,273,330 to 332

R2   Griggs, Jesse - Estate - 348 to 358

R3   Grigg, Jesse - Estate - 259,353 to 358, 416,463

M1(1)   Gregory, James - Estate of - 103

R24   Gregory, Ruth Small - Inc. - 24 - 437,443

R26   Grey, Laura Lee H. - Change Name - 26 - 287,288

M1(2)   Griffin, Daniel - Estate - 72,130,166,190,445,166

R11A   Griffin, Daniel - Estate - 308 to 327

R12A   Griffin, Daniel - Decd. EState - 367 to 383

R13   Griffin, George & Eloise McCarthy Griffin, et al vs. Fayette Co. - 513 thru 526

R17   Griffin, George - Decd. - 210, 211

M1   Griffin, Lee - 358

M10   Griffin, Lee - Decd. Estate - 541

W1A   Griffin,   - 335,491,492

M7   Griffin, T. M. - guardian - 472,296,501

R7   Griffin, Thomas M. - Guardian - 372

M3   Griffin, Tracy - Estate - P. 38,39,40,41,50,51

M1(2)   Griffin, Troy - 488,497,516,517,585,611,624,634,635,637,649,656,657

M1   Griffin, Troy - 545

M2   Griffin, Troy - Estate - 18 to 23, 126

R2   Griffin, Troy - Estate - 540 to 543

R3   Griffin, Troy - Estate - 457, 458

W1A   Griffin, Troy - 448,449,465 thru 469,522,524,667,672 thru 674,715,753,770

R13   Grimsley, A. M. - Decd. - 444

R14   Grimsley, A. M. - deceased Estate - 216 thru 228, 326 through 329

W2   Grimsley, A. M. -   - 102,103

M8   Grimsley, Felix - Decd. Estate - 309

R8   Grimsley,Delix A. - Decd. Estate - 340,341

R24   Grimsley, Felix A. - Dedd. - 24 - 219,228

W2   Grimsley, Felix A. - Will & Proof - 526,27

       Grimsley, Harriette M.   - 487,490

R28   Grimsley, Harriette M. - 28 - 774,781,917,919

R17   Grimsley, John Clifford - Estate - 158,161,340

W2   Grimsley, John Clifford -   - 297,298

M2   Guin, Elze - Estate - 677,686,687,709,726

R2   Guin, Eliza - Estate - 340 to 347, 508 to 527, Michael Guin

M1(2) Guin, G. D. - 589,606

R11A   Guin, G. D. - Estate - 346,348

W1A   Guin, G. D. -   - 661 thru 666

W1   Guin, I? C. -   - 281

M7   Guin, Maurice - Decrss recovering diabitis of man - 467

R27   Guin, Maurice - 27 - 45,53

M2   Guin, Michael - Estate - 685,686

M3   Guinn, Michael - Estate - P. 36,37,49,86,87,88,89,185,190,192,193,334 to 337

R3   Guin, Michael & Eliza - Estate - 74 to 76, 358,363,377,378

R10   Guin, P. C. - Decd. Estate - 276,277,278,279,280

M3   Guin, Perry E. = Declaration adopting James Nichols - et al - P. 635

W1A   Gunp, Wms. - 447,448,456 thru458,478,492,493,517,518,715,753,770   .

R15   Gullett, George H. - Decd. 82, 85

W2   Gullett, George H. - 164,165

M10   Gunter, Mars. Annie White - guardian - 288,289,334,343,344,345,346,347,419

R11   Gunter, Mrs. Annie White - gdn. - 525,526,528,584,585,585,587,594,595,596,597

R13   Gunter, Marvin G. - Estate - 90,194

W2   Gunter, Marvin G. - 64

M2   Gurley, J. W. - Estate - 207,520 to 521,536,537,563

W1A   Gurley, J. W. - 171

R2   Gurley, James W.- Estate - 155 to 156

R2   Gurlays, James W. - Estate - 10 to 13, 42 to 45

R23   Guthrie, John - Decd. - 23 - 967,970

R8   Guyton, Arby - Decd. - Simon Guyton, admr - 583

M8   Guyton, Awbray, - Decd. Estate - Mrs. Senie Guyton, admrx. - 488

R2   Gwyn, Joanna E. - Estate - 14, 15

M2   Gwyn, James E. - Minor Jacob Chines, guardian - 518, 528,529

R11A   Gwyn, Morris - 328,335

M1(2)   Gwynn, William - Estate - 487,494,505,506,514,515,516,553,554,555,556,638,
                                                    702,703,714

M2   Gwyn, Wm., - 98

M2	Hagen, James J. - guardian for A.K.Stuart - 225
R11A	Hager, Jonahan - 382, 387
R21	Hagood, James Alfred - 21 - 211,214,363,364
M9	Hales, J. T. - father of 3 minors petition for fund in court of Ala. Power Co. - 345 - Fee Bk. G - 9 - 131
R20	Haley, Clara - Decd. Estate of - 20 - 202,208
W2	Haley, Clara E. - Will & Proof - 380,381
M1(2)	Haley, M.A.E. - Estate S. Haley , guardian - 611,617
W1A	Haley, Mary A. E. - S.Haley, guardian - 2,3,5,107
M2	Haley, Seckem - Guardian for minor heirs of M.A.E.Haley - 78,483, to 486
M8	Hall, James K. Vardman - name changed to Smith, adopted by T.A.Smith - 70
R27	Hall, L. C. - 27 - 654,662
W3	Hall, L. C. - Will Proof - Vol. 3 - 298,301
R13	Hall, Mary - Estate - 257,258
R16	Hall, Ollie - Decd. - 353,355
W2	Hall, Ollie - 273
R16	Hall, Samuel B. - Incompetent - 375,378
R14	Hall, V. G. - Decd. Estate of - 363 thru 367
R25	Hallman, Arrie - 25 - 975,979 - Vol. R26 - 5
R26	Hallman, Arrie - 26 - 587,592
M9	Hallman, Cynthia - decd. Estate - 377,378
R10	Hallman, Cynthia - Decd. Estate - 212,213
M9	Hallman, D. M. - Minor disabilities removed - 17
R20	Hallman, Henry Leroy - Dedd. Estate of - 20 - 227,231
R21	Hallman, Henry Leroy - Decd. Est. - 21 - 84, 94
M9	Hallman, Zora - Minor - 147,148
R9	Hallman, Zora - Minor - 329,157,158
M10	Hallmark, J. H. - etal condemnation of lands vs. Fayette Co., Ala. - 351,352, 353,354,355
M10	Hallmark, J. T. - Decd. Estate - 406,407,408
M4	Hallmark, W. F. - Guardian for J.T. & A.H.Hallmark - 125,142,143

R4	Hallmark, W. F. - guardian for Jas.T. & A.J.Hallmark - 312
M3	Hallmark, William H. - Estate - 379,380,397,714
R2	Hallmark, W. H. - Estate - 314 to 316
R25	Ham, Elizabeth K. - Incompetent - 25 - 521,524
R21	Ham, Fenton Harvey - Decd. Estate - 21 - 95,98,159,174
M3	Ham, Henry - Deceased Estate - p. 686,689,690,714,715
M4	Ham, Henry - Estate - 138,161,174 to 177
R4	Ham, Henry - Decd. Estate - 14 to 19, 30 to 36, 241 to 248
M1	Ham, H. J. - 30,31
M1	Ham, J. B. - 29, 30
M1(1)	Ham, Spias - Estate of - 65,77,97,98,106,107
M3	Ham, William - Deceased Estate - P.620,624,638,639,640,641,656,657
M4	Ham, William - Decd. Estate - 28,34 to 37,101,310,323,349,389,492,522,514
R4	Ham. Wm. - Decd. Estate J.B.Ham, Admr. - 23 to 29,76 to 92, 510
R14	Hamby, Edward Franklin - Deceased - 174,175,176
W2	Hamby, Edward Franklin - 91,92
M(3)	Hamby, George W. - Estate of - 550,551,552
M10	Hamby, John A. - Decd. Estate - 250,254,255,256
R11	Hamby, John G. - Decd. Estate - 466,477,478
R14	Hamby, John G. - Deceased - 174 thru 182
W2	Hamby, John G. - 5
R25	Hamby, Lillie M. - Incompetent - 25 - 720,730
	Hamby, Lily - 421
R24	Hamby, Myrtle B. - Incompetent - 24 - 703,709
R25	Hamilton, Betty Marle - Minor - 25 - 394,397
M1(1)	Hamilton, James P. - Estate of - 138,149,344,364,388,389
R25	Hamilton, Joseph Hollis - Decd. - 25 - 390,393
R25	Hamilton, Joseph Wayne - Minor - 25 - 402,405

R23	Hamilton, Robert F. - Decd. - 23 - 753,756
M10	Hamner, A. J. - Decd. Estate - 335
M10	Hamner, A. J. - sale of lands - 336,337
M10	Hamner, A. J. - 338, 339,340,341
R11	Hamner, A. L. - Estate - 587
R11	Hamner - A. L. - Estate - sale of lands - 588
M4	Hamner, Elizabeth - Insane - 357
M2	Hamner, H.W.J. - Estate - 280 to
M10	Hamner, Luard - Decd. Estate - 15
R10	Hamner, Luard - Decd. Estate - 573,574
R28	Hamner, Marion Snow - 28 - 550,551
	Hamner, Marion Snow - 403,405
M9	Hancock, John G. - adoption Virginia Hancock - 254
M9	Hancock, John G. - adoption Frances Hancock - 25-
R24	Handley, Buel - Decd. - 24 - 974,977
R16	Handley, Lidia - Incompetent - 381,85
R17	Handley, Lidia - Incompetent - 356,360
M4	Handley, Mary, St. - Guardian - 495
M4	Handley, Mary -_____ for Pro ___ & d.___ among Joint Owners - 447,472,482
M4	Handley, Sarah - non Comp ___ - 509,510
R14	Haney, Charlie - Decd. Estate - 197,198,310,311
R11A	Haney, William P. - 388,392,409,411
R3	Haney, William P. - Estate - 131,132,376,439
R11A	Hankins, Thomas - 373,378
W2	Hankins, Uridine J. - Will & Proof - 302
R17	Hankins, Uridine J. - Decd. Estate - 200, 205
R23	Harbin, Danny - Minor - 23 - 670,674
M9	Harbin, Felix - guardian Fred McDonald - 435,436
R10	Harben, Felix - guardian for Fred Dowell McDonald - 423
M10	Harbin, Grocer C. - Incompetent - 449

R13	Harbin, Grover C. - Incompetent - 5,6,7,8,9,10,11,12,13,14,15,16
R14	Harbin, Grover C. - Incompetent - 103 thru 108
R15	Harbin, Grover C. - Incompetent - 497,500
R17	Harbin, Grover C. - Incompetent - 3,6,463,64,65,66,67,68,69
R18	Harbin, Grover C. - Incompetent - 335
R20	Harbin, Grover C. - Incompetent - 20 - 765,781
R22	Harbin, Grover C. - Decd. - 22 - 561,567
R22	Harbin, Grover C. - Decd. - 22 - 795,804
M8	Harbin, J. L. - Estate - 44, 50
R7	Harbin, J. L. - Decd. Estate - 454
M10	Harbin, Louis Harbin - Decd. Estate - 326
R11	Harbin, Louis David - 573
M1	Harbin, Wm. A. - Apprentice to L.B.Harbin, Sr. - 50
M4	Hardleys, William, Newt & John - Ex-Habreas, Corpus & bail - 318
M9	Harkins, - Estate of Lige & Millie - 481
M9	Harkins, Caroline - decd. Estate - 42,43,56
R9	Harkins, Caroline - Decd. Estate - 162,163
M8	Harkins, D. A. - et al joint owner - 200,216
M8	Harkins, D. A. - et al. Joint Owner - 197,202,205,206,215,226,227,235,239 to 244
R8	Harkins, D. A. - et al. joint owners - 240
M1(2)	Harkins, E. M. - Decd. Estate - 11,50,73,74,215,216,217,296,297,298,301,351 352,388,389,411,412,541
M2	Harkins, E. M. - Estate of J.T.Harkins, Admr. - 540,552,562,587
R12A	Harkins, E. M. - Decd. Estate - 512 to 522
R2	Harkins, E. M. - Estate - 138 to 140
R3	Harkins, E. M. - Estate - 265, 266
R13	Harkins, E. Max - Estate - 91,94
W1A	Harkins, E. M. - 238 thru 244, 285 thru 287, 577,683
W2	Harkins, E. Max - 61
M9	Harkins, H. G. - guardian - 502
W1A	Harkins, Jas. G. - R. M. McClain, guardian - 78

R10   Harkins, Lige & Millie - Minor Estate - 381, 386

R17 (M7) Harkins, Rufus Mastes - Azzie Metcalf apprentice - 171,172

R17   Harkins, (Hankins) Uridisa J. - Decd. Estate - 200, 205

R9   Harkins, W. B. - Decd. Estate - 116

M6   Harkins, Walter - Estate - 10,11,14,15,78

R6B   Harkins, Walter - Decd. Estate - 152 (Vol. 10 to 210)

M9   Harkens, Wm. B. - Decd. Estate - 40,41,55

M1(1)   Harkins, William S. - Estate of - 264,267,268,282,283,300,505,532

M9   Harkins, Will S. - Decd. Estate - 485

M10   Harkins, Will S. - Decd.   Estate - 210

R10   Harkins, Will S. - Estate - 381

R11   Harkins, Will S. - Decd. Estate - 374

R18   Harkness, K. L. -   - 533,540

W2   Harkness, K. L. - Will & Proof - 336,337

R1A   Harrell, Elijah - Estate - 377 to 380, 701 to 703

M3   Harris, Adlia - Estate - P. 84

R2   Harris, Adlia - Estate - 105 to 113

M2   Harris, Adline - Estate - 610,611,613 to 615

M9   Harris, Alfred J. - Decd. Estate - 231,303

R9   Harris, Alfred J. - Decd. Estate - 478, 479

R10   Harris, Alfred J. - Decd. Estate - 70

R11A   Harris, B. Lewis - 357, 362

R11A   Harris, Churchbull I. = 364, 369

R4   Harris, David S. - Decd. Estate - 135 to 139, 142

M1(2)   Harris, Estate - 723,727,750,(3), 751,(3)

M2   Harris, Edwin, - Estate - 432 to 439, 401 to 405, 572,578, to 581

R2   Harris, Edwin - Estate - 100 to 105

W1A   Harris, Edwin -   - 55 thru 58 thru 60, 199a

M2   Harris, F. D. - Estate - 149 to

R7(M7)   Harris, Geo. S. - Decd. Estate - 528

M8	Harris, George S. - Estate - 3,6,18,65,171,187,212
R8	Harris, George S. - Decd. Estate - 236
R7	Harris, George S. - Decd. Estate M.W.&D.S.Harris, Admr. - 416,520
M1(1)	Harris, James C. - Estate of - 64,130,144,157,158,173,316,331,343,446
W1A	Harris, L. D. - 150 to -
M2	Harris, Moses - Estate - 643,644,645,663,664,680
M3	Harris, Moses - Estate - P.282,283,306 to 308
R2	Harris, Moses - Estate - 195 to 205
R3	Harris, Moses - Estate - 286,287,310 to 315
R25	Harris, Pauline W. - Decd. - 25 - 629,637
	Harris, Pauline W. - Will - 17, 20
R15	Harris, Ray - Et al - guardianship - 24 thru 29
R15	Harris, Robert J. - Incompetent - 420,21
R16	Harris, Robert J. - Incompetent - 359,61
R17	Harris, Robert J. - Cert. of Competency -475
R20	Harris, Robert J. - Incompetent - 20 - 265,346
R14	Harris, Sy ? - et al - Guardianship - Mrs. Helen Norris, guardian - 410,412
M8	Harris, W. L. - guardian Marion Marie Payne - 573,578,588
M9	Harris, W. T. - special Judge of Probate in Will D.Harkins, Estate - 494
R9	Harris, W. T. - guardian of Marion Mae Payne - 62
M2	Harrison, Robert - 188
M2	Harrison, Robert - Estate, E.M.Chambless, guardian for Sultana Harrison - 196
M2	Harrison, Robert - Estate, Isaac Perry & M.E.Chambless, guardian Petition to sell lands - 328
M2	Harrison, Robert - Decd. Estate, M.E.Chambless, Admr. - 335 to 339,388 to 394 340 to 342,703,740,756,757
M3	Harrison, Robert - Estate - P.130,131,200,308,309,319,333,348 to 351
M5	Harrison, Robert W. - Minor T.M.Reese, guardian - 9, 12
R3	Harrison, Robert - Estate - 284,285,348 to 350,364,384 to 393,417
R5	Harrison, Robert W. - Minor heirs of Robert Harrison - decd. - 360,361
W1A	Harrison, Robert - 146 to 150

M(3)	Harten, Amanda - Estate of - 578, 579
M1(2)	Harton, F. L. - adoption of child - 151, 152
R11A	Harton, Green T. - 392, 397
M1(1)	Harton, Hardy - Estate of - 292,298,300,321,322,339,567,568
R5	Harton, James A. - 328
M2	Harton, James H. - Decd. Estate, John B.Sanford & Josephine E.Harton, Admrs. - 356,357,358 thru 363,263,365,366,423,424,367 to 369,567,568,588 to 590,651, 652,653,664,(661)662,673,692,710
M3	Harton, J. H. - Estate - P.241,242,388,420
M4	Harton, J. H. - Estate - 64,65,67,325,634,637
R2	Harton, James H. - 74 to 79, 246 to 251
R3	Harton, James H. - Estate - 171,172,261,262,621
R4	Harton, James H. - Decd. Estate - 524
M1(2)	Harten, John D. - Decd. Estate - 27,28,573,94,95,595
M2	Harten, John D. - Estate - 28
M2	Harten, J. D. - Estate, J.J.Taylor, guardian for minor heirs of P.D.Harton 137 to
M3	Harton, John D. - Estate - P.74,76,77
R12A	Harton, John D. - Decd. Estate - 597, to 601
R3	Harton, John D. - Estate - 178, 379
R2	Harton, John D. - Estate - 544 to 546
W1A	Harton, John D. - 648 thru 651, 106
M2	Harton, L. L. - Estate - 220
R2	Harton, L. L. - Estate - 7, 8
W1A	Harton, L. L. - 195
M7	Harton, Nancy F. - Estate - J.B.Harton, admr. - 93,94
M5	Hassell, Myles B. - Decd. Estate - 100, 113
R5	Hassell, M. B. - G.T.Hassell, Admr. - 444, 445
R13	Hassell, R. V. - Estate - 494, 496
M9	Hassell, W. J. - Decd. Estate - 480, 481
R10	Hassell, W. J. - Decd. Estate - 443, 444
W1	Hassell, W. J. - 297
R27	Haughton, James C. - 684, 692

Haughton, James C. - Vol. 3 - 307, 309

W1   Harvey, Mr. Eliza -   63

R2   Harvey, William - Estate - 153,154,240 to 245

M2   Har-ey, William D. - Estate - 590,591,595,649,668,669,689.690,774

M3   Harvey, William D. - Estate - P. 28, 29

M1(2) Harvey, Wm. P. - Decd.'Estate - 301,309,600

M2   Harvey, W. P. - Estate, J. C. Moore, Admr. - 332, 668

M(3) Harvey, Wm. P. - Estate of - 131,132,133,134,463 to 482,387 to 392

R12A Harvey, William P. - Decd. Estate - 565 to 573

W1A   Harvey, W. P. - 658, 660

M10   Hawkins, John - Decd. Estate - Decd. Estate - 13, 14

R10   Hawkins, John - Decd. Estate - 580,581,582,583

R28   Hawkins, Theron - 28 - 833,834

M9   Hay, Lillian - guardian for Frances Hugh Hay - 240,349

R9   Hay, Lillian - guardian, Frances Hugh Hay - 510, 511

R10   Hay, Mrs. Lillian - guardian - 157

M10   Hayes, R. - Decd. Estate - 89,90,91,102,108

R11   Hayes, R. - Decd. Estate - 176,177,178,179,180,181,182,183,212,213,214,215,
                                                                       226 to 229

M10   Hayes, V. C. - et al. joint owner - 89,90,91

R11   Hayes, V. C. - et al. sale fo- div. - 176,177,178,179,180,181,182,183

M4   Hays, Isaac K., - Minor, H.B.Propst, special guardian - 331

M9   Hays, R.L. - Decd. Estate - 481

R28   Hellers, George N., Jr. - 28 - 784,789

      Hellers, George N., Jr. - 491,495

M5   Henden, A. J. - Decd. Estate - W.A.Hendon, Admr. - 145, 163

M4   Henderson, Elizabeth - Decd. Estate - 111,120,131,132

R4   Henderson, Elizabeth - Estate - 210 to 213

M4   Henderson, _____ - Minor heirs of W.G.Baker - Guardian - 157

R4   Henderson, L. P. - Heirs of Wm. G. Baker - guardian - 316

M1(2) Hendric, Berry - Estate - 678,680

M2   Hendricks, Berry - Estate - 593, 596

M3	Hendrix, Barry - Estate - P.377,387,413,497,583,716	
M5	Hendrix, Berry - Estate of - 173	
R2	Hendrix, Berry - Estate - 90 to 96	
R3	Hendrix, Berry - Estate - 590 to 598	
R4	Hendrix, Berry - Decd. Estate - 95 to 99,107 to 110	
W1A	Hendrix, Berry - 30 thru 32	
R21	Hendrix, Dexter - Decd. Estate of - 21 - 148, 158	
W2	Hendrix, Dexter - Will & Proof - 440,441	
R1A	Hendrix, Lucius A., - Estate - 211, 212,(112), 517	
M(3)	Hendrix, Lucius B. - Estate of - 335,334,333,575,576	
R11A	Hendricks, Lucius H. - 378,381	
M2	Hendrick, Reubin - Estate - 212 to	
W1A	Hendrics, Reuben - 173	
R23	Henley, John - Estate of - 23 - 902,910	
E2	Henley, John - Will & Proof - 513,514	

280,351

M7	Henry, B. - guardian for Estate of Minor children of Simpson Lindsey, Decd. -	
R7	Henry, B. - guardian - Estate, Minor heirs of Simpson Lindsey, Decd. - 156	
R10	Henry, B. - 513,514,515	
W1	Henry, B. - 326	
R21	Henry, Dorthea - Minor - 21 - 239,243	
R19	Henry, Johnny James - 19 - 99, 106	
W2	Henry, Johnnie James - Will & Proof - 340, 341	
R20	Henry, J. R. - Decd. Estate of - 20 - 187, 194	
W2	Henry, J. R. - Will & Proof - 391-92	
M6	Henry, Joseph - Estate - 98	
M1(1)	Henry, Samuel - Estate of - 67	
R19	Henry, Vista - 19 - 107,168	
R20	Henry, Vista - Decd. Estate of - 20 - 669,676	
W2	Henry, Vesta - Deceased, Will & Proof - 346,347	
R13	Henson, Dora - Estate - 503 to 506	

R17	Henson, Richard A? - Decd. Estate - 100,108,321
M10	Herbert, Henry T.C., Sylvester & Roosevelt (Minors) - 448
R14	Herbert, Roosevelt - Minor - 134 thru 137
R13	Herbert, T. C. - Gdn. final settlement, etc. - 383, 384
R13	Herbert, T. C., Sylvester & Roosevelt - Minors - Estate - 167
R24	Herren, E. C. - Decd. - 24 - 503,510
W2	Herren, E. C. - Will & Proof - 554, 555
R17	Herren, R. C. - Decd. Estate - 123,126
M1(1)	Hester, David G.W. - Estate of - 91,92,97,108,123,145
M7	Hester, David G.W. - Decd., Jane Norris - Petition - 49,50,63,64
W1	Hester, David G.W. - 98
R14	Hewitt, Curtis J. - Decd. Estate of - 438,439,440
W2	Hewitt, Curtis I - 130
M2	Hewett, John N. - 628,629,639,717,722
M3	Hewett, J. N. - Estate - P. 92,93,94,95,96,318
R2	Hewett, John N. - Estate - 163 to 170, 382 to 384, 530 to 532
R3	Hewit, John N. - Estate - 289 to 367
	Hewitt, Lovie Lee - 64, 66
M1(1)	Hickman, John - Estate of - 5,20,21
M(3)	Hicks, Irvin - Estate of - 556,557,558
R11A	Hicks, Ervin - 362, 363
R11A	Hill, I. W. M. - 370, 373
R27	Hindman, Claudine - 27 - 571,584, Vol. 28, P. 15, 25
R28	Hindman, Bradley Claudine - 28 - 393 (claim)
R28	Hindman, Bradley Claudine - 28 - 189,201, (393 claim)
	Hindman, Bradley Claudine - 358
R7	Hindman, L. S. - guardian - 70
M7	Hindman, L. S. - guardian L.A.Hindman - 229
R18	Hinson, Richard A. - Decd. Estate of - 483,528
R19	Hinson, Richard A. - Estate of - 19 - 815, 848
W2	Hinson, Richard A. - 290,291,292,293

W2   Hinson, Dora N. - 88, 89,90

M4   Hinton, S. V. = appointment Speċċal Coronor -   133

M4   Hinton, Sam - Insane - 527

M9   Hiram, Dora - Admr., W.H.Naugher (Dora Hinson) - 462,490

M10   Hiten, Charles E. - incompetent, Estate - 30,39,74,75,111,152,153,210,211,212, 218,279

M10   Hiten, Chas. E. - Incompetent - appointment & Acceptance of gdn. at letim - 341,342,389,390,401,402,403,492

M10   Hiten, Charles E. - Incompetent - 560,561

R11   Hiten, Charles E. - Incompetent - Estate - 21,22,47,48,49,50,147 to 151,238, 345.346,372,373,427,509

R11   Hiten, Charles E. - Imcompetent, settlement - gdn. - 591

R13   Hiten, Charles E. - Application to sell land for reinvestment, etc. - 103 thru 109

R13   Hiten, Charles E. - Incompetent - Gdn. final settlement & appointing T.L.Lindsey, New Guardian - 94,103

R13   Hiten, Charles C. - Application to sell lands for reinvestment, etc.-110 thru 114

R14   Hiten, Charles E. - Incompetent - Estate of - 29 thru 36

R15   Hiten, Charles E. - Incompetent - 116,117

R12   Hiten, Charles E. - Incompetent - 250

R18   Hiten, Charles E. - Inc. - 229, 238

R20   Hiten, Charles E. - Decd. Estate of - 20 - 153,158

R19   Hiten, Charles E. - Inc. - 19 - 335,338,229,238

M9   Hiten, J. C. - guardian - 273,293,344,280,281

M10   Hiten, J. C. - guardian of - 30, 39

M9   Hiten, J. C. - guardian - 416,417

R9   Hiten, J. C. - guardian for Charles E. Hiten - 120

R10   Hiten, J. C. - guardian - 16,51,52,53,150,153,218,219,344,345,346,358

R8   Hiten, J. R. - Ministerial Certificate - 306

M7   Hiten, Mary C. - Decd. Estate - 102

M7   Hiten, Mary C. - Decd. Estate - 102

R24   Hiten, Mollie - Decd. - 24 - 159,174

W2   Hiten, Mollie - Will & Proof - 522

M7   Hocutt, Floyd - Minor hild of Susan Eliza Sylman - adopted & name changed Jo' H. Hocutt - 420

M10   Hocutt, Leo - Decd   ate - 420

W1	Hocutt, L. G. - 230, 231
M9	Hocutt, L. T. - Decd. Estate - 154, 155
R9	Hocutt, L. T. - Decd. Estate - 337 to 340
R25	Hocutt, Lovie Lee - 25 - 891,899
M9	Hocutt,, Lucy, guardian - 259, 260
R9	Hocutt, - guardian - 541,546
R28	Hodges, Betty LaVerne - 28 - 39,46,100,101
	Hodges, Betty LaVerne - Vol. 3, 333,337
R24	Hodges, Dorothy - Incompetent - 24 - 668, 680
R24	Hodges, Harry - Minor - 24 - 686, 690
R24	Hodges, Sandra - Minor - 24 - 681,685
R29	Hodges, Sandra - 29 - page 16
W1A	Hogan, Wm. J. - Jas. I. Hogan, guardian - 3,4,
W2	Hoehn, A. U. - 119
M1(2)	Hogan, James J. - guardian - W.J.Hogan - 610
R6B	Hole, Susan - Decd. Estate - 536
R1A	Holliman, J. C. - Bond - 729
R7	Holliman, J. F. - Decd. Estate - Will - 286
W1	Holliman, J. F. - 117
M8	Holliman, J. I. - guardian - 347
R8	Holliman, J. T. - guardian - 380
M2	Holliman, P. Holliman, guardianship - 591
W2	Holliman, Virgie Lee - 480,481
R22	Holliman, Virgie Lee - Decd. - 22 - 373,403
M10	Holliman, Virginia - Decd. Will - 135,136
R11	Holliman, Virginia - Estate Will - 303
W1	Holliman, Virginia A. - 354,355,356
M3	Holliman, William P. - Estate - P. 199,233,234
R3	Holliman, Wm. P. = Estate - 257,258
R28	Hollingshead, James Wilbert - 28 - 639,646

R24   Hollingsworth, Arthur E. - Decd. - 24 - 340,347

W2   Hollingsworth, Arthur E. - 545

R27   Hollingsworth, Cora - 27 - 641,647

M8   Hollingworth, H. T. - fines paid to Judge of Probate - 401,402

      Hollingworth, James Wilbert - 429 (Hollingshead?)

W1   Hollingsworth, Jeptha - 12, 13

M5   Hollingsworth, Jessie - Decd. Estate - 124,130,131,133

R15   Hollingsworth, John A. - Decd. 243,246,340,341,342

W1   Hollingsworth, John A. - 220,222

W2   Hollingsworth, John A. - 176, 177

M8   Hollingsowrth, John R. - Decd. Estate - 561,568,569

R9   Hollingsworth, Jn. R. - Decd. Estate - 48

M9   Hollingsworth, M. G. - Decd. Estate - 484, 504

M9   Hollingsowrth, M. G. - Estate - 504

M10   Hollingsworth, M. G. - Estate - 110,115

R10   Hollingsworth, M. G. - Decd. Estate - 437

R11   Hollingsworth, M. G. - Decd. Estate - 235,236,256,257

W1   Hollingsworth, M. G. - 301

M5   Hollingsworth, Pierce - Estate - 245, 246,265

M3   Hollingsworth, Samuel - Estate - P. 384,414

R3   Hollingsworth, Samuel - Estate - 579 to 585, 629,630

M4   Hollingsworth, Thomas - Estate of dower proceedings - 582,584

M6   Hollingsworth, Zilpha - Estate - 24,26,30

R28   Hollis, Brett H., Jr. - 28 - 261

      Holling, Brett H., Jr., - 383

M10   Hollis, David - Decd. Estate 476,477,478

R9   Hollis, David - guardian - 141

W2   Hollis, David - 321

R18   Hollis, Felix - 541,552

R19   Hollis, Felix - 19 - 50,603,607

M10   Hollis. Dr. J. S. - Decd. Es   464

R14	Hollis, Dr. J. S. - Decd. Estate - 26,27,28
M9	Hollis, Pauline - 26
R20	Hollis, Reed Ann - Decd. - 20 - 617,622
W1	Hollman, Mrs. Cynthia - 263,264,265
M7	Hollman, J. F. - Decd. Estate - 418,419,420
M4	Holly, Rles - Declaration to revovering child - 307
W1	Holly, Sally - 97
R18	Holt, Samuel V. - Incompetent - 151,168
R13	Honeycutt, Arthur J. - Incompetent - 25,33,408,410
R14	Honeycutt, Arthur J. - Incompetent - 51 thru 60
R16	Honeycutt, Arthur J. - Incompetent - 407
R19	Honeycutt, Arthur J. - Incompetent - 19 - 623,745
R21 -	Honeycutt, Arthur J. - Incompetent - 21 - 1 - 66
R22	Honeycutt, Arthur J. - Incompetent - 22 - 454,503
R24	Honeycutt, Arthur J. - Incompetent - 24 - 105,142,510,540
R26	Honeycutt, Arthur J. - Incompetent - 26 - 233,272,441,460
R27	Honeycutt, Arthut J. - Incompetent - 27 - 412,420
R25	Honeycutt, Arthur J. - Incompetent - 25 - 406,436
R25	Honeycutt, Charlotte Belinda - change name - 25 - 706,707
R13	Honeycutt, J. D. - Estate - 22
R13	Honeycutt, J. D. - Declaration of fatherhood - 371
W2	Honeycutt, J. D. - 59, 60
R11A	Honeycutt, L. G. - 401,405
M10	Honeycutt, Loyd T. - Incompetent - Estate - 416,417,418
R19	Honeycutt, R. C. - Estate of - 19 - 901,915,333,362
W2	Honeycutt, R. C. - Eill & Proof - 370, 371
R17	Honeycutt, Verna, Mrs. Gdn. Bond - 327
R28	Honeycutt, Verna - Guardian Arthur - Vol. 28 - 155,180
R25	Hood, S. M. - Decd. - 25 - 821,829

Hood, Samuel M. - Will & Proof - 54A, 54B

M1(1)   Hoodenpyl, M. D. - Estate of - 88,90,93,108,142,171,180,191,393,394,618,619

R18   Hooker, J. Earl - Estate of - 1 - 18

W2   Hooker, J. Earl - Will & Codicil & Proof - 321,22,23

R12A   Hopson, Edmond - Decd. Estate - 749 to 752

W1A   Hopson, E. - 288,289,330,331,339 thru 347,654,655,709,719,745,751,752

M1(2)   Hopson, Edward - 340,341,356,358,359,417,383,384,396,397,403,404,648,667,668,
                           683,694,679,705,658,662

R3   Hopson, Edward - Estate - 717

M1(2)   Hopson, (Hopson)   - Estate, final settlement - 707,708,709

R14   Horn, Frank - Decd. Estate - 191,192,193

R11A   Horn, Jesse - 405,409

R17   Horn, Rosezema - Decd. Estate - 109,112

W2   Horn, Rosezema - 289

R11A   Horne, James B. - 55, 60

R1A   Horner, Jesse - Estate - 227 to 229, 572, to 578, 721 to 724

R17   Horten, J. E. - Decd. Estate - 32

R11A   Horton, Hardy - 31,23,348,357,411,412

R1A   Horton, Harry - Estate - 588 to 595

M6   Horton, Nancy F. - 526, 527

R24   Houston, Jesse Barnes - Decd. - 24 - 924,931

W2   Houston, Jesse Barnes - Will & Proof - 568-63

M9   Howard, William L. - Decd. Estate - 27

R9   Howard, William T. - Decd. Estate - 145

M8   Howell, Emmeline - Decd. Estate - 367,371,380,381,391

R8   Howell, Emmaline - Decd. Estate - 418

M8   Howell, Clark - Minor - Estate - 434,456

R8   Howell, Clark - Minor, Estate - 490

R15   Howel, Clark - 127,131

M1(1)	Howton, Abran - Estate of - 499,537 to 539
M(3)	Howton, Abran - Estate of - 591,592
M3	Howton, Abraham - Deceased Estate - P.573,585,608,609
M4	Howton, Abraham - Estate of - 19,73,292,583
M5	Howton, Abraham - Decd. Estate, Mat Howton, Admr. - 26,48,49,159,171,197,200, 205,243,307,311,312,334,354
M7	Howton, Abraham - Decd. Estate - 417
R4	Howton, Abraham - Decd. Estate - 144 to 157, 460 to 464
R5	Howton, Abraham - Decd. Estate - 303
R6B	Howton, Abraham - Estate - 68,73
R7	Howton, Abraham - Decd. Estate - 282
R1A	Howton, Abram - Estate - 739
M8	Howton, Felix - Decd. Estate - 520,545,549,553,557,561,579,591
M9	Howton, Felix - Decd. Estate - 21
R9	Howton, Felix - 22,29,100
R1A	Howton, Jesse - Estate - 142
M10	Howton, S. M. - Decd. Estate - 109
R11	Howton, Silas M. - Decd. Estate - 229,230,231,285,286,287,288,289,290,291,292
M4	Hubbard, Elizabeth M.- Estate of - 63,68
R4	Hubbard, Elizabeth M. - Estate - 100 to 106
R17	Hubbert, Andrew Jackson - Court Proceedings - 139,146
R21	Hubbert, A. J. - Unsound Mind - 21 - 67,74
R21	Hubbert, A. J. - Unsound Mind - 21 - 75, 83
R23	Hubbert, A. J. - Inc. - 23 - 806,811
R23	Hubbert, A. J. - Inc. - 23 - 812,837
R28	Hubbert, A. J. - 28 - 847,858
	Hubbert, A. J. - Deceased - 3,4

R27	Hubbert, A. L. - 27 - 361,373,400
	Hubbert, A. L. - Will & Proof Cert. - 256,259
R24	Hubbert, Bessie - Decd. - 24 - 481,488
W2	Hubbert, Bessie - Will & Proof - 548,549
M3	Hubbert, George M. - Estate - P. 445,675,687, (1881)
M4	Hubbert, George M. - Estate - 9,10,38,39,47,65
R3	Hubbert, G. M. - Estate - 625 to 627
R4	Hubbert, George M. - Estate - 111 to 123
M10	Hubbert, G. W. - De-d. Estate - 33,34,145,146 332
R11	Hubbert, G. W. - Decd. Estate - 28,29,30,332,333,581
R22	Hubbert, J. B. - Estate of - 22 - 117,133
W2	Hubbert, J. B. - Will & Proof - Will - 329,355,356
R20	Hubbert, J. Murry - Decd. Estate of - 20 - 641,668
W2	Hubbert, J. Murry - Will - 375
R20	Hubbert, Juanita - Inc. - 20 - 77, 88
M8	Hubbert, R. F. - guardian - 547
R8	Hubbert, R. F. - guardian - 584
R25	Hubbert, Silas, Se. - Decd. - 25 - 708,719
	Hubbert, Silas, Sr. - Will & Proof - 39,41
R27	Hubbert, Vadus - 27 - 375,381
	Hubbert, Vadus - Will & Proof - 260, 264
M9	Hudging, Robert - guardian - 439
R10	Hudging, Robert - guardian - 290
W2	Hudson, Eugene Wilson - 77
R13	Hudson, Hobson Eugene - 339 thru 344, 424 to 426
R28	Hudson, Melba Jean - 28 - 790,793
R23	Huffman, Arnie J. - Minor - 23 - 705,716
R26	Huffman, Arnie J., Jr. - 26 - 305,316
	Huffman, Arnis J. - 194, 197

R24	Huffman, Bertha B. - Decd. - 24 - 691,695	
R23	Huffman, Doris Ann Mealer - Decd. - 23 - 647,651	
M10	Hughes, Dock - Decd. Estate 35,36,92	
R11	Hughes, Dock - Decd. Estate - 34,35,36,185,186,187	
M1(1)	Hughey, William - Estate of = 250	
M8	Hull, Mabel - Minor - adoption by H. Francis Pinkerton - 63	
R25	Humber, Annie - Inc. - 25, 935,947	
R26	Humber, Annie - 26 - 153,161	
	Humber, Annie - 126,128	
R7	Humber, G. W. - etal - joint owner - 492	
M10	Humber, Harold P. - Decd. Estate - 252	
R11	Humber, Harold P. - Decd. Estate - 468,469	
M10	Humber, L. E. - Decd. Estate - 313	
R11	Humber, L. E. - Decd. Estate - 560,561	
M7	Humber, L. P. - Decd. Estate - 150,151,249,271,272,273	
M7	Humber, L. P. - Decd. Estate - 150,151,158,159,164,165,166,267,271,272,273	
R6B	Humber, L. P. - Decd. Estate - 520,521,522,544 to 548,549,550 to 553	
M4	Humber, R. H., Jr. - Es. - 112,113	
M2	Humber, R. W. - Mortgage to Horace Dodson - 145	
M8	Humber, S. W. - et al. joint owner - 9,11,16,17,23,26 to 29	
R23	Humber, W. H. - 23 - 911,920	
W2	Humber, W. H. - Will & Proof - 504,505	
R11A	Hunter, Robert - 398, 401	
M8	Hurley, Mary - Decd. Estate - 253, 255	
R8	Hurley, Mary - Decd. Estate - 274	
W1	Hurley, Mary - 220,222	
R24	Hurst, J. T. - Decd. - 24 - 257,269	
W2	Hurst, J. T. - Will & Proof - 528	
M10	Hush, Hardy B. - Decd. Estate - 579	

M2	Hutton, William - Estate - 446 to 448,506 to 511,539,559,572,573,585
R2	Hutton, Wm. J. - Estate - 141 to 143,476 to 479
	Hutto, William Thomas - 48,53
M9	Huttonm, Mattie - Decd. Estate - 430,431
M8	Hyde, C. B. - Decd. Estate - Mrs. Pearl Hyde, Admrx. - 463
M9	Hyde, C. B. - Decd. Estate - 220
R9	Hyde, C. B. - Decd. Estate 447,448,449
M1(2)	Hyde, C. M. - 541,553,670,672,703
R3	Hyde, C. M. - Estate - 282
W1A	Hyde, C. M. - 25,26,28,29
W1A	Hyde, C. M. - 576,588,589
M9	Hyde, F. H. - Decd. - 414
M10	Hyde, F. D. - Estate - 251,379
R10	Hyde, F. D. - 379,380
R11	Hyde, F. D. - Decd. Estate - 467,468
R3	Hyde, J. C. - 61 to 73
M2	Hyde, James H. - Guardian for heirs of T.Griffin Estate - 47
M2	Hyde, Jeremiah - Estate - 664,665,666,667
M3	Hyde, Jeremiah - Estate - P.184,197,198
M6	Hyde, J. T. - guardian for Minna & Thos. H. Hyde - 28
R16	Hyde, Lena Swinwood - Decd. - 323-25
W2	Hyde, Lena Swinewood - 27,72
M9	Hyde, Pearl - guardian - 286,287
R10	Hyde, Pearl - guardian - 38 to 41
R14	Hyde, Mrs. Pearl, Marie & Edd - et al, vs. City of Fayette - 86 thru 98
R11	Hyde, Mrs. S. F. - Decd. Estate - 151,152
M10	Hyde, Mrs. S. T. - Decd. Estate - 75
R24	Hyder Hosea Dean - Decd. - 24 - 903,908

W2   Hyder, Hosea Dean - Will & Proof - 564

Hyder, James Bertin - Original filed in Marion County - 398

M1(1)   INCORPORATION of Fayetteville, Petition - 116,129,401

R23   Ingle, Allie - Incom. - 23 - 839,844

W1A   Ivins, Isaam W. - 534,536,611

M1(2)   Irvin, Isham W. - 521,522,572,676,679,693

R15   Ivy, Evelyn Glover - Decd. - 508,510

R19   Ivy, Evelyn Glover - Estate of - 19 - 809,811

M7	Jackson, Jesse F. - Decd. Estate - 98,110	
M10	Jackson, George - Decd. Estate - 111	
R11	Jackson, George - Decd. Estate - 241,242	
M7	Jackson, Jesse F. - Decd. Estate - 98,99,110	
M10	Jackson, William A. - Decd. Estate - 294,295	
W2	Jackson, William H. & Lucy J. - 11	
R11	Jackson, William H. - Decd. Estate - 533,534,535	
W2	James, Dock W. - Will & Proof - 488,89	
R23	James, Dock W. - Decd. - 23 - 559,567	
M9	James, Isaac - Decd. Estate - 191,192	
R9	James, Isaac - Decd. Estate - 399,400,401,402	
M1	January Term - 1881 - 164	
M1	January Term - 1885 - 270	
M1	January Term - 1886 - 299	
M1	January Term - 1887 - 329	
M4	Jeffries, Bud - name change to Ples Holly - 307	
R23	Jeffries, Dorothy C. - Decd. - 23 - 798,801	
M2	Jeffries, E. A. - guardian for Rexannah & J.H.A.Thornton - 12	
	Jeffries, James F. - Will - 9,13	
R26	Jeffries, James - 26 - 8, 17	
R26	Jeffries, James F. - 26 - 8, 17	
R11A	Jeffries, Josiah P. - 435,439	
R23	Jeffries, Kenneth B. - Decd. - 23 - 802,805	
W2	Jeffries, Thomas M. - Will - 411	
R20	Jeffries, Thomas M. - Decd. Estate of - 20 - 461,467	
M10	Jeffries, Miss Virginia - Decd. Estate - 583	
M8	Jeffries, V. V. - Decd. Estate - 436,437	
R8	Jeffries, V. V. - Decd. Estate - 494	

W1	Jeffries, V. V. - 201
M9	Jeffries, William T. - Decd. Estate - 156,157,158,185
W1	Jeffries, Wm. T. - 234
R9	Jeffries, William T. - Decd. Estate - 341,342
M5	Jeffreys, E. A. - guardian - 21
M9	Jenkins, John S. - Decd. Estate - 234,235,236
R9	Jenkins, John S. - Decd. Estate - 485,486,487
R15	Jenkins, John Thomas - Charles Ray, Dessie Rhee - 47,51,219,220
R20	Jenkins, John Thomas - Removal of guardian, etc. - 20 - 809,855
R23	Jenkins, John Thomas, Chas. Ray & DessiRhee - Minors - 23 - 899,901
M1(2)	Jenkins, Lewis W. - Decd. Estate - 373,374
R11A	Jenkins, Lewis W. - 412 to 427
R12A	Jenkins, L. W. - Decd. Estate - 672, to 677
M9	Jenkins, Thos. N. - Decd. Estate - 57
R9	Jenkins, Thomas U. - Decd. Estate - 188, 189
W2	Jenkins, Ulysses C. - Will & Proof - Probate C.R. - Vol. 19A - 539,542
R19	Jenkins, Ulysses C. - 19 - 533, 542
M10	Jenkins, V. R. - Decd. Estate - 168,169,170,171,172
R11	Jenkins, U. R. - Decd. Estate - 375,376,377,378
M1(1)	Jennings, Nancy - Estate of - 254,489,513,574
M(3)	Jennings, Thomas - Estate of - 300,301,302
R1A	Jennings, Thomas - Estate - 217 to 220, 731
R11A	Jennings, Thomas - 444,447
M10	Jewell, Guy D. - guardian - 550
W1	Jinkins, John S. - 386
M9	Johns, Era - a Minor decree releasing of disabilities of non age - 147
M9	Johns, G. W. - Decd. Estate - 215,216
R9	Johns, G. W. - Decd. Estate - 442,443

W1	Johns, G. W. - 245
M8	Johnson, Bud - adopted by John Wright & name changed to Bud Wright - 340
	Johnson, Carrie - Copy of Will - Vol. 3 - 231,233
R27	Johnson, Carrie - Decd. - 27 - 1,43 - Will - Vol.3,pg.231 - Proof,pg.233
R12	Johnson, Ellie - Deceased - 277,280,286,287
W2	Johnson, Ellie - 268
R25	Johnson, Evaline - Inc. - 25 - 198,204
M1(2)	Johnson, Frances, substitution o Marriage licenses - 118 (Robert Johnson & Frances Mobley, issued 8 Dec. 1860, MG Peter McGee, Esq. 9 Dec. 1860
M1(2)	Johnson, George - Decd. Estate - 556,148,149,190,191,411,426,429,438,439,440, 252,411,474,475,476,477,205,206,207,208,209,210
W1A	Johnson, George - 259,284,285,323 thru 328,391 to 393,424 thru 428
R12A	Johnson, George - Decd. Estate - 236 to 252, 664 to 669
R22	Johnson, Jacob Emmett - Decd. - 22 - 404,422
M(3)	Johnson, James - Estate of - 345,346
R1A	Johnson, James - Estate - 635 to 640
W2	Johnson, Jim - Will & Proof - 556
R15	Johnson, Joe A. - Decd. - 86,89
M1(1)	Johnson, John - Estate of - 474
R1A	Johnson, John - Estate - 533 to 534
M9	Johnson, J. W. - Decd. Estate - 511,523
R10	Johnson, J. W. - Estate - 506,506,508
M1(2)	Johnson, Lemuel - Estate - 654,665,666
W1A	Johnson, Lemuel - 20,21,22 to 25
R15	Johnson, Mattie E. - Non Corpus Mentes - 431,435
R16	Johnson, Mattie E. - Non Corpus Mentis - 420,24
M3	Johnson, M. C. - Habus Corpies - P. 158
M10	Johnson, Millard - guardian for Inez & Elsie Johnson - 235,245,246
R11	Johnson, Millard - guardian - Inez & Wlsei Johnson - 445,446,447,448,461
M2	Johnson, Moses T. - Guardian for Roxannah & J.H.A.Thornton - 10

R25   Johnson, Ozie - 25 - 560,577

M2   Johnson, P. M. - Estate - 308 to

M6   Johnson, Sallie W. - Minor child to W.H.Terry - 320,321

R18   Johnson, Shannon - Estate of - 18 - 258,262

M2   Johnson, Thomas - Estate - 618,619,620,637,682

M4   Johnson, Thomas - Decd. T.D.Enis - Admr. - 308,512,517,521

R2   Johnson, Thomas - Estate - 178 to 185

R3   Johnson, Thomas - Estate - 168,169

R5   Johnson, Thomas - Decd. Estate - 150

W2   Johnson, Thomas G. - 66

R13   Johnson, Thomas G. - Estate - 196,197

        Johnson, Thomas G. - Copy of Will - Misc. Vol. 3 R1 - 115

R15   Johnson, Virgie E. - Decd. - 422,431

M(3)   Johnson, William - Apprentice Bond - 260,261,228,237,236

M(3)   Johnson, William - Estate of - 236 to 238

R11   Johnson, William - Minor Estate - 145,146,251,582,583

M10   Johnson, William (Willner) - Minor Estate - 73,119,333

R11A   Johnson, William - 449,451

M10   Joiner, Harrey - Estate - 6

R10   Joiner, Hassey - Decd. Estate - 549

M8   Jones, Anner - (T) I - Decd. Estate - 296

M10   Jones, Mrs. Annie - Decd. Estate - 103,104

R11   Jones, Jrs. Annie - Decd. Estate - 216,217

W1   Jones, Mrs. Annie - 346

R11A   Jones, Benjamin - 440,444

W2   Jones, Charlie - Will & Proof -   389

R14   Jones, Charlie - et al, vs. City of Fayette - 86 thru 98

R19   Jones, Charlie - Estate of - 19 - 921,930

M8	Jones, Chester - adopted by A.H.Alexander, name changed to Chester Alexander 464
M8	Jones, Clyster - adopted by J.A.Brown - 458
M4	Jones, Della - name changed to Jan Tollie Eeds - 591
M8	Jones, Dora - mother of Nora Reese - Minor - 362
M5	Jones, Dudley T. - Insane - 202
M7	Jones, Earl - Decd. Estate - 522,538
M8	Jones, Earl - Decd. Estate - 2
W1	Jones, Earl - 122
R7	Jones, Earl - Decd. Estate - 438
R26	Jones, Easby - 26 - 81,88
R26	Jones, Easby - 26 - 79,89
	Jones, Easby - Will - 87,92
M4	Jones, Elizabeth, J. S. - Decd. - Estate - W.W.Jones, Afmr. - 628
R5	Jones, Elizabeth J. - Decd. Estate - 495 to 496
M3	Jones, E. P. - P.290,291,412
R3	Jones, E. P. - Estate - 307 to 309, 584 to 586
R4	Jones, E. P. - Decd. Estate - 180 to 185, 186 to 188
R5	Jones, E. P. - Decd. Estate - 100
R15	Jones, Fred - Decd. 152,153
R11	Jones, George G. - Decd. Estate - 401, 402
M10	Jones, George H. - Decd. Estate - 193
M10	Jones, Glover - et al. Petition for sale - 49,50,51,52,53
W2	Jones, Glover - 214,215
R11	Jones, Glover - et al. petition for sale - 82,83,84,85,86,87,88
R15	Jones, Glover - Decd. = 557, 560
R16	Jones, Glover - Decd. - 59,61
M1(2)	Jones, H. R. - Decd. Estate - 60,204,715,734
M2	Jones, H. R. - Estate - 70,478 to 482

R12A	Jones, H. R. - Decd. Estate - 383 to 385
M3	Jones, Iza Ida - et al. - p.452
R3	Jones, Iza, Ila - et al. - 623,624
M8	Jones, James G. - of unsound mind - 37, 39
R7	Jones, James G. - Non Compas Mortem - 504
R27	Jones, J. Frank - 27 - 879, 885
M5	Jones, James J. - Estate Berry G. Jones, Admr. - 88,91,416,417,420
R5	Jones, James J. - Decd. Estate - 111
M4	Jones, Dr. James J. - Estate of - 162,167,172,173,184,192,193,219,225,404,425
R4	Jones, James J. - Decd. Estate - 272 to 287
R25	Jones, Jason - Declaration of legitimation - 25 - 697,698
M10	Jones, Jasper - Decd. Estate - 49,50,51,52,53
R11	Jones, Jasper - Decd. Estate - 82,83,84,85,86,87,88
M8	Jones, John J. - Decd. Estate - 587
M9	Jones, John J. - Decd. Estate - 25
M4	Jones, J. P. - Estate of - 61,78,79,151,182,278,394,405,412,413,414
R21	Jones, Joseph C. - Decd. Estate of - 21 - 939,942
R13	Jones, J. T. - Estate - 290,291
R9	Jones, John T. - Decd. Estate - 88, 535
M10	Jones, J.W.R. - Estate - 1,53
R10	Jones, J.W.R. - Decd. Estate - 546,547,548
R11	Jones, J.W.R. - Decd. Estate - 89,529
W2	Jones, Mrs. J.W.R. - 12
M10	Jones, Mrs. J.W.R. - Decd. Estate - 290,291
R11	Jones, Mrs. J.W.R. - Decd. Estate - 530
R24	Jones, Leon B. - Will - 24 - 1, 34
W2	Jones, Leon B. - Will (see Roberts record Vol. 24 - 1-34)
R1A	Jones, Martha A. - Estate - 294 to 299
M9	Jones, Melissa P. - et al. joint owners - 247 to 249,255 to 257

R9	Jones, Malissa P. - et al. joint owners - 521,524,528,535
R23	Jones, Nannie Elizabeth - Decd. - 23 - 791,797
W2	Jones, Nannie Wlizabeth - Will & Proof - 506,507
W2	Jones, Newton Emory - Will & Proof - 306, 308
R17	Jones, Newton Emory - Decd. - 384,395,470,674 (474?)
R13	Jones, Robert Isaac - A Minor - 381,82
M8	Jones, Ruby - adopted by Shad R. Kimbrell - $ 457
W2	Jones, T. J. - Will & Proof - 508,508
R23	Jones, T. J. - Decd. - 23 - 845,852
M9	Jones, T. W. - Estate - 270,271
R9	Jones, T. W. - Decd. Estate - 227,229,230
M8	Jones, Verie Nelle - adopted by W. E. Roberts - 457
M1(1)	Jones, William - Estate of - 9,18,19,23,24,25,44,146,429,431,462, to 467, 607,609,613
M1(2)	Jones, William - 542,545,571,572
M(3)	Jones, William - Estate of - 275 to 280,344,279,278,277,276,275,260,261
M(3)	Jones, William - - 531,532,533
W1A	Jones, William - - 608,609,610
R1A	Jones, William - Estate - 108 to 116,165
R1A	Jones, William - Estate - 623 to 628
R11A	Jones, William - 72,74,447,448
M2	Jones, W. W. - guardian for James J. & Benny G. Jones - 26
M4	Jones, W. W. - Guardian - 148,160,189
W1A	Jones, W. W. - guardian of A.M.L.Bell - 16,17
R21	Jordan, Mann Pugh - 769,818
R21	Jordan, Mann Pugh - 826,828
M9	Judge - Special Judge of Probate in Estate of Well S. Harkins - Decd. - 494
M7	Julian, Jake F. - Guardian for Lizzie & Milton Julian - Minor heirs of Frank Julian - 169
M7	Julian, Jake F. - guardian for Lizzie & Miller Julian - 169

R6B   Julian, Jake F. - Guardian, Lizzie & Milton Julian - 565,566,567

M7   Julian, Jesse W. - Petition to sell lands - 35 to 45

M1   July Term - 1882 - 184

M1   July Term - 1883 - 224

M1   July Term - 1885 - 284

M1   June Term - 1882 - 182

M1   June Term - 1883 -

M1   June Term - 1884 - 252

M1   June Term - 1885 - 280

M1   June Term - 1886 - 313

M1   June Term - ~~122~~ 1889 - 402

W2	Kaplan, Elizabeth H. - Certified Copy of Will - 310,311
R26	Karrah, Tommie W. - 26 - 427, 439
	Karrah, Tommie W. - 155, 157
M10	Keene, Frank Dee - Minor Estate - 151
R11	Keene, Frank Dee - Minor Estate - 343, 344
M8	Keenum, Frank - Decd. Estate exemption to widow Nancy F. Keenum - 524,536
R9	Keenum, Frank - Decd. Estate - 36
M9	Keenum, Nancy F. - Decd. Estate - 328,329
R10	Keenum, Nancy F. - Decd. Estate - 115, 116
W1	Keenum, Nancy F. - 256
M6	Keller, John - Decd. Estate 189 to 192
M6	Keller, John - Estate of - 351,352,374,375,381,540,571,572
R6B-	Keller, John - Decd. Estate - 460 et al - 476 to 479
M8	Kelley, Andrew J. - Decd. Estate of Lucy E. Kelley, Admr. - 477,567,590
M10	Kelley, Dan C. - Estate - 8
R10	Kelly Dan C. - Decd. Estate - 579,580
R8	Kelley, D. J. - Decd. Estate - Lucy Kelly, Admrx. - 495
M4	Kelly , Daniel W. - Substitution of Record of Deed - 429,432
R11A	Kelly, Edmond - 451, 465
R12A	Kelly, Edmond - Decd. Estate - 120
M9	Kelly, J. H. & W. B. - et al, joint owners sale of division - 257,258
M10	Kelly, James H. - Incompetence - 88,98,146,147,152,280,281,282
R9	Kelley, J. H. & W. B. - et al. point owners - 537,538,to 541, to 546
R11	Kelly, James H. - Incompetent - Estate - 184,185,197,333,334,335,336,345,513 t 519
M9	Kelley, J. Newton - Admr. Estate - 97,98,100,101
M9	Kelley, Jeff - et al. joint owners - 59,65,66,67
R9	Kelley, Jeff - et al. joint owners - 192,193,200 to 204,205,206
R9	Kelly, Newton J. - Admr of Estate - 266,267,268,269

M4   Kelly, Presly - Decd. Estate - T.E.Goodwon Sheff & Adm. - 322,393,402,403,415,
                                                                  446,464,506

M5   Kelley, Presly - Estâte - 78,84,85,86,87

R4   Kelly, Pressly - Decd. Estate - 388

R5   Kelley, Pressly - Dedd. Estate - 386

R15   Kelley, R. W. - Estate - 114,115

R27   Kelley, W. W. - 27 - 836,853

        Kelley, W. W. - 320,321

M1(2)   Kemp, Aaron - Decd. Estate - 66

W1A   Kemp, Aaron - 257,258

R1A   Kemp, E. J. - Apprentice Bond - 336 to 338

M8   Kemp, Sarah Elisabeth - Decd. Estate - 550,560

M7   Kemp, John B. - Decd. Estate - 350,353,366

R7   Kemp, J. B. - Decd. Estate - 224

W1   Kemp, John B. - 114

M8   Kemp, J. H. - et.al. joint owner - 455,459,475,479

R25   Kemp, Jesse Richard - 29 - 20

        Kemp, Jesse Richard - 529

R8   Kemp, Sarah Elizabeth - Decd. Estate - 500

W1   Kemp, Sarah Elizabeth - 218, 219

M9   Keyzer, J. W. - Decd. Estate - 228,292

R9   Keyzer, J. W. - Decd. Estate - 469,470

R10   Keyser, J. W. - Decd.Estate - 50

M2   Kidd, Avery - Mortgage to M.J.Bryant - 100 (marked through)

R12A   Kidd, A. W. - Decd. Estate - 253 to 260

M5   Kilgore, George - Decd. Estate - A.Kilgore, Admr. - 259,266,275,277,278,376,
                                                            310,377

K6B   Kilgore, George - Decd. Estate - 40, 174

M8   Killingsworth, J. C. - et al. Joint owners - 101,128,138,166,167

R8	Killingsworth, J. C. - joint owner application to sell for division - 40
M9	Killingsworth, M. D. - Estate - 102,128, 129
R9	Killingsworth, M. D. - Decd. Estate - 303,304
W1	Killingsworth, M. D. - 157
M7	Killingsworth, Walter - et al joint owners - 131,149,156
R6B	Killingsworth, Walter - et al, Final N____ - 500 to 506
M9	Killingsworth, W. D. - Decd. Estate - 486,487,488
R10	Killingsworth, W. D. - et al. joint owners - 402 to 406
M9	Killingsworth, W. J. - Estate - 51
R9	Killingsworth, W. J. - Estate - 178
M6	Kimbrell, - Estate, minor - R.D.Kimbrell, guardian - 463 to 466
M4	Kimbrell, A. J. - Decd. Estate Of J.T.Kimbrell - Admr. - 573,574,602,614,630
M5	Kimbrell, A. J. - Estate of J.T.Kimbrell, Admr. - 99, 101 to 105
R5	Kimbrell, A. J. - Decd. Estate - 301,316 to 320
M7	Kimbrell, Della - et al. joint owners - 232,238,252
R7	Kimbrell, Della - et al, joint owner petition to sale - 71 to 76
R28	Kimbrell, Henry G. - 28 - 212,216
	Kimbrell, Henry H. - 371
R16	Kimbrell, Lester - Decd. - 139,141,203,204
R20	Kimbrell, Meek - Estate of - 20 - 144,152
W2	Kimbrell, Meek - Will & Proof - 393
M3	Kimbrell, Nancy - Estate - p.574,593,720
M4	Kimbrell, Nancy - Decd. Estate - 8,9,168,169,170,184,194 to
R3	Kimbrell, Nancy - Decd. Estate - 705 to 708,742 to 750
M7	Kimbrell, Peyton G. - Decd. Estate - 740,253,254,255,(240)
R7	Kimbrell, Peyton G. - Decd. Et al. - 110
W1	Kimbrell, Peyton G. - 110, 111
M1(1)	Kimbrell, Royal - Estate of-348,358,408

R1A	Kimbrell, Royal - Estate - 290 to 293 - Inclusion
M8	Kimbrell, Shad R. - declaration adopting Ruby Jones - 3 yrs.age - 457
M6	Kimbrell, Susan J. - Decd. Estate - 436 to 458,552,553
M10	Kimbrell, Thomas Hampton - Decd. Estate - 296,297
R11	Kimbrell, Thomas HHampton - Decd. Estate - 536,537,538,539
W2	Kimbrell, Thomas Hampton - 10,13
M7	Kimbrell, William H. - Decd. Estate - 198
R7	Kimbrell, William H. - Decd. Estate - 40
R11A	Kincannon, Rainey F. - 465,466
R24	King, Betty Gay - Minor - 24 - 943,947
R26	King, Brenda Kay - 26 - 897,926
R26	King, Betty Gay - 26 - 927,957
R24	King, Brenda Kay - Minor - 24 - 936,939
R24	King, Cynthis N. - Decd. - 24 - 932,935
R24	King, Judy Inez - Minor - 24 - 940,943
R26	King, Judy Inez - 26 - 866,896
M8	Kirk, J. F. - guardian - 169,177,181
M1(1)	Kirkland, Archibald - Estate of - 38,39,40,41
R1A	Kirkland, Archibald - 407, to 409
M10	Kirkland, B. D. - Decd. Estate - 397
M5	Kirkland, John C. - Decd. Estate - 42,43,58,61,62
R5	Kirkland, John C. - Decd. Estate - 548 to 552
W1	Kirkland, John C. - 67, 68
M8	Kirkland, John E. - Decd. Estate - 452,453,461
W1	Kirkland, John E. - 208
M8	Kirkley, Albert Cx - Decd. Estate - 586
M9	Kirkley, Albert C. - Estate - 4,5,16
R9	Kirkley, Albert C. - Decd. Estate - 84
R23	Kirkley, B. R. - Decd. - 23 - 490,494

W2   Kirkley, B. R. - Deceased, Will & Proof - 475

R26   Kirkley, Lois - 26 - 289,296,536,770,774

        Kirkley, Lois D. - Will & Proof - 136,37,38

M10   Kirksey, Earl - Estate - 314,550

M10   Kirksey, Earl - Incompetent - 550

R11   Kirksey, Earl - Estate - 562

E17(M)? Kitchens, A. M. - guardian - 406,494,495

R26   Kittle, William Lee - 26 - 74,78

M10   Kivette, Mrs. M. E. - Decd. Estate - 494,495,496

W2   Kivette, Mrs. M. E. - 36

R15   Kizzire, Alie T. - Decd. 542,546

R16   Kizzire, Aline T. - Decd. - 97,108,144,145

R23   Kizzire, Midie Lee - Decd. - 23 - 929,936

W2   Kizzire,-Maide Lee - Will & Proof - 517,518

R25 -   Knight, Nettie - Incompetent - 25 - 847,842

        Kuykendall, C. M. - Deceased - 456

R15   Kuykendall, Rise - Setting apart homestead - 307,314

R21   Lagrone, W. H. - Decd. - 21 - 429,478

M7   Lambert, M. A., vs. M. Davis -

M7   Lambert, Rena - adoption of Y.P.N. Fortenberry - 236,237

R24   Lane - John Wesley - Decd. - 24 - 879,889

W2   Lane, John Waley - Will & Proof - 874,875

M9   Langston, Adaline - Estate - a person of unsound mind - 488, 489

M9   Langston, C. W. - guardian Adaline Langston - 488, 489

R10   Langston, C. W. - guardian - 420 et al.

R23   Langston, C. W. - Decd. - 23 - 721,728

W2   Langston, C. W. - Will & Proof - 492,493

M6   Langston, J. B. - Estate of decd. - 182 to 188

M1(1)   Langston, Jesse J. - Estate ef - 204,207,211,218,223,229, 250,259,266,316,344,
                345,354,365,366,373,402,403,436,604,611
M9(3)   Langston, Jesse J. - Estate of - 505,506,507,508,509

R1A   Langston, Jesse J. - Estate Of - 502,524, to 527,749 to 751

W1   Langston, John B. - 68

M5   Latona, Town of - Incorporation Proceedings - 196,198,799

M1   Laudergram - 555

R2   Laurimore, John - Estate - 570 to 580

W1A   Lawrence, Alesc. - 629, to 633

M1(2)   Lawrence, Alexander - Estate - 57,58,59,60,123,141,142,191,192,193,285,564,
                578,579
R12A   Lawrence, Alexander - Decd. Estate - 173 to 179,399 to 406,779 to 781

R3   Lawrence, Alexander - Estate - 273

R11A   Lawrence, Alexander - 518,519

R25   Lawrence, Annie Mae - Inc. - 25 - 842,848

R17   Lawrence, Horace Rowland - change of name - 365

R16   Lawrence, Jerry Dale - Minor - 369,370

R19   Lawrence, Jerry Dale- Minor - 19 - 807,808

R25   Lawrence, Leather N. - Inc. - 25 - 668,674

R21   Lawrence, Mattie - Inc. - 21 - 05,416

R22   Lawrence, Nodie Little - Decd. - 22 - 423,426

R22   Lawrence, Nodie Little - 22 - 434,453

M9   Lawrence, O. C. - settlement with Tusaaloosa Cooperage Co. & of Empersation
                                                        Law - 4

R15   Lawrence, Rayburn L. - Estate - 561,63

R16   Lawrence, Rayburn L. - Estate of Deceased - 371,372,412

R15   Lawrence, Wallace P. - Decd. - 272,275,337,388,339

M3   Lawrimore, John - Estate - P.136,137,165,166,215,221,222,224,239, to 241,273,
                                           311, to 313, 314,315

R3   Lawrimore, John - Estate - 326 to 340, 372

M1(2)   Lawrimore, W. G. - Substitution of Justice Bond - 119

M8   Lawson, James D. - Decd. Estate - 514

R11A   Lee, A. Nancy - 94,98,127,136,516

M8   Lee, Ethel - Decree removing d____ of non age - 566

M10   Lee, J. J. - Decd. Estate - 303,304

R11   Lee, J. J. - Decd. Estate - 552

W2   Lee, J. J. - 7

M1(2)   Lee, James - Decd. Estate - 165,166,194,196,359,160,197,307

M3   Lee, James - Estate - p.55, 56

M2   Lee, James - Estate - 202 to 206, 318,319,320,603

M4   Lee, James - Decd., G.W.Richards, Admr. - 260,306,312,338,344,358,583,604,605
                                                      606.

M4   Lee, James - Jno. C. Moore, exec'ter - 560,566

R12A   Lee, James - Decd. Estate - 415 to 422, 655 to 658

R3   Lee, James - Estate - 258,259

R5   Lee, James - Decd. Estate - 310

W1   Lee, James - 1

W1A   Lee, James - 159

R2   Lee, James & William - Estate - 116 to 119

M7   Lee, Mary R. - guardian for Ethel & Effie Lee, Minor heirs of C.F.Lee, Decd.
                                                           497

R7   Lee, Mary R. - guardian for Ethel & Effie Lee - 396

M(3)   Lee, Nancy A. - Estate of - 127 to 131,483,484,485,486,487,488,489,490,491,492

M9   Lee, Sam - guardian Mattie Hutten (Person of unsound mind) -178,314,315

R9   Lee, Sam - guardian Mattie Hutton (unsound mind) 454,455

R10   Lee, Sam - guardian of Mattie Hutton - unsound mind - 87,88,89,295,296,297,298

M1(2)   Lee, William B. - Decd. Estate - 165,166,198,199,200,201,202

M2   Lee, William B. - Deceased Estate - 406,603,604,605

R12A   Lee, William B. - Decd. Estate - 409 to 414

M7   Legg, Gustavus - Decd. - A.B.Legg, Admr. - 325,326,355,351,358

R7   Legg, Gustavus - Decd. Estate - Albert B. Legg, Admr. - 220

R25   Liles, John William - Decd. - 25 - 578,584

M7   Lindsey, Bessie & Lovie May - Minor heirs of John Lindsey, Decd. - F.N.Patter-
                                                                          son, gdn. - 389
M8   Lindsey, C. B. & other joint owners to sell property for dividion - 396,397,
                                                                    398,408,422,424,427
R8   Lindsey, C. B. & others - joint owners - 466

R14   lindsey, Eugenia - Decd. - 567, 573

W2   Lindsey, Mrs. Eugenia - 137

R13   Lindsey, Huston - Estate - 372 thru 374

M7   Lindsey, Ida - guardian for Jakie Katrinia Lindsey, minor heir - Jake Lindsey,
                                                                          decd. - 433
R7   Lindsey, Mrs. Ida - guardian for Jakie Katerman Lindsey - Minor - 320

M8   Lindsey, Isabell - etal joint owners - 325,334,335,338,348,356

R8   Lindsey, Isabelle - et al, joint owner - 358

M4   Lindsey, Joseph E. - Dora, minors, W.M.Lindsey, guardian - 268

M10   Lindsey, J. H. - Decd. Estate of-21

R9   Lindsey, J. H. - Estate - order granting letters - 484,548

M4   Lindsey, John K. - et al, minors - 90,252,256

M4   Lindsey, John K. - Minor over 14, B.D.Williams, guardian - 276,627

M10   Lindsey, J. L. - Decd. Estate - 567

R11A   Lindsey, L. - Estate - 69, 70

M6   Lindsey, Levi - Estate - 201 to 206

M8	Lindsey, Meek - Minor over 18 - 375
M4	Lindsey, Newton H. & Thomas E. - Minors (Dock B.Williams gdn.)- 277 - J.T. Williams, gdn. - 548
M5	Lindsey, N. H. & T. E. - Estate - 224,372
M7	Lindsey, Simpson N. - Decd. Minor heirs of - B.Henry, gdn. - 280,298,299
R7	Lindsey, Simpson - Decd. Estate - Minor heirs B.Henry, gdn. - 156
M4	Lindsey, Thomas G. = Decd. Estate - 223,224,241,242,252,266,584,598,599,600, 601 - settlement
R4	Lindsey, Thomas G. - Decd. Estate - 351 to 359, 495 to 499
R5	Lindsey, Thomas G. - Decd. Estate - 305
R19	Lindsey, T. L. - Estate of - 19 - 311,318
W2	Lindsey, T. L. - Will & Proof - 358
M(3)	Lindsey, William L. - Estate of - 135,136,137,138
R4	Lindsey, Wm. M. - guardian for John K. et al - 238 to 239
M8	Lindsey, Mrs. Zora - guardian for Minor Heirs - 214
R8	Lindsey, Mrs. Zora - guardian - 224
R25	Lifcer (Lipcer), Carl Willie - change of name - 25 - 292,293
M3	Liquar Prohibition - P. 245,253
R24	Little, Alton - Decd. - 24 - 651,654
R24 -	Little, J. N. - Inc. - 24 - 854,860
M10	Livingston, Artie Leed, - Decd. Estate - 443
M9	Livingston, Bessie Mae - guardian, Willard Livingston - Minor - 506
R10	Livingston, Bessie (Berree) Mae - guardian - 486
R10	Livingston, Georgia Mae - Minor - E.W.Walters - 442
M9	Livingston, Loyd Danny - Minor - 505
M10	Livingston, Lloyd Danny - Minor - 457
R10	Livingston, Lloyd Deny - Minor H.W.Crawford, guardian - 441,284
R14	Livingston, Lloyd Danny - Minor - 238,239,240,358
M8	Loe, J. A. - guardian for Verdall Loe - Minor - 71

R8   Loe, J. B. - guardian of Estate of Verdelle Loe, Minor - 10

R11A   Loftis, David - 467,488

M1(1)   Loftis, Lemuel - Estate of - 99,127,175

M(3)   Loftis, Lemuel - Estate of - 576,577

R1A   Loftis, Lemuel - Estate - 651

R11A   Loftis, Lemuel - 508,512

M6   Logan,   - Application for order to sell personal property - 548
                                            Order for Notice - 549
M6   Logan,   - Appraisement Bill Fayette Co. - 542

M6   Logan,   -   Bill Marion Co. - 544

M6   Logan,   - Inventory of administration H.V.Bostick - 502 to 505

M6   Logan,   - Order for sale of personal property - 550 - Report of sale -
                                                                            551
M6   Logan,   - Petition for letter Administration - 498 to 502

M8   Logan, Freelin - adopted by W.Carroll Sparks - 421

M10   Logan, Freeland - et al (Condemnation of lands) 508,509,510,511,512,513,514,515,
                                                            516,517

R21   Logan, G. W. - Deceased - 21 - 372,378

W2   Logan, G. W. - 406

M4   Logan, Martha A. & - guardian for U.S.,A.W. & J.W. - 316

R4   Logan, Martha A. - guardian for 3 minors - 480

M4   Logan, N.B. - Estate - 30,106

R4   Logan, N. B. - Decd. Estate - 170 to 174

M6   Logan, R. B. - Decd. Estate - 354,415 to 426

M6   Logan, R. B. - Decd. Estate - Petition of letters administration - 427,428

M6   Logan, R. B. - Decd. Estate - Designation of W.R.Enis - Admr. - 428

M7   Logan, R. B. - Estate - 90,91

W1   Logan, R. B. - 173

R23   Lollar, Rufus Theron - Decd. - 23 - 589,590

M(3)   Long, Ephraim, - Estate of - 330

- 100 -

R23   Love, Robert R. - Decd. - 23 - 971,983

W2   Love, Robert R. - Deceased, Certified Copy - 515,516

M1   Lovett, Alvah - 28, 29

M5   Loutherwood, Martha Ann - adoption & change of N_____ - 111

R11A   Lowe, Marcus W. - 512,516,517

M2   Lowerey, A. B. - Estate - 708m, 709

R3   Lowery, A. B. - Estate - 134,135

R25   Lowery, Annie V. - Decd. - 25 - 585,592

       Lowery, Annie V. - Will - 5, 8

M1(2) Lowrey, B. F. - Decd. Estate - 44,45,46,77,593,594

M4   Lowrey, Benjamin F. - Decd. Estate - 1,2,26,69,80,88,328,334,336,337

R12A   Lowrey, B. F. - Decd. Estate - 618 to 623

R4   Lowry, Benj. F. - Decd. Estate - F.M.Lowry, Admr. -   324 to 333

W1A   Lowery, B. F. - 644 to 648

R23   Lowery, Loyd - Decd. - 23 - 628,631

R11A   Lowery, Mathis N. - 498,505

R25   Lowery, Sandra - Inc. - 25 - 969,974

M10   Lucas, J. H. - Decd. Estate - 497,498,499,597,598

W2   Lucas, J. H. - 36

M10   Lucas, Pleasie, Joseph M. - et al. joint owners - 590,591,592,593,594

W2   Lucas, S. U. - 2, 3

M10   Lucas, S. W. - Decd. Estate - 174,176,257

R11   Lucas, S. W.? - Decd. Estate - 384,386,425,426,479

M1(2) Lyles, Thomas V. - Decd. Estate - 65

M(3)   Lyles, Thomas V. - Estate of - 349,348,347,346,318,317,316,315,314,578

R11A   Lyles, Thomas V. - 488,497,505,507

R23   Lynn, Ella Howton - Decd. - 23 - 608,613

W2   Lynn, Ella Howton - Will & Proof - 491

R22   Lynch, Clayton A. - Decd. - 22 - 106,116

W2   Lynch, Clayton - Deceased, Certified copy of Will (see book 22, P,108,111)

M10   Lyons, Jim - Decd. Estate - 285

R11   Lyons, Jim - Decd. Estate - 522,523

M8   McArthur, H. S. - Decd. Estate - 532

M9   McCaleb, Alex - Decd. Estate 252,253

R9   McCaleb, Alex - Decd. Estate - 529,530

W1   McCaleb, Alex - 248

M5   McCaleb, Alfred C. - Estate - T.S.McCaleb, Admr. - 227,232,241,261,262,277

R16(15) McCaleb, A. C. - Decd. - 468,476

R6B   McCaleb, Alfred J. - Decd. Estate - 16

R17   McCaleb, Alfred - Decd. Estate - 423,442

R23   McCaleb, Alfred - Decd. - 23 - 233,238

R16   McCaleb, Andrew Jackson - Deceased - 34,35

M10   McCaleb, H. B. - Decd. Estate - 463

R17   McCaleb, Hester - Estate Decd. - 245,459,460

M10   McCaleb, James F. - Dedd. Estate of - 451,452,453

W2   McCaleb, James F. & Reginia C. - 15 (28-29)

W2   McCaleb, James F. & Reginia C. - Will & Proof - 386,387

M8   McCaleb, J. T. - Decd. Estate - 384,386,387

R8   McCaleb, J. T. - Decd. Estate - 426

W1   McCaleb, J. T. - 136,137

R19   McCaleb, Regina C. - 19 - 608,619

R15   McCaleb, Ruth Ezell - Decd. E. - 533,35

R23   McCaleb, Sleetie - Inc. - 23 - 640,646

M9   McCaleb, Tim - Decd. Estate - 301

M10   McCalebm Tim - Decd. Estate - 32,32

R10   McCaleb, Tim - Decd. Estate - 64, 65

R11   McCaleb, Tim - Decd. Estate - 23,24,25,26,27

R13   McCarthy, Vera & Children - et al. vs. Fayette Co. - 513 thru 526

R28   McCaleb, Warrne I - 28 - 802

        McCaleb, Warren I. - 502

M10   McCaleb, W. C. - et al, condemnation of lands vs. Fayette Co.,Ala. -351,2,3,4,5

M10   McCaleb, W. C. (Condemnation of lands) vs. Fayette Co.Ala. - 356,7,8,9

M8   McCaleb, W. F. - Estate & Other - 271,272

M(3)   McCay, William, Mort - 263

M1(2)   McClain, G. R. - Guradian for James Harkins - 76

M1(2)   McClure, John - Decd. Estate - 291,640,45 655

M(3)   McClure, John - Estate of - 311,310,309,308,307,517,518,519,520

R11A   McClure, John - 71,72

M1   McClure, J. W. - 25, 26

M(3)   McClure, John W. - Estate of - 500,501,502,503,504

R1A   McClure, Joseph - Estate - 135 to 141,735

R20   McClure, William C. - Estate of - 20,29,36

W2   McClure, William C. - Will & Proof - 384,385

M2   McCollough, Joseph E. - Estate - 174

R11A   McCollough, William H. - 549,551

R28   McCollum, Arthur C. - 28 - 109,115

        McCollum, Arthur C. - 347,349

R24   McCollum, Geneva, Faymon,Jr., & Glenda Sue, Minors - 24 - 249,252

M1(2)   McCollum, G. W. - Decd. Estate - 305,306,307

M1(2)   McCollum, G. W. - 353,354,375,376,377,378,379,553,562,563,565

R12A   MCCollum, G. W. - Decd. Estate - 579 to 587

W1A   McCollum, G. W. - 595,596

M10   McCollum, Jake - Decd. Estate - 573

W1A   McCollum, Joseph - 133 to 135 to 143

R8   McCollum, M. B. - guardian, C.R.Wheeler - 170

M8   McCollum, M. C. - guardian for C.K.Wheeler, Minor - 69, 178

M2   McCollum, Newman - Estate - 299 to 302

M(3)   Newman - Estate of - 581,582

M3   McCollum, Newman - Estate - P. 443,471,514,535,568,569,570,571

R1A   McCollum, Newman - Estate - 413 to 423, 652 to 654, 745 to 748

R11A   McCollum, Newman - 519,528

R3   McCollum, Newman - Estate - 461,462,651 to 672

M5   McCollum, Newman L. - Estate (F.L.McCollum, Admr.   182,194

M4	McCollum, N. T. - Estate - 46,80,105
R4	McCollum, N. T. - Decd. Estate - 190 to 196
M4	McCollum, Samuel - non Em-Mertis - 478,479,486
M5	McCollum, Samuel - Non Corpus Metes - 73,81,166
M5	McCollum, Samuel - Decd. Estate of L. F. McCollum, Admr. 89
R5	McCollum, Samuel - Non Corpus Metes - 530 to 536
M4	McCollum, William - Estate - 439,449,469,474,475,487,492,504
M5	McCollum, William - Estate - 209,290
R5	McCollum, William - Decd. Estate 90, 242
R6B	McCollum, William - Decd. Estate - 80 et al.
R6B	McCollum, W.H. - Bond in Sollomon Castleberry Estate - 262
M1(2)	McClung, Jonas - Decd. Estate - 332,333,335,336,381,382,406,649,694,564,578, 579,658,659,696,697,698
R12A	McClung, Jonas - Decd. Estate - 685 to 690
W1A	McClung, Jonas - 201 to 205,209,593,594,706,747,748
R15	McCombs, Jerry - Decd. - 285,289,350,352
W2	McCombs, Jerry - 184
R26	McCombs, Lula M. - 25 - 297,306 - Will 3 - 139
	McCombs, Lula M. - Will & Proof - 139,140,142
R18	McConnell, Arthur - Estate of - 18 - 406,412
W2	McConnell, Arthur - Deceased, Will & Proof - 342,343
M7	McConnell, D. O. - Condemnation of lands for public road - 515,516,517,518,519 520
M10	McConnell, Daniel O. - Decd. Estate of - 376,377
R14	McConnell, D. O. - Decd. - 72 thru 75, 510,513
M7	McConnell, Ernest - Disabilities of ___ off relieved by Decree in Chancery-457
R10	McConnell, J. Murray - Decd. Estate - 239,240
R17	McConnell, Joseph - et al. - 82,87
M9	McConnell, M. Murray - Decd. Estate - 391
R14	McConnell, Oise C. - Decd. - 76 thru 78, 514,517
R16	McConnell, Thomas O. - Decd. - 160,163

W2   McConnell, T. O. - 251,252,253

M1(1)   McConnell, Thmmas P. - Appointed County Admr - 120

R6B   McConnell, Thomas P. - 338 to 342,326 to 330

R11A   McConnell, Thomas P. - 555

W1   McConnell, Thos. P. - 80

W1   McConnell, Thos. P. - 86

M1(2)   McCool, E. E. - Estate - 618,620,641,687

M2   McCool, E. E. - Estate - 122

W1A   McCool, E. E. - 6,7,8,9,11,12,20,38

R25   McCool, Frank - Decd. - 25 - 675,679

R17   McCool, George F. - Decd. - 29, 31

M1(1)   McCown, John 2nd. Estate of - 154,155,156,157

M10   McCoy, Mrs. D. O. - Decd. Estate - 85,86,150

R11   McCoy, Mrs. J. O. - Decd. Estate - 172,173,336

W1   McCoy, Mrs. S. O. - 336

M6   McCracken, A. D. (J) - Decd. Estate - 524,525

R6B   McCracken, A. J. - 468 - etal.

W1   McCracken, A. J. - 100

M7   McCracken, J. T. - etal. joint owners - 300,301,303,310,311,312,313,314,320,321,
                                                           322,323,324

R26   McCray, Jack (_____ ___) - 26 - 312,313

M1(1)   McCrary, Thomas - Estate of - 78,79,80,81

M1(1)   McCraw, Mary - Estate of - 202,232-233

M(3)   McCraw, Sarah A. - Estate of - 341,340

R1A   McCraw, Thomas - Estate - 434 to 440

R11A   McCraw, Thomas - 545,548

M1(2)   McCullough, Williamson H. - Decd. Estate - 110,111

M2   McCullough, W. H. - Estate - 74 to 77, 315

R12A   McCullough, W. H. - Decd. Estate - 328 to 331

R25   McCutcheon, H. E. - Decd. - ? - 541,547

          McCuthceon, H. E. - Will -] 16

M10   McDaniel, Walter L. - Decd. Estate - 587

M2	McDonald, Alexander - Estate - 796,797,798
M3	McDonald, Alexander - P.13,57,266,326 to 329
R2	McDonald, Alexander - Estate - 409 to 419
R3	McDonald, Alexander - Estate - 287,345,348
M10	McDonald, G. W. - Decd. Estate of - 388
M9	McDonald, J. E. - Decd. Estate - 474,475
R10	McDonald, J. E. - Decd. Estate - 425
R18	McDonald, Hal P. - Estate of - 18 - 92,132
R23	McDonald, Hal P. - Deceased - 23 - 277,291
R14	McDonald, Jeff & W. vs. Fayette County - 350 thru 357
M7	McDuff, Aggie & Lewis - Minors - 372,511,512
R7	McDuff, Aggie & Lewis - Minor J. E. Woodard, guardian - 230
R28	McEachein, Marilyn S. - 28 - 920,923
M10	McFadden, Lucile Miller - Minor Estate - 42
R11	McFaddin, Lucille Miller - Minor - 56,57
R19	McGee, Dinella - Estate of - 19 - 916,920
M2	McGee, Peter - guardian for A.Cole - 46
M1(2)	McGill, Thomas - Estate Rachel McGill, Adm. - 723,726,727,755
M2	McGill, Thomas - Estate - 84
R3	McGill, Thomas - Estate - 286
W1A	McGill, Thos. - 56,57,89
R21	McGough, J. C. - Decd. - 21 - 489,495
W2	McGough, J. C. - will & Proof - 402-403
R25	McGough, McKinley - Decd. - 25 - 856,859
M10	McGowen, G. B. - Decd. Estate of - 17 -
R10	McGowen, G. B. - Decd. Estate - 574,575,576
R13	McGowen, G. B. - Estate - 402,427 to 434
M8	McGraw, J. F. - Admr. of B.H.Smothers Estate - who was gdn. in this court - 85,92
M7	McGuff, Claude - male child 8 yrs. old adopted by J.R.Skelton - 502
R15	McGuff, Rufus - Estate - 36,37

R28   McKee, Melba Jean - 28 - 790,793

M1(2)   McMinn, D. D. - 526,527,531,545,546,556,557

M2   McMinn, D. D. - Estate - 24

W1A   McMinn, Drury - 546,547,557,583,591,592

R21   McNease, Alma Lee - Decd. - 21 - 864,875

W2   McNease, Alma Lee - Will & Proof - 459,460

R15   McNees, D. A. - Decd. - 379,81

W2   McNees, D. A. - 221,222

R17   McNees, Harold C. - an Incompetent - 147,154,155,199,326

R19   McNees, Harold C. - Incompetent - 19 - 813

R22   McNees, Harold C. - Incompetent - 22 - 299,310

R22   McNees, Harold C. - Inc. - 22 - 733,794

R24   McNees, Harold C. - Inc. - 24 - 277,323

R25   McNees, Harold - Inc. - 25 - 326,367

R15   McNees, Harold C. - Incompetent - 547,549

R24   McPherson, Jesse Elmer - Decd. - 24 - 241,244

R25   McPherson, Jesse Elmer - Decd. - 25 - 205, 226

M7   McReynolds, T. H. - Decd. Estate - 422

R7   McReynolds, T. H. - Decd. Estate - 290

M10   McNeil, Walter Scott - Decd. Estate - 195,196,197

R11   McNeil, Walter Scott - Decd. Estate - 407,408,409

W2   McNeil, Walter Scott - 1

R14   Madden, A. C. - Decd. Estate of - 203,204,205

W2   Madden, A. C. - 96

R24   Maddox, Josie - Decd. - 24 - 487,502

W2   Maddox, Josie - Will & Proof - 550,551

R13   Maddox, Loyal Baker - Proceedings to have declared of unsound mind, etc. - 262
                                                                          thru 266

R19   Maddox, Loyal Baker - Inc. - Vol. 19 - 227,309

M1(2)   Maddox, Mary Jane - substitution marriage record - 26 - widow of H.J.Maddox.

M10   Maddox, S. E. - Decd. Estate - 321,322,323,324

R11   Maddox, S. E. - Deceased - 569,570

W2   Maddox, S. E. - 18, 19

R16   Maddox, W. M., Sr. - Decd. - 54,58

W2   Maddox, W. M., Sr. - 231

R21   Maddox, W. W. - Decd. - 21 - 496,504

W2   Maddox, W. W. - Will & Proof - 405

R16   Madison, A.D. & Flora Mae Gilliam - Minor - 129,131 - Sale of Land - 196,200,
                                                                          339,342

R27   Madison, Calven - Minor - 26 - 477,480 or 877,880

M6   Madison, G. A. to W. T. Madison -

M6   Madison, G. A. - Decd., Petition Probate Will - 404,405,405,507,508,510,511,512
                                                513,514,515,516,517, to 521

M7   Madison, Ga. A. - Decd. - Letter Testamentary - 17

M7   Madison, G. A. - Decd. Estate - Exe. Bond W.T.Madison - 17

M7   Madison, G. A. - Estate - 196,203,204

W1   Madison, G. A. - 178

R13   Madison, G. R. - Estate - 332,336

R26   Maddison, Jossie Lee - 26 - 709,715

        Maddison, Josei Lee - 208,211

R27   Madison, Lester L. - 26 - 465,469 - Vol. 27 - pg. 253,260

M7   Madison, Sarah E. - guardian for Sallie Madison, Minor - 170,195,175,179

R6B   Madison, Sarah E. - guardian Sallie Madison, Minor - 568,569,570, to 573

M7   Madison, W. T. vs. B.N.Madison - 16,18 to 21

M(3)   Mahan, William - Estate of - 295 to 296

R1A   Mahan, William - Estate - 241 to 244, 655 to 661

R11A   Mahan, William - 48,55,554,555

M6^   Manasco, Joseph E. & Franklin - W.C.Manasco - 469

M1   March Term

M1   March Term - 1882 - 173

M1   March Term - 1883 - 202

M1   March Term - 1895 - 587

M7   Marion, E. E. - Decd. Estate, Mrs. Jane Atchiey, Extrx. - 181,184

R5   Marlyoung, James M.- Decd. Estate - 557 to 560

R8   Markham, J. D. - guardian - 354

M8   Markham, - for Lydia A. Markham, minor heirs - 315

M9   Mariam, S. E. - guardian - 138

M(3)   Markamson, Martha - Estate of - 583,584,585

        Marx, Jack - original on file Lowndes Co., Micc - 515

R15   Mathes, Ethel Kathleen - Decd. - 362,68

W2   Mathes, Ethel Kathleen - 194,195

W2   Mathes, G. R. (Prob. Ct. Recd. Vol. 13, pg. 207, 208)

M10   Mathis, Nathan - Decd. Estate - 117,147,148

R11   Mathis, Nathan - Decd. Estate - 258

R13   Mathes, S. R. - Decd. Will of - 207,208

R21   Matthews, George Lester - Decd. - 21 - 743,746

M4   Matthews, Jerome - guardian - 567

M10   Matthews, Jerome - 25,26,27,28

R11   Matthews, Jerome - Decd. Estate - 7,8,9,10,11,12,13,14,15,16

M10   Matthews, Lee - Decd. Estate - 328

R11   Matthews, Lee - Decd. - 575

M5   Matthews, Lewis - Declaration adopting 3 children & change of name - 69

R11   Matthes, Nathan (col) - Estate - 326,327,328

M1   Matthews, R. C. - 26,27

M3   Mathews, Samuel - Estate - P. ?7 to 230, 243, 400,418

R3   Mathews, Samuel G. - Estate - 184 to 196, 481

M4   Mathews, Steward - Declaration legitimatizing - 553

M(3) Mattison, George B. - Estate of - 573,574

M8   Mattox, C. P. - et al. joint owners - 554, 559,563,571

R9   Mattox, E. P. & other heirs of G.W.Norris - et. al. joint owners - 56

R11A Mattox, Joseph - 528,529

R1A   Maxley, A. S. - Estate - 445 to 454

R20   Maxwell, Ethel - Unsound Mind - 20 - 167,178

R15   May, Carrie L. - Decd. - 572,575

W2   May, Carrie L. - 219

M4   May, George - Estate - 81,82,83,99,100,119,150,366,376,382,83,84,85

R4   May, George - Decd. Estate - 200 to 209

M4   May, Lewis F. - Estate - 103,200,216

R4   May, Lewis F.- De-d. Estate - 160 to 165

R21   May, Olen - Inc. - 21 - 517,531

M9   May, W. A. - guardian - 58,495

R9   May, W. A. - Guardian account - 476, order & decree - 477, Bond 485

R10   May, W. A. - guardian - Washington F. May - 130,143

R9   May, M. F. - guardian - 190,191

M1   May Term - 1882 - 179

M1   May Term - 1883 - 213

R25   May, William Louise May - 25 - 245,251

M10   May, W. F. - Incompetent - 44,65,110,116,163,165,187,204,347,8

M10   May, Washington F. - Incompetent - 349,370,371,459,528,542

R11   May, Washington F. - Incompetent - 61,62,63,64,65,66,122,123,124,232,233,364,367,
                                            368,403

R11   May, Washington F. - Incompetent - 601,602,603

R11   May, Washington F. -Incompetent - Estate - 598,599,600

R13   May, Washington F. - Incompetent - 68,71,259,260,261,435,436,437,438

R14   May, Washington F. - Incompetent - 48,49,50

May, Washington F. - Estate of - 336,339

R15   May, Washington F. - Incompetent - 451,56

R10 or 15 - May, Washington F. - Incompetent - 195,345,352

R17   May, Washington F. - Incompetent - 378,383

R19   May, Washington F. - Inc. - 19 - 765,772

R22   May, Washington F. - Inc. - 22 - 163, 189

R24   May, Washington F. - Inc. - 24 - 397,418

R26   May, Washington F. - Inc. - 26 - 204,232

R27   May, Washington F. - May Bond (See May below) - 27 - David Enslen - 405

R27   May, Washington F. - 27 - 480,488 - Vol. 28, 187,188,Vol. 28, 857,892

R23   Maberyy, Nades L. - Decd. Estate of - 23 - 923,29 927

W2   Mayberry, Nades G. - Will - see Probate Rec. Vol. 23 - 924,2925

M9   Mayfield, P. P. - Estate - 505

R10   Mayfield, P. P. - Decd. Estate - 488,489

R23   Mealer, Leslie Franklin & Lesa Ann, - Minors - 23 - 745,748

M8   Medders, S. A. - et.al. joint owner - 126,144,192

R8   Medders, S. F. - et. al. joint owners - 57

M7   Meharg, James T. - guardian for 3 minor children Jesse B. Neville - 154,455

M8   Meherg, J. T. - guardian for Neville heirs - 210

R6B   Meherg, J. T. - guardian J.B.Neville - Minor heirs - 539,540

R8   Meherg, J. T. - guardian (Neville (Sims) Heirs _ 222

M4   Melton, Elishu - Decd. Estate - 254,258,259,280

R4   Melton, Elihu - Decd. Estate - 450,456

R23   Melton, Karen Denise - Minor - 23 - 591,594

M1(1) Meriweather, Joseph & Elizabeth - Estate of - 447,486

M1(1) Merritt, John - Estate of - 479,490,544,588,606,618

R1A   Merritt, John - Estate - 299 to 307

R11A   Merrett - John - 532,534

R15   Metcalf, Fred - Decd. - 62,63,278,80

M2   Metcalf, Lewis - lein note to D. S. Harris - 154

M7	Metcalf, Ozzie - apprentice Rufus Harkins - 171,172
R15	Metcalf, Willie Mae - Decd. - 56,57,266,67
M10	Michael, Isaac - Decd. Estate - 409
R21	Michael, Isaac - Decd. - 21 - 505,508
R21	Michael, Nathan - Decd. Estate - 21 - 747,750
M6	Middleton, Earnest - Minor J.R.Sizemore - guardian - 466,467
R15	Miles, Leon Bradford - Incompetent - 60, 61
R16	Miles, Leon Bradford - Incompetent - 14
R18	Miles, Leon B. - Incompetent - Vol. 18,110,778 - Vol. 19, 407,412
R21	Miles, Leon B. - Inc. - 21 - 751,768
M2	Miles, R. P. - Estate - 285,783,784,798,799
M3	Miles, Robert P. - Estate - P.24, 315,342,343,352, to 354
M4	Miles, R. P. - Estate of - 43
R2	Miles, Robert P. - Estate - 401 to 408
R3	Miles, Robert P. - Estate - 394 to 400
	Miller, Blanche Waldrop - 93,125
M7	Miller, D. H. & wife, Maude Miller - adoption of Verna Maude Miller - 369,370
M7	Miller, Eugene Brewster, decree recovering diabitis of ___ age - 468
R9	Miller, Hulda - of unsound mind - 217
M6	Miller, Jacob G. - Decd. Estate - 363 to 371, 396 to 400
R26	Miller, John Robert - 26 - 531,535
R28	Miller, John Robert - 28 - 527,541
M9	Miller, Lucile - Minor - 85
R9	Miller, Lucile - Minor Estate of - 239,240,241
W2	Miller, Margret - 40
M9	Miller, Micajah H. - Decd. Estate - 80
R9	Miller, Micajah H. - Decd. Estate - 228,254,255
M7	Miller, R. H. & Maude - declaration daopting Verner Gladys Otts - 140
M7	Miller, R. H. ___ of James Barnes Otts apprentice re___ - 212

M9   Miller, Rhoda - non corpus mentis - W.O. Colling - guardian - 81

W2   Miller, Ward R. - Cert. copy of Will, see Deed Record Vol. 121 - 240,241

R13   Mills, Roy J. & Junina Mirian - 451,452

R20   Mills, Thomas Quinton - Decd. Estate of - 20 - 223,226

R14   Mims, Jessie Davis - Incompetent - 81 through 85

R16   Mink, Clara Jean & Earnest James - Minor - 189,195

R11A Minton, Isaac - 556,557

R28   Mitchell, Florence D. - 28 - 116,142

      Mitchell, Florence D. - 350,353

M6   Mitchell, Isaac J. - Estate - 42,44,46

R6B   Mitchell, Isaac J. - Decd. Estate - 195 to 204

M9   Mitchell, Harvey J. - Decd. Estate - 223

R9 Mitchell Harvey J. - Decd. Estate - 458,459

R28   Mitchell, Henry G. - 28 - 70,100

      Mitchell, Henry G. - 43,46

R24   Mitchell, Lingee - Decd. - 24 - 229,234

R21   Mitchell, Roma - Decd. - 21 - 509,516

W2   Mitchell, Roma - Will & Proof - 431

R14   Mitchell, R. T. - Decd. Estate of - 183 thru 187

R15   Mitchum, Claude - Decd. 409-16

W2   Mitchum, Claude - 198,199

R28   Mitchum, Elaine - 28 - 716,720

      Mitchum, Elaine - 452,455

R17   Mobley, W. N. - Decd. - 22,24,284

W2   Mobley, W. N. - 286

M10   Molloy, Elizabeth & Dorothy - Minors - Estate - 84

R11   Molloy, Elizabeth & Dolly   - Minor Estate - 171,172

M2   Monroe, Wm. - Estate, J.S.Moore, Adm. - 303,632,634,654,662,681,693,694

R21   Monroe, William Wright - Decd - 21 - 417,429

M5   Montgomery, James Madison - Estate - 179,190,191,193

M6   Montgomery, James M. - Estate of - 284,285,286

W1   Montgomery, James M. - 21,22,23

M3   Montgomery, Thomas - P.293 to 298

R3   Montgomery, Thomas M. - Estate - 291 to 295

M8   Moon, E. B. - Decd. Estate - 184,186,189

M5   Moore, Mrs. A. A. - Petition of dower - 360

R24 Moore, Annie Mae - Inc. - 24 - 270,276

M9   Moore, Brazzie M. - et al. joint owners & oral examination - 267 to 269,345,359,
                                                     360,361,362

R10 Moore, Braxzie M. - et al. joint owners to sell land - 173,174,175,176

M1(2) Moore, Carson H. - decd. Estate - 66,193,194,229,374 to 379,484,485,653m667

R11A Moore, Carson H. - 542, 545

W1A Moore, Carson H. - 220 to 223,444,713,714

M3   Moore, D. W. - P.196,316,323

R3   Moore, Daniel W. - Estate - 343,344

R23 Moore, E. M. - Decd. - 23 - 749,752

M1(1) Moore, Henry - Estate of - 139,140,299,390,477,485,510

 M1(2)Moore, Henry - Decd. Estate - 329,330,360,361,415

M2   Moore, Henry - Estate, J.H.Moore, Adm. - 503 to 505,537,693,761

M3   Moore, Henry - Estate - P.9 to 11,382

R1A Moore, Henry - Estate - 468 to 470,647 to 648

R11A Moore, Henry - 530,532

R12A Moore, Henry - Decd. Estate - 721 to 726

R2   Moore, Henry - Estate - 46

R3   Moore, Henry - Estate - 114 to 120,628

R3   Moore, Henry - Estate - 628

W1A Moore, Henry - 281

M9   Moore, H. L. - Decd. Estate - 71,74

M8   Moore, H. T. - Decd. Estate - 583

R9   Moore, H. T. - Decd. Estate - 80

M4	Moore, Ira W. - Decd. Estate - 1,397,398,406	
R5	Moore, Ira W. - Decd. Estate - 76,77,78,79,80,81,82	
M2	Moore, James - Estate, J.B.Sanford, Admr. - 227,373,471 to 474,374 to 376,620	
M3	Moore, James - Estate - P.398,399,410,411,412	
R1A	Moore, James - Estate - 643	
R2	Moore, James - Estate - 154,155	
R3	Moore, James - Decd. Estate - 477 to 480	
M10	Moore, James David - Decd. 45, 46	
R11	Moore, James David - Decd. Estate - 69,70,71	
W1	Moore, James David - 332	
M5	Moore, James H. - Decd. Estate - 358,359,361	
R6B	Moore, James H - Decd. Estate - 131	
R6B	Moore, James H. - Decd. Estate - 161,162	
W1	Moore, James H. - 33	
R27	Moore, Jan Elizabeth - 27 - 819,834	
R18	Moore, James W. - Est. of - 529,532	
M10	Moore, Jim H. - et. al. (Condemnation of lands) - 508,509,510,511,512,513,514, 515,516,517	
M5	Moore, John C. - Decd. - Thomas E.Goodwin, Admr. - 20,22,34,57,58,82,83,95,181, 346	
R5	Moore, John C. - Estate - 370	
R6B-	Moore, John C. - Estate - 5	
M10	Moore, John M. - Decd. Estate - 562,63,64,66	
W2	Moore, John M. - 43	
M1(1)	Moore, John P. - Estate of - 209,212,242,259,356,357	
R1A	Moore, John P. - Estate - 118 to 121	
R1A	Moore, John P. - Estate - 650	
R11A	Moore, John P. - 26,27	
M1(1)	Moore, Lewellen, - Estate of - 11,426,456 to 461	
M8	Moore, Lizzie - et. al. joint owners - 398	
R8	Moore, Lizzie - et al. point owners - 450	

M3	Moore, M. A. J. - Estate - P.194,316,324,325,326,459,463
M3	Moore, M.P.B. - Estate - P. 195,315,322
M9	Moore, Mexeco - guardian for Melvin Moore, Minor - 75
R9	Moore, Mexico - guardian for Melvin Moore, Minor - 217
R3	Moore, M. V. B. - Estate - 341, to 342
R3	Moore, Moses A. J. - Estate - 342,343,418,419,511 to 514
R18	Moore, Rilla - Estate of - 169,180,651,663
R19	Moore, Rilla - Estate of - 19 - 849,900
W2	Moore, Rilla - Will & Proof - 327,28
R25	Moore, Robert Lee - Decd. - 25 - 266,276
	Moore, Robert Lee - Will & Proof - 45,47
M9	Moore, Thos. A. - Decd. Estate - 426
R10	Moore, Thomas A. - Decd. Estate - 273,274
M10	Moore, T. J. - (Lonnie Moore guardian of Est. Thelma, Lester,Adalene & Buster Howton -Estate-247
R11	Moore, T. J. - Estate of - Lonnie T. Moore, Adm. - 435,462
M8	Moore, T. R. - father of Douglas & Francis Moore, Minors - 564
R10	Moore, Tollie R. - joint owners - 7,8,9
M10	Moore, W. A. - Decd. Estate - 465
R4	Moore, Walter G. - Power of Atty. - 360
M1(2)	Moore, Wm. - Estate - 796
M3	Moore, William - Estate - P. 78,79
R2	Moore, William - Estate - 251 to 258
R3	Moore, William - Estate - 143 to 145
W1A	Moore, William - 80
M9	Moore, Zack - Decd. Estate - 189,190,246
R9	Moore, Zack - Decd. Estate - 356,397,398,518 to 521
W1	Moore, Zack - 239
R25	Morgan, Bobbie J. - Minor - 25 - 277,297
R25	Morgan, Bobbie Jean - Minor - 25 - 687,696

R20   Morgan, L. G. - Guardian Settlement - 20 - 856,884

R18   Morgan, Nancy Carol & Boby Jean , Minors - 195,198

R23   Morgan, Nancy Carol & Bobbie Jean, Minors - 23 - 245,276

R25   Morgan, Nancy C., Minor - 25 - 298,323

R27   Morgan, Nancy Carol - 27 - 421,433 (Vol. 28 - 893,895

      Morgan, O. C. - Deceased Cert. Copy of Will - 1

M7   Morgan, Susan Emma - Decd. Estate - 540

M8   Morgan, Susan Emma - Estate - 1,5

R7   Morgan, Susan Emma - Decd. Estate - Leon M.Dodds, Ex. - 434

W1   Morgan, Susan Emma - 124

R13   Morgan, Willis F. - Estate - 453,454,455

W1A   Morns, Certificate - 298,297

R24   Morris, Johnny Lee - Decd. - 24 - 717,720

R29   Morris, Myra Sue - Dr. Anthony - 760,764 - Guardianship

R18   Morris, Rhonda Lee - Minor - 457,460 (Vol.19) 162,172

W2   Morris, Sabastian N. - 94

M9   Morris, Theresa - Decd. Estate - 131

R9   Morris, Theresa - Decd. Estate - 451

R7   Morrison, E. E. - Decd. Estate, Jane Atchley, Ex. - 10,11

W1   Morrison, E. E. - 105

R25   Morrison, James Clifton - 25 - 262,265

R27   Morrison, Mary Anis (Avis) - 27 - 633,636

R9   Morrison, S. E. - guardian - 318,319

M1(1) Morrow, James M. - Estate Of - 142,133,148,151,163,179,262,283,427,469,470,489
                                                                    503,504,556

M(3) Morrow, James A. - Estate of - 342,343,497,498,499,500

M2   Morrow, James E. - Estate - 235,285,678,679,704,705

M3   Morrow, James - Estate - P.60,61,119,123 to 125,375

R1A   Morrow, James M. - Estate - 99 to 106

R3   Morrow, James M. - Estate - 150 to 157,279,280

R11   Mosley, Brady - et. al. sale o joint owners property - 109,110,111,112,113,11
                                                                    115
M10   Mosley, Grady - et. al. sale f division -   61,62,63

R1A   Moseley, Hustin S. - Estate - 123 to 126

M5   Mosley, James O. - Decd. Estate , Wm. G.Mosley, Admr. - 148,153,228

R25   Mosley, R. L. - Decd. - 25 - 875,882

       Mosley, R. Lee - 58,60

R26   Moss, Ernest H. (Letters) - 26 - 825

R17   Moss, Hubert Floyd - Minor - 267,73

M3   Moss, John B. - Decd. Estate - P. 461,468

R3   Moss, John B. - Estate - 606 to 616

R26   Moss, Walter L. - 26 - 826,831

       Moss, Walter L. - Will & Proof - 214,215,218

       Mothershed, N. T. - Will & Proof - 223,26

R23   Moucha, Alice - Decd. - 23 - 521,537

W2   Moucha, Alice - Will & Proof - 474,479

R21   Mouchett, Enoch Dan - Decd. - 21 - 479,488

W2   Mouchett, Enoch Dan - 417

R11A   Mouchetta, James L. - 551, 553

R11A   Moxley, A. J. - 18, 19

M1   Mozingo, Isaac A. F. - 385

M10   Murphy, Marjorie Benton - adoption by Mr. & Mrs. T. J. Wright - 316

M1(1) Murray, James - Estate of - 202,217,231,277,493,525, to 528

M2   Murray, Mary - 723,2x2 729,768,769

M3   Murray, Mary - Estate of J.C.Moore - Extr. - P.141,142,153,154,185,279,286 to
                                                            318,593   289
M5   Murray, Mary - Decd. - 59,68,69

R7   Murray, Mary - Estate - 385 to 392

R3   Murray, Mary - Estate - 25,26,29 to 35,251 to 253,291,364,378,440

M1(1) Murray, Nancy A. - Estate of - 49,224,245,263,275,276

R1A   Murray, Nancy - Estate - 343 to 345

M1(1) Murray, Richard G. - Estate of - 119,120,147,150,203,225,228,278,284,294,301,420
                                                 421,435,449,450,502

R11A Murray, William P. - 535,541

R14   Musgrove, Frances Rebecca - Minor - 528,529

R6B   Musgrove, Robert L. - Decd. Estate - 426,427,428

M3   Musgrove, William - Deceased Estate - P. 453

R24   Myers, James Douglas - Decd. - 24 - 444,454

W2   Myers, James Douglas - Will & Proof - 552,553

R11A Nall, Bradley - 558,569

      Nalls, Decater - 77,79

R25   Nalls, Decater - 25 - 987,999

R26   Nalls, Decater - 26 - 419,421

M2   Nall, John - Pay Lein - 154

R26   Nalls, Lucille - 26 - 1,7

M1(1) Nall, Martin - Estate of - 13,14,15

M1(2) Nall, Nathan - Decd. Estate - 12,13,87,88,89,90,91,92,93,94 to 97,240,265,285
                         to 289,469,481 to 483,501,502,724,725,735,736 to
                                    743,740 - 7

M2   Nall, Nathan - Estate - 155,702,703,736

M3   Nall, Nathan - Estate - P.121,127,149 to 152,345 to 347,517,237,259

R2   Nall, Nathan - Estate - 562 to 569

R3   Nall, Nathan - Estate - 58 to 60,266,267,281,373 to 376, 414,627

R12A Nall, Nathan - Decd. Estate - 149 to 165, 376 to 378, 607 to 613

W1A   Nall, Nathan - 439 to 443,474 to 477, 754,755,764

R14   Nalls, Rastus M. - Decree Legitimizing child - 241

R27   Nalls, Sharon R. - 28 - 143,148

M1(2) Nalls, Silas - 493,522

M2   Nall, Silas - Estate - 42

M3   Nall, Silas - Estate - P. 132,155,156

R3   Nall, Silas - Estate - 380 to 384

      Nalls, Silas - 81-84

R26   Nalls, Silas - 26 - 18,58

W1A   Nalls, Silus - 480 to 484,505,506,536

      Nalls, Troy - 518

R29   Nalls, Troy   29 - 1 - 15

M1(1) Narimore, Joseph - Estate of - 93

W2   Naugher, Pauline - 54

W2   Naugher, Pauline - 57

M10   Naugher, William H. - Decd. Estate - 19,20

M9   Naugher, William H. - Mrs. Dora Henson, Admrx. - 462,490

M8   Naugher, William T. - unsound mind - 287,289,293

M8   Naugher, William T. - Decd. Estate - 490,496,497

R8   Naugher, William T. - unsound mind - 300, Decd. Estate - 586

W1   Naugher, Wm. T. - 210

M10   Neal, Mrs. Geo. Willingham - et.al. (Condemnation of lands) - 508, to 517

M1(1) Neal, Green - Estate of - 75,76

R1A   Neal, Green, Estate - 65 to 71

R21   Neal, Icye Beatrice Freeman - Inc. - 21 - 849,852

M9#) Neal, Janette - Apprentice - 592

R11A Neal, Janetta - 68

M1   Neal, John V. - 32,34

M(3) Neal, Littleton M. - Apprentice - 590

R11A Neal, Littleton M. - 68

M10   Nelson, Belton - Incompetent - Estate - 71,77,78,82,148,167,168,202,205,211

M10   Nelson, Belton - Incompetent - 399,400,426,427,493

R11   Nelson, Belton - Incompetent - 140,141,143,156,157,158,166,167,304,305,306,307,
                                     338,339,371,372,414 to 418,422

R28   Nelson, Carlos - 28 - 558,564

M9   Nelson, Carrie - Guardian - 272,318

M9   Nelson, Mrs. Carrie - guardian - 508

R9   Nelson, Mrs. Carrie - guardian for Belton Nelson - 66,68

R10   Nelson, Carry - guardian - 14,16,94

R10   Nelson, Carrie - guardian - 491, et. al.

R21   Nelson, Claude - Decd. Est. of - 21 - 835,848

W2   Nelson, Claude - Will & Proof - 456,457

R15   Nelson, Columbus - Decd. - 58,59

R27   Nelson, Donald W. Aaron - 27 - 124,132

M7	Nelson, F. A. - Decd. exemption to widow M.A.Nelson - 408,411
R7	Nelson, F. A. - Decd., M.A.Nelson, Widow - 270
M4	Nelson, Jasper - exports for bail - 319
M8	Nelson, R. L. - guardian - 269,511,513
R8	Nelson, R. L. - guardian - 286
M9	Nelson, R. L. - guardian'- 187,188
R9	Nelson, R. T. - guardian - 393,394,395
R8	Nelson, T. J. - Estate - 550
M8	Nelson, Mrs. T. J. - et.al. joint owner - 472,478,484,486,531,537
R27	Nelson, W. Aaron - 3 - Will 234, Proof 237
M9	Nelson, W. J. - Decd. Estate - 39
R9	Nelson, W. J. - Decd. Estate - 160,161
M6	Neville, Jesse B. - Decd. Estate - 208,209,210,211
M6	Nevillw, Jesse B. - Decd. Estate - W.H.Blankenship - guardian - 214, 215, 216, 217
M7	Neville, Jesse B. - Minor heirs of James T. Meherg - guardian - 154
M7	Neville, Jurnie - decree releasing minor of disabilities of ---age - 456
M9	Newman, Almedia - et. al - 149,150
R9	Newman, Alemedia - et. al. - 330,331,332
R20	Newman, Dessie Kay - Decd. Estate of _20 - 257,259
R21	Newman, Floyd C. - Decd. Est. of - 21 - 853,863
M10	Newman, J. P. - Decd. Estate - 143,144,212,213
R11	Newman, J. P. - Decd. Estate - 329,330,421,422,428
W1	Newman, J. P. - 357
R15	Newman, J. Walker - Decd. - 465,67
W2	Newman, J. Walker - 206,207
M1(1)	Newman, Reubin - Estate of - 248,451
M(3)	Newman, Reuben - Estate of - 521,522,523
R1A	Newman, Reubin - Estate - 345 to 348, 644
M5	Newton, A. K. - guardian - 175 (195)

R9   Newton, Mrs. Caine - Decd. Estate - 147

M9   Newton, Mrs. Carrie - Decd. Estate - 30

R23   Newton, Claude W. - unsound mind - 23 - 484,487

R8   Newton, E. B. - Decd. Estate - 180

W1   Newton, E. B. - 131

        Newton, Felix - 174,180

        Newton, George H. - 181,194

R16   Newton, Henrietta - A Minor - 487,91

M9   Newton, John Henry, Jr. - Decd. Estate - 532

R10   Newton, John Henry, Jr. - Decd. Estate - 535,536

M9   Newton, John Henry, Sr. - guardian - 127

R9   Newton, John Henry - guardian - 301,302

R5   Newton, N. K. - guardian - 552 to 554

M10   Newton, Olin E. - Decd. Estate - 117,118,200,201,213

R11   Newton, Olen E. - Estate - 242,243,411,412,413,428

M5   Newton, P. M. - guardian - 13,30,31,302

                    R.
R16(15?)Newton, Bernice - Decd. - 169,172

W2   Newton, R. Bernice - 263

        Newton, Reubin - 172,173

M10   Newton, Robert D. - Decd. Estate - 217

R11   Newton, Robert D. - Estate - 434

M1(2)   Nichols, Catherine - guardian forminor heirs 6f D.C.Nichols - 620

W1A   Nichols, Catherine - guardian foo minors - 13

M9   Nichols, Carry - Ministerial Certificate - 84

R13   Nichols, Doris Edral - Petition to restore maiden name - 289

M1   Nichols, E. S. - 35,36

M2   Nickols, John - Estate,M.A.Nichols, guardian - 524,533,534

R23   Nichols, John C. - Decd. - 23 - 389,396

M9   Nichols, Louis G. - Decd. Estate - 440

M10   Nichols, Louis G. - Decd. Estate - 455,456

R10   Nichols, Lewis G. - Decd. Estate - 283

R15   Nichols, Louis G. - Decd. - 8,18

R14   Nichols, Lucille & Willard - et.al. vs. City of Fayette - 86 thru 98

M1(2)   Nichols, M. A. - guardian - 621

M8   Nichols, Margaret - declaration adopting 2 children   - 412

M1(2)   Nichols, Mary Ann - guardian - 544 (?)

W1A   Nichols, Mary Ann - guardian - 72

M1(2)   Nickols, Robert - 502 thru 509, 512,582,723,732

M2   Nickols, Robert - Estate - 422,421 order to -

M3   Nichols, Robert - P. 231,232

R2   Nichols, Robert - Estate - 36 to 39

R3   Nickols, Robert - Estate - 255,256

W1A   Nichols, Robert - 497 to 504,532,534,760

M1(2)   Nickols, William - Decd. Estate - 2,29, to 33,74,112,113,121,122,145,671,677

M1(2)   Nichols, William - Estate, appointment of guardian - 686

M2   Nickols, William - Estate, J.L.Walton, Admr. - 553,564,574 to 577

M3   Nickols, William - Estate - P. 692

R2   Nickols, William - Estate - 144 to 148

R3   Nickols, William - Estate - 288,724

R12A   Nickols, William - Decd. Estate - 121 to 127,261,to263,375 to 381,

W1A   Nichols, William - Guardian, Wm. Strong - 38

M1(2)   Norman, Isaac - 573,574,577,578,628,634,640,641

M2   Norman, Isaac - Estate - 4

W1A   Norman, Isaac - 513 to 515, 527 to 529, 578, to 579,680

M9   Norris, E. G. - Decd. Estate - 171

R9   Norris, E. G. - Decd. Estate - 365,366

R14   Norris, Grant - Estate of - 124,125

M6   Norris, G. W. - decd. Estate - 102,103,104 to 109

M8   Norris, G. W. - et.al. by joint owners, C.P.Mattox, Et.Al. - 554

M9   Norris, G. W. - Decd. Estate - 289

R6B   Norris, G. W. - Estate - 230 - et.

R10   Norris, G. W. - Decd. Estate - 44 to 46

R9   Norris, Luther B. - Decd. Estate - 20

R6B   Norris, M. A. - Decd. - 331,332,333

R20   Norris, Randall - Minor - 20 - 243,256

M5   Norris, Thomas J. - Decd. Estate - 70,75,77

W1   Norris, Thos. J. - 9

M6   Norris, Tom - decd. Estate - 219

R6B   Norris, Tom (cold) - Estate - 313,314

R24   Norris, Viola - Inc. - 24 - 581,587

M9   Norris, Virgie L. - Admrx. Estate of, Luther B. Norris - Decd. - 13

M1(1)   Northam, Eli T. - Estate of - 330,340,359,597,617

R1A   Northam, Eli T. - Estate - 75 to 82

M(3)   Northam, John S. - Estate of - 243 to 255,

R1A   Northam, John S. - Estate - 503 to 510, 615,616,617,669 to 675

M4   Northam, Susan F. - Insane - 191

M4   Horthcutt,   :A.L. - J.M.Stewart, Admr. of C.C.Stewart - 613

M2   Notthcutt, H. L. - 39 to

M5   Northcutt, H. L. - Estate - 1

R5   Northcutt, H. L. - Estate - 331 to 337

R16   Northwest Ala. Gas Dis. Inc. - 23,26

M1   November Term - 1882 -

M1   November Term, 1893 - 565

M1   November Term - 1884 - 260

M1   November Term - 1885, - 291

R17   Nuckols, Dorothy - Destate Deceased - 443-48

R15   Nuckols, Paul - Decd. - 461,64'

W2   Nuckols, Paul - 205

M8   Oakley, W. B. - et. al. joint owners - 14,22,23,30,34,35

R7   Oakley, W. R. - et.al. joint owner proceeding sale petition & division - 444

M1   October Term - 1882 - 189

M1   October Term - 1885 - 290

M7   Odell, James F. - adopting & changing name of Lee Edney to Robert Lee Odell-365

R26   Odom, Betty Gay - 26 - 927,957

M1(1)   Ogdon, Francis - Estate of - 345,346,354,355,359

M8   Olive, Frank - decree removing disability of non age - 170

M8   Olive, Frank & Bessie - Minors J.D.Taylor - guardian - 38

R7   Olive, Frank & Bessie - Minors,J.D.Taylor - guardian - 508

M10   Olive, Geo. Franklin - decd. Estate - 153,154,178,180,181,182,183

R11   Olive, George Franklin - Decd. Estate - 348,387,389,390

M10   Olive, G. W. - decd. Estate - 600

W2   Olive, R. A. - Will & Proof - 361

R19   Olive, R. A. - Deceased Estate of - 19 - 343,368

M4   Olive, Robert C. - declaration adopting & changing name of child - 617

M7   Olive, Velma - Minor - Estate paid to her father W.J.Olive - 532,533

R25   Olive, W. D. - Decd. - 25 - 382,385

R13   Oswalt, Annie Ruth - Minor, etc. - Tetition of Gdn. to sell lands, etc. - 223 to
                                                                 228, 365 to 368
R14   Oswalt, George R. - Estate of - 313

M9   Oral Examinations Notice to residents our of Fayette - 290

M9   Oral Examination notice to residents out of Fayette County - 318

M9   Order appointing Commission to set apart exemption & order appointing Guardian
            ad___ to minors recorded in Probate Court Record - 434

W2   Oswalt, J. H. - 53

R14   Oswalt, J. H. - Estate of - 313

R14   Oswalt, J. H. - Decd. Noah C.Oswalt, Adm. - 522,527

R15   Oswalt, James H. - Decd. - 76,81

M7   Oswalt, J. H. - as sheriff, guardian for Isaac Cotlan, Minor - 287,290,291,396

R7   Oswalt, J. H. - Sheriff & guardian of Isaac Cotton, Minor - 84 to 86

M7   Oswalt, J. H. - guardian as sheriff for Estate of Curtis & Florence Reeves -
                                              344,324,426

M7   Oswalt, J. H. & Addie - Adopting & changing name of George Roberts - 80

M7   Oswalt, J. H. - as sheriff - guardian forEstate of Mary Elizabeth & Wm.L.Watkins,
                                              Minors _ 263

W2   Oswalt, Joseph Alexander - 99

R14 Oswalt, Joseph Alexander - Deceased - 170 thru 173

M9   Oswalt, J.W.Ward - Decd. Estate - 162, 163,164

M9   Oswalt, J. Ward - Decd. Estate 9 insolvent) - 233, 234

R9   Oswalt, J. Ward - Decd. Estate - 350,351,352,353,354,481,482

R24 Oswalt, Lois - Inc. - 24 - 574,580

R26 Oswalt, Lois - 26 - 525,530,543,49

W2   Oswalt, Mattie Lee - Will & Proof - 565,566

R21 Oswalt, Mattie Lee, Unsound Mind - 21 - 819,826

R21 Oswalt, Mattie Lee - Incompetent - 21 - 827,834

R24 Oswalt, Mattie Lee - Decd. - 24 - 896,902/999

R24 Oswalt, Ollie - Inc. - 24 - 696,702

M8   Oswalt, W. H. - Decd. Estate - 441,448

R8   Oswalt, W. H. - Decd. Estate - 503,504

R5   Otts, X J. Banner & Abijah Paul Otts to R.H.Miller - 414

R27 Otts, Robert Neal - 27 - 799,803

M7   Otts, Rudolph Hobson - adopted by D. O. White - 77

M7   Otts, Verner Gladys - adopted by R.H. & Maude Miller - 140

M8   Owen, George W. - Estate - 570,575

R9   Owen, George W. - Decd. Estate - 46

M9   Owen, James David - adoption of R. M. Sparks - 408

M7   Owen, Ju-e - Decd. Estate - 503,509,521

R8   Owen, Judie - Decd. Estate - W. B. Owen, Admr. - 144

M8   Owen, Judy - Decd. Estate - 17,55,71,113,134,180,182,183,193

M1(1) Page, James - Estate of - 254,272,620

M1(1) Page, James - Guardian - 367

M3   Palmer, Alexander - Estate - P. 230,231

R3   Palmer, Alexander - Estate - 229 to 231

M1(2) Palmer, Alexander W. - Decd. Estate - 133,158,187,188,234,235,337,338,339,524,
                                                                        539,540
R12A Palmer, A. W. - Decd. Estate - 364 to 367, 782 to 785

W1A   Palmer, A. W. - 573,575

R7   Palmer, J. C. - et.al. joint owner for sale of distribution - 550,554

R8   Palmer, J. C. - et.al. joint owners sell for division (Thos.D.Palmer Est.) - 1

M8   Palmer, J. R. - et. al. joint owners - 48,52,66

M8   Palmer, J. R. - et.al. joint owners - application for order to sell property
              for distributxion - 84,90,110,114

M1(1) Palmer, Thomas - Estate of - 57,60,62,71,95,426,468,469

W1   Panter, Richard - 151,152

R9   Papazan, C. L. - decd. Estate - 455,456

M9   Papazan, L. C. - Decd. Estate - 281, to 284, 222

R10   Papazan, L. C. - Decd. Estate - 30 to 35

M9   Papazan, T. J. - Decd. Estate - 222,223,228

R9   Papazan, T. J. - Decd. Estate - 456,457

M7   Parker, Ada - Widow of R.R.Parker - Decd. Minor children - 504,505,506

M9   Parker, M. - Decd. Estate - 304,305

R10   Parker, M. - Decd. Estate - 72, 73

W1   Parker, M. - 254

R7   Parker, R. R. - Decd. Estate - 400

M7   Parks, Mrs. Martha C. - Decd. Estate of - 469,470,471

R7   Parks, Martha C. - Decd. Estate - 350

W1   Parks, Mrs. Martha C. - 120,121

M9   Parks, M. F. - Decd. - 64,77,79

R9   Parks, M. E. - 218,219 (M.L.)

W1   Parks, M. L. - 223,224

R17   Parks, Martha M. - Minor   12,13

M8   Parks, Mrs. Sula - guardian - 137   (10

R8   Parks, Sula - guardian - 140,455

R27   Parrish, Eloise - 27 - 534,557.

W3   Parrish, Eloise - Will & Proof & Cert. - 289,292

R26   Parrish, William A. - 26 - 273,282

W3   Parrish, William A. - Will & Proof - 132 - 134

R13   Pasley, J. M. - Decd. Estate - 140

R2   Pate, A. - Estate - 490 to 497

R3   Pate, A. - Estate - 268,269

M4   Pate, Al. - guardian - 205

M10   Pate, A. L. - Decd. Estate - 107,109,156,157,158,160,161,162,308,309,310,398

M10   Pate, A. L. - Decd. Estate - 398

R4   Pate, A. L. - guardian - 270

R11   Pate, A. L. - Decd. Estate - 223,224,225,231,259,353,354,355,356,358,553,554,
                                            555.556,557,558

M3   Pate, Archibald - Estate - P. 14, to 16, 23,24,41,42

R15   Pate,   J. W. - Decd. Estate - 118,119

R24   Pate, J. W. - Decd. - 24 - 661,663

M9   Patterson, A. E. - Decd. Estate - 177,178

M8   Patterson, Belton - et. al. joint owner - 440,4440443,445

R8   Patterson, Belton - et. al. joint owners - 512

M9   Patterson, B. F. - Decd. Estate - 201

R27   Patterson, Claude - Decd. - 27 - 147,155

M10   Patterson, Cora - Minor Estate - 66

R11   Patterson, Cora - Minor Estate - 124, 125

R9   Patterson, Dora Et. Al. - 416,417,418

M9   Patterson, Ella - guardian - 270

R10   Patterson, Ella - guardian - 11, 12

M9   Patterson, Felix - Petition of T.M.Patterson - 18,20,23

M7   Patterson, J. A. - Decd. Estate - J.N.Patterson, Admr. - 206

R7   Patterson, J. A. - Decd. Estate - 24

M9   Patterson, J. L. - Decd. Estate - 32

M9   Patterson, John L. - Decd. Estate - 94

R9   Patterson, John L. - Decd. Estate - 126,185,186,187

M7   Patterson, J. N. - guardian for persons & Estate of Bessie & Louisa May Lindsey
                                                                        389
R7   Patterson, J. N. - guardian for Bessie & Livie Lindsey, Minor heirs of J.F.Lindse
                                                            Decd. - 236
R24   Patterson, Lizzie H. - Inc. - 24 - 992, 998

R27   Patterson, Lucy E. - 27 - 669,678, (Vol. 28) page 102 - 106

W3   Patterson, Lucy E. - Will & Proof - 302 - 306

M10   Patterson, Lucy F. - Estate of - 3,38,39

R11   Patterson, Lucy F. - Decd. Estate - 42,43,44,45,46

M10   Patterson, Moses - Minor Estate - 44

R11   Patterson, Moses - Minor Estate - 59, 60

R9   Patterson, Nancy Ann - Decd. Estate - 423,424,425,426

W1   Patterson, Mrs. N. A. - 236, 237

M9   Patterson, Mrs. N. C. - Decd. Estate - 186, 205

M1(2)   Patterson, Samuel J. - Decd. Estate - 131,217,218

R11A   Patterson, Samuel J. - 599 to 621

R12A   Patterson, S. J. - Decd. Estate - 758 to 762

M10   Patterson, Samuel F. - Estate of - 20,21,57,105,142,253,259

M10   Patterson, Samuel F. - Estate of - 428,429,430,468,553,554,556

R11   Patterson, Samuel F. - Incompetent - Estate - 98,101,218,220,323,324,325,470,471,
                                            472,483,484,485,486

R13   Patterson, Samuel F. - Incompetent - 77,82,313, thru 321

R14   Patterson, Samuel F. - Incompetent - 62 thru 71, 330 thru 333, 474 thru 477

R15   Patterson, Samuel F. - 66,70, 262

R16   Patterson, Samuel F. - Incompetent - 518,19

R17   Patterson, Samuel F. - Incompetent - 66, 81

R19   Patterson, Samuel F. - Inc. - 19 - 204,226

R22   Patterson, Samuel F. - Inc. - 22, 671,732

R24   Patterson, Samuel F. - Inc. 24 - 432,436

R26   Patterson, Samuel F. - Inc. - 26 - 775,824,833,858, Vol. 27, 262,263

R27   Patterson, Samuel F. - Inc. - 27 - 269,285, Vol. 28, 437,448

R27   Patterson, Samuel F. - 382,395

M9   Patterson, Tom - guardian of Samuel F. Patterson - unsound mind - 198,500,238,
                                                              302,303,366

M9   Patterson, Tom - guardian New Bond (11001) - 509

R9   Patterson, Tom - Bond - 318 (518)

R10   Patterson, Tom - guardian - 67 to 69,190 to 191, 554 to 559

R10   Patterson, Tom - guardian - 11000 Bond - 503,580

R17   Patterson, Tom - Decd. - 37,41

W2   Patterson, Tom - 281,282

R9   Patterson, T. P. (R) - Decd. Estate - 256

R9   Patterson, T. W. - guardian - 113,114,499 to 502,503,504, to 507,508

R19   Patterson, Victor S., Sr. - 19 - 173,182

W2   Patterson, Victor S. - Will & Proof - 348,349

R9   Patterson, W. E. (N.E.)? - Decd. Estate - 376,381

R24   Patterson, W. Theron - Inc. - 24 - 956,962

M8   Patton, W. D. - Decd. Estate - 106

R8   Patton, W. D. - Decd. Estate - 50

M8   Patton, Will - Decd. - J.W.Maddox, Admrx. 233

R8   Patton, Will - Decd. Estate - J.W.Maddos, Admr. - 260

M8   Patton, Willie - Decd. - L-vi Patton, Admr. - 236,237

R8   Patton, Willis - Decd. Estate - - Levi Patton, adm. - 262

R24   Payne, James A. - Inc. - 24 - 455,467

R27   Payne, James A. - 27 - 600,609

M6   Pearson, Frank - Decd. Estate - 88

M9   Pendley, Alice (Aline) A., - Mother of Agnes Pendly, Minor - 291

R24   Pendley, Bessie - Decd. - 24 - 637,644

W2   Pendley, Bessie - Will & Proof - 557,558

R24   Pendley, Doyle & Lelia vs. J.D.Scrivner - 24 - 561,573

M9   Pendley, Grady - et. al. joint owners - 288,311,312

R10   Pendley, Grady - et. al. joint owner - 42,43,83,84,86

R27   Pendley, Howard et.al. vs. Ala. Power Co. - 27 - 959,1011

R15   Pendley, Linda Jean, Thomas Marlow & Jimmy Allen - Minors - 187,88

R16   Pendley, Virgil - Decd. - 176,77

R1A   Pennington, Joseph - Estate - 498 to 500

R11A   Pennington, Joseph - 71

R21   Peoples, Bessie - Decd. Estate of - 21 - 973,987

W2   Peoples, Bessie - Will & Proof - 462,463

M8   Perkins, Franklin P. - Decd. Estate - 562

R9   Perkins, F. P. - Decd. Estate - 94

R17   Perkins, Henry Frank - Incompetent - 236,241

R20   Perkins, Henry Frank - 20 - 783,807

M9   Perkins, Jamie & Henry Dobbs - Minor over 18 joint owners - 321

M1(2) Perkins, Moses - Decd. Estate - 572,573m576,580,581,584,585 thru 596,626, 6, ?,
                                      45,29,68, & 2, 687,701,764,766,59
M2   Perkins, Moses - Estate - 252,569,682,683,684

M3   Perkins, Moses - Estate - P. 97,98,110,111,112,113,121,122,203, to 209

R2   Perkins, Moses - Estate - 158,480, to 489

R3   Perkins, Moses - Estate - 18 to 24, 27,28,288,372,724

W1A   Perkins, Moses - 612 to 614,617 to 628,640 to 644,651 to 657,677,678,734,749 to
                                      751, 761,185
M1(1) Perkins, William - Estate of - 488,451

M7   Perry, B.J.A. - father of Lydia, Lela & _____Perry - 371

M8   Perry, Della - mother of Buford & Adele Perry, - Minors - 508

M2   Perry, Isaac - guardian for minor Celia Harrison & Others - 52

M2   Perry, Isaac - guardian for W.J.Harrison - 208

M4   Perry, Isaac - guardian for E. Henderson heirs - 111,120

R9   Perry, L. W. - guardian - 140

R10   Perry, S. W. - guardian for Elton G. Perry - Final Settlement - 160,161

M9   Perry, T. W. - guardian Elton Perry N. - 25,4,7,

R13   Perry, T. W. - Estate - 403,407

M5   Perry, Wiley - Estate - 394, 5,396,398,399,414

M9   Peters, T. M., Sr. - Decd. Estate - 350

R10   Peters, T. M., Sr. - Decd. Estate - 158

W1   Peters, T. M., Sr. - 261,262

R16   Pettis, Pierce R. - Decd. - 142,143

M1(1)   Petty, Andrew J. - Estate of - 605,614

M(3)   Petty, Andrew J. - Estate of - 170 to 175

R1A   Petty, Andrew J. - Estate - 31, to 40, 268 to 289,400 to 405, 633 to 634

R11A   Petty, Andrew J. - 18

M1(1)   Peyton, Daniel - Estate of - 141,503,512,557,558

R24   Phillips, Gara Olene - Decd. - 24 - 861,865

M(3)   Phillips, John - Estate of -231 to 235

R1A   Phillips, John - Estate - 258 to 262

M8   Phillips, Joseph Edward - Decd. Estate - 527

R8   Phillips, Joseph Edward - Decd. Estate - 560

R10   Pickett, Dora - et. al. joint owners - 7,8,9,

M10   Pike, Henry G. & Nancy V. - Minors - 430

R26   Pinion, Abb A. - 26 - 89,95

M8   Pinion, A. W. - Decd. Estate of C.H.Pinion, Admr. - 502

R9   Pinion, A. W. - Decd. Estate - 8

M10   Pinion, E. C. - Decd. Estate - 137,138,194,205 to 207,208

R11   Pinion, E. C. - Decd. Estate - 308,309;310, to 314,404,405,423

M9   Pinion, Icie - adopting Charles Wesley Maddox - 392

M4   Pinion, James - Decd. Estate - 220,490,508,543,587,608,631

M4   Pinion, James - Decd. Estate - 490,501,508,515,563,589,608,631

M5   Pinion, James - Estate - 320

M7   PInion, J. N. - Estate of - Trans. of purchase - 374

R5   Pinion, James - Decd. Estate - 170 to 175

M10   Pinion, James N. - et.al.joint owners - slae of lands - 140,156,163,164

R11   Pinion, James N. - et.al.joint onwers - sale of lands - 317,318 to 322, 358

M9   Pinion, Lizzie - guardian - 158,159,160

R9   Pinion, Lizzie - guardian - 342,345

M9   Pinion, Mary E. - Estate - 519,520,521

R10   Pinion, May E. - Decd. Estate - 518 to 527

M4   Pinion, Newton J. - Decd. Estate - 491,488,590,610,633

M7   Pinion, Newton - Decd. Estate - 374

R5   Pinion, N. J. - Decd. Estate - 140

R7   Pinion, Newton - Decd. Estate - 112

R24   Pinion, Ora - Decd. - 24 - 664,667

M8   Pinion, W. E. - Estate of - Lizzie Pinion, Admrx. - 512,584

M9   Pinion, W. E. - Decd. Lizzie Pinion - Admrx. - 1

R9   Pinion, W. E. - Decd. Estate - 16

R17   Pinkerton, Billy Gene - Decd. - 96,97

R14   Pinkerton, Bobbie Jean - Minor - 444,449

M8   Pinkerton, H. Farris - Declaration adopting Mabel Hull - 63

M4   Plyler, D. F. - Petition to petition - 580,592, to 595

M8   Plyler, James Wesley - Decd. Estate - 449

M1(2)   Plyler, Nancy - guardian of minors - 666

R3   Plyler, Nancy - Estate - 183,184

W1A   Plyler, Nancy - guardian - 710,711

M1(2)   Plyler, Phelt - Decd. Estate - 177 thru 181,447,448,471,656,664,665,701

M4   Plyler, Phelt - Estate - 561,564,576,577,578,580

M5   Plyler, Phelt - Decd. & koint owners - 180

M7   Plyler, Phelt - decd. Estate of J.Q.Brady, Admr. - 356,364,368,430,431,432

R12A   Plyler, Phelt - Decd. Estate - 533 to 540

R7   Plyler, Phelt - Decd. Estate - J.R. Bradley, admr. - 210

W1A   Plyler, P. D. - 363,742

M8   Poe, Andy & Miley Poe - Estate - 58,59

R10   Poe, Ethel - et. al. minors - 76

M7   Poe, G. W. - et.al. joint owner: proceeding to sell land for promotion & ____
                                                        464,465,473

R7   Poe, G. W. - et.al. joint own   340.364

R23   Poe, Lona - Decd. - 23 - 675,683

W2   Poe, Lona - Will & Proof - 494

R24   Poe, Marion Calvin - Decd. - 24 - 362,370

W2   Poe, Marion Calvin - 543,544

M1(2)   Poe, Oliver P. - Decd. Estate - 83,84,182,183,418,419,399,400,___,434,435,503,
                          525,526,530,534,543,565,575
M(3)   Poe, Oliver P. - Estate of - 323,322,321,320,319,318,585,586,553,554

R1A   Poe, O. P. - Estate - 707 to 711

R11A   Poe, Oliver P. - 570,584

R12A   Poe, O. P. - Decd. Estate - 774,775

R3   Poe, O. P. - Estate - 280,281

M2   Poe, Simeon - Estate, Blakeney & Jones Admr. - 538,539,544 to 546,566,606,726,
                          740,762 to 766
M3   Poe, Simon - Estate - P. 90,102 thru 109

R2   Poe, Simon - Estate - 56 to 73, 265 to 269, 464 to 468

R3   Poe, Simon - Estate - 280

W1A   Poe, O. P. - 290 to 297,539,540,543,545,550,551,553,560,614

R15   Poe, T. J. - Incompetent - 134,136,210,213,237,237, Decd. Est. 540,541,590,595

R16   Poe, Toney - Decd. - 388,89, 410,411

R17   Poe, Toney - Decd. - 33,36

M9   Poe, Wash ℬ - Decd. Estate - 307

W2   Pollock, Jacob - 144 thru 147

W2   Pollock, Julia - 140 thru 143

M(3)   Ponder, Malcomb - Estate of - 338,561,562,426 to 438

R1A   Ponder, Malcomb - 545 to 549

M5   Pope, Era - Decd. Probating Will - 344,375

W1   Pope, Ira - 35

M10   Porter, Billy, Bernice & Dupree - (Condemnation of lands) - 500 thru 508

M10   Posnack, Frances Tobie - Estate - 24,25,234,243

R17   Porter, Franklin & Rebecca - Minors - 7,11

R20   Porter, Frankie & Rebecca, Minors - 20 - 685,690

R22   Porter, G. Eulice - Decd. - 22 - 651,670

W2   Porter, G. Eulice - Will & Proof - 472,473

R17   Porter, Homer - Deceased - 1,2

M8   Porter, Jewell - Minor heir of R.G.Walker, Decd. - J.W.Sanders, guardian - 484

M2   Porter, John - Estate S.A.Walden, admr. - 526,568,569,630,706,707

R2   Porter, John - Estate - 171 to 177

R3   Porter, John - Estate - 94 to 101

R21   Porter, Lela Mae - 21 - 960,967

M9   Porter, Richard - Decd. Estate - 122,123,124

R9   Porter, Richard - Decd. Estate - 298,299,300,301

M5   Porter, Samuel H. - Estate - 126,134,135

R5   Porter, S. H. - Decd. Estate - 454

R6B   Porter, Samuel H. - Decd. 398 thru 407

W1   Porter, Samuel H. - 14,15,16

M9   Posnack, Sarah Yergin - guardian - 264,386

R10   Posnack, Sarah Yergin - guardian - 2,3,216,217

R11   Posnack, Mrs. Sarah Yergin - Gdn. - 5,6,7,441,442

M9   Posnack, Tony - Decd. Estate - 263,390

R10   Posnack, Toney - Decd. Estate - 1,2,234,235,236

M2   Porter, William - Estate - 760

M3   Porter, William - Estate - P. 174,188,189,200,201

R3   Porter, William - Estate - 102 to 113

R14   Powers, David A. - Decd.'- 518 thru 521

R14   Powers, David A. - Est. Application for Letters of Administration, Will Conveyed-
                                                                                 587,590
W2   Powers, David A. - 131,132

R13   Powers, Levi L. - Decd. Estate - 533 thru 543

R14   Powers, Levi L. - Estate of - Decd. Minnie Ethel & Mildren Powers - Incompetent -
                                                                                 554,557
R24   Powers, Mildren - 24 - 773,815

R13   Powers, Minnie Ethel & Mildred - Incompetent, Estate - 416 to 419,544 to 546

R15   Powers, Minnie Ethel & Mildred - Non corpus Mentes - 321-326, 596,5_9

R16   Powers, Minnie Ethel & Mildred - Non Corpus Mentis - 1, - 10

R24   Powers, Ethel / Inc. - 24 - 721,772

R27   Powers, Minnie Ethel - Inc. - 27 - 196,215,252,407,411

R27   Powers, Minnie Ethel - 27 - 350

R28   Powers, Ethel - 28 - 912,916

M10   Powers, William A. - Decd. Estate - 373,473,474,475

M10   Powers, William A. - Decd. Estate - 490,491

M1(1) Powell, Ezekiel - Estate Of - 51

M1(2) Powell, E. R. - Decd. Estate - 118,158,453,454,467,603,612

R11A   Powell, Ezekiel R. - 585,599

R12A   Powell, E. R. - Decd. Estate - 640 to 646

W1A   Powell, E. R. - 409 to 422

R7   Powell, J. W. - guardian, Clara & Carie Powell, Minors, in McIntosh Co.,Okla. - 226

R1A   Powell, R. A. M. - Estate - 230 to 232,455 to 467,554 to 558,755 to 765

M8   Powell, R. F. - Decd. - S.E.Maddox, Admr. - 191,188,203,209,254,268,262,288,294, 295,301,316,319,321

M8   Powell, R. F. - Decd. - Proceeding to sell land for division - 393,402,416,421, 423,425

M9   Powell, Reuben F. - Decd. Estate - 308

R8   Powell, R. F. - Decd. Estate - S.E.Maddox, admr. - 194, Sale Div. - 440

R10   Powell, Reuben F. - Decd. Estate - 77, 78

M7   Powell, Sarah E. - guardian of stste of minor heirs of Robert Logan, Decd. - 116

R6B   Powell, Sarah C. - guardianship - 484,485

M9   Pratt, Sam, Jr. - vs. The Tuscaloosa Cooperage Co. - 50

R9   Pratt, Sam, Jr. - vs. The Tuscaloosa Cooperage Co. - 177

R25   Presley, Durward Morrell - Decd. - 25 - 476,485

W3   Presley, Durward Morrell - Will & Proof - 42, 44

M8   Prewitt, Thelma - Minor - E.E.Thomason, guardian - 563

M3   Price, John C. - Estate - P.438,456,465,466,467,485,576,598

M4   Price, John C. - Estate - 45,48,66,77,82,84,85,92

R3   Price, John C. - Estate - 515 to 537

R4   Price, John C. - Decd. Estate - 73 to 76,93 to 94, 124 to 131

R18   Price, M. B. - Est. of - 18 - 445,449

W2   Price, M. B. - Estate of - 324,325

R17   Price, Pearl Milan - Decd. - 133,137

R18	Price, Pearl Milan - Est. of - 18 - 181,189
W2	Price, Pearl Milan - Will - 295,296
M3	Price, Reubin - Estate, M.C.Davis, gdn. & Etc. - P.372
M4	Price, Mrs. Sarah - Insane proceeding - 320
M4	Price, Mrs. Sarah A.L. - Exemption - 377
M3	Price, William - Estate - P.33,34,35,45,56,134,133,129,126,127,157,85,292 to 293
M3	Prince, William - Deceased James T. Prince, gdn. for Geo. R. - P. 521 521
M7	Price, William - Decd. Estate of Thos. G.Price - Administration - 264
R2	Price, William - Estate - 526 to 529
R3	Price, William - Estate - 46 to 52,306,307,368 to 372
R7	Price, William - Estate Thos.G.Price, Admr. - 108
M5	Prince, Charles - Estate of M.C.Davis - guardian - 252
M4	Prince, Reubin - Decd. Estate - 11,29
M2	Prince, Wm. - Estate G.W.McDonald, gdn. for minor heirs - 324,325,606,698,713M
M2	Prince, Wm. - Estate - 779
R2	Prince, William - Estate - 153
R3	Prince, William - 129 to 131,182
R15	Pritchet, C. A. - Decd. - 446,449
R17	Pritchett, C. A. - Decd. - 46
W2	Pritchett, C. A. - 202,203
M4	Prohibition in Berry Beat # - 7
M7	Prohibition Election - 82,83
M7	Prohibition Election - 173,182
M4	Prohibition Fayette C. H., Ala. - 635,639
M4	Prohibition in Lee Beat - 12
M3	Prohibition, Liquar - p.245,253
M4	Prohibition at school house near Fayette Depot - 616,626
M9	Propst, C. D. - guardian - 296
R10	Propst, C. D. - guardian - 57
M9	Propst, Daniel F. - Decd. Estat - 265
M9	Propst, D. F., Sr. - Decd. Es+ - 374,375

R10   Propst, Daniel F. - Decd. - 3,4

R10   Propst, D. F. - Decd. Estate - 196,205

R12A   Propst, Fanny - Decd. Estate - 614 to 617

M1(2) Propst, Fanny - Decd. Estate - 37,64,146

M10   Propst, G. C. - guardian - 35

R11   Propst, G. C. - Gdn. - 32,33,34

M10   Propst, Lenora Sue & Mina Louise - Minors, Estate of - 576,577,587

R13   Propst, Lenora Sue & Mina Louise - Minors Sale of timber - 130,131,132

R14   Propst, Lenora Sue & Mina Louise - Minors - 37 thru 40

M9   Propst, Susie E. - Decd. Estate - 285

R10   Propst, Susie E. - Decd. Estate - 36,37

R28   Propst, Thomas C. - 28 - 647,654

W3   Propst, Thomas C. - 433,436

M4   Quarantine Order - 556

R17   Rainey, D. A. - Decd. Estate - 453,58

W2   Rainey, D. A. - Will & Proof - 314,315

R25   Rainey, Clarence - Inc. - 25 - 680,686

M8   Rainey, Sam - Decd. Estate - Mrs. Annie Rainey, Admrx. - 75

R25   Rainey, Tony Randall - change of name - 25 - 474,475

R28   Raley, Theron A. - 28 - 1,4

M10   Raley, V. V. - Decd. Estate - 461,462

W2   Raley, U. V. - 30

R27   Ramsey, Evelyn Jean - 27 - 679,683

M1(2) Randell, John E. - Decd. Estate - 210,211,212,213

R11A   Randell, John E. - 621,632

R12A   Randall, John E. - Decd. Estate - 670 to 672

M10   Randolph, Mrs. Martha C. - Estate - 118,119,214,215

R11   Randolph, Mrs. Martha C. - Decd. Estate - 246,247,259,260,429,430 to 433

M9   Randolph, Rosa E. - guardian - 454,491

R10   Randolph, Rosa Lee - 347,348,349,350,427

M7   Randolph, Virgil E. - Estate of - 86,87,95,96

W1   Randolph, V. E. - 102,103,104

R8   Raney, Sam (Tom) - Decd. Estate - 166

R24   Rasberry, J. F. - Decd. - 24 - 175,183

W2   Rasberry, J. F. - Will & Proof - 524,25

M1(2) Ray, Alexander - Estate - 617,625,631

M2   Ray, Alexander - 1, 676

M7   Ray, Alexander - Decd. Estate - 414,416

R11A   654x657 Ray, Alexander - 654,657

R3   Ray, Alexander - Estate - 267,268

R7   Ray, Alexander - Decd. Estate - 280

W1   Ray, Alexander - 115,116

W1A   Ray, Alexander - 675,15

M10   Ray, David Fletcher - Minor, Estate - 118,374

R11   Ray, David Fletcher - Minor Estate - 245,246

R13   Ray, David Fletcher - A Minor - 72,74

R14   Ray, David Fletcher - Minor - 112,113

M1(2) Ray, Duncan - Decd. Estate - 119

R22   Ray, J. A. - Decd. - 22 - 315,319

W2   Ray, J. A. - Will & Proof - 447,48

M10   Ray, Thomas - Decd. Estate - 261,262,263,264,265

R11   Ray, Thomas - Decd. Estate - 489,490

M9   Reaves, Ella Martha, Ruby & Frances - Minors - Estate - 88

R9   Reaves, Ella Martha, Ruby & Francis, Minors, Estate - 248,249,250

M9   Reaves, Robert E. L. - Decd. Estate - Felix F. Shirley - Admr. - 82,219

R9   Reaves, Robert E. L. - Estate - 232,445,446

W1A   Redaish, James - 390,496,560,568,694

R27   Redden, Fronie M. - 27 - 588,599

M1(2) Redus, James - Decd. Estate - 1,2,13 thru 21,106,204,506,507,517 to 519,532,
                                                    557 to 559,651,506
M2   Redus, James - Estate - 32,519,522,529,530,695

M3   Redus, James - Estate - P. 187

R12A   Redus, James - Decd. Estate - 179 to 193,376,743

R2   Redus, James - Estate - 16,17,30

R3   Reddus, James - Estate - 141 to 143, 290

M1(2) Redus, Miller - Decd. Estate - 28,226,227,228,528,529,530,344,345,370,372,395,
                                                    573,574
R12A   Redus, Miller - Decd. Estate - 275 to 284,713 to 720,795,796

W1A   Redus, Miller - 252,547,549

M2   Reed, Hugh - Estate - 191

M3   Reed, Hugh - Estate - P. 175,176

R3   Reed, Hugh - Estate - 166 to 168

W1A   Reed, Hugh - 154

M1(1) Reed, Joseph - Estate of - 555,571,579

M10   Reese, H. A. - Decd. Estate - 98,209

R11   Reese, H. A. - Decd. Estate - 199 to 205,424

M10   Reese, Mary Susan - Decd. Estate - 202,203,204

R11   Reese, Mary Susan - Decd. Estate - 419,420

W2 Reese, Mary Susan - 4

M8 Reese, Nora - Minor heirs of T.M.Reese Estate & daughter of Dora Jones - 362

R27 Reese, P. W. - 27 - 351,360

W3 Reese, P. W. - Will - 265,216

M1(2) Reese, T. M. - substitution Justice Bond - 21

M5 Reese, Terrell M. - guardian of R.W.Harrison - 9,12

M7 Reese, Terrell M. - Estate of - 126

M8 Reese, T. M. - Decd. Estate - Albert L. Reese, Admr. - 297,302,306,312,331,342

R6B Reese Terrell M. - Decd. Estate - 514, 515

R8 Reese, T. M. - Decd. Estate - 322

M7 Reeves, Curtis & Florence - Minor - Estate - 324,426

R7 Reeves, Curtis & Florence - Minor H.H.Oswalt, sheriff, guardian - 200

M7 Reeves, Florence - Minor heir of Charlie Reeves, Decd. H.M.Webster, guardian-42!

M8 Reeves, Florence - Minor - H.M.Webster, guardian - 82,83

M8 Reeves, Mollie E. - Estate & Will - 447,454

R8 Reeves, Mollie E. - Decd. Estate - 524

W1 Reeves, Mollie E. - 206,207

M3 Reeves, S. A. - Estate - P. 283 to 285

R3 Reeves, S. A. - Estate - 225 to 229

W2 Renfroe, Archie D. - Will & Proof - 415

M8 Renfro, Cora - Mother of Sam Renfro - et. al. Minor to have certain funds to d_
                     102,103

M9 Renfro, Cora - Guardian - 202,203

R9 Renfro, Cora - Guardian - 418,419,420,421,422

R14 Renfro, Murray, Sr. - Deceased - 236,237

R28 Renfroe, Susie - 28 - 725,727

R1A Report of Grand Jury - 768

R11A Reynolds, Alcy M. - 637,644

M1(1) Reynolds, Benjamin E. - Estate of - 34,101,112 to 115,482,530,531

M1(2) Reynolds, John J. - Estate - 727,758,777

M2	Reynolds, J. J. - 118,594,595,598	
R11A	Reynolds, John J. - 93,645,651	
R2	Reynolds, John J. - Estate - 114 to 116	
W1A	Reynolds, J. J. - 97 to 109	
R25	Rhodes, Leona Moore - Decd. - 25 - 638,648	
W3	Rhodes, Leona Moore - Will - 21,27	
M2	Rice, Japtha - Zack Savage Admr. - 541 to 544,557,570,571,584,585,592,659,660, 674,786	
M3	Rice, Jeptha - P. 247,260 to 266	
M4	Rice, Jeptha - Zack Savage Admr. - order to ____ little - 315	
R2	Rice, Jeptha - Estate Ω - 80 to 89	
R3	Rice, Jeptha - Estate - 179,180,283284,295 to 298,376,633	
R15	Rice, L. V. - Decd. - 491,496	
W2	Rice, L. V. - 210,211	
M2	Rice, M. F. - Deed to James York - 144,145	
R14	Richards, Elizabeth, Anne - Minor Estate of - 15,16	
M4	Richards, Horace G. -et.al. petition for sale for petition - 212,213,217,218,237, 238,239	
R15	Richards, H. H. - unsound mind - 281,284	
M1(1)	Richards, James T. - Estate of - 454,473	
M2	Richards, Jefferson A. - Estate - 549,551,602,607,616,623,624,633,658	
R3	Richards, Jefferson, A. - Estate - 259,260	
R2	Richards, Jefferson A. - Estate - 49 to 55,159 to 162,270, to 272	
R4	Richards, Jefferson A. - et. al. Estate of - 492 to 493	
R14	Richards, Jefferson A. - Decd. Estate of 359,361	
W2	Richards, Jefferson A. - 112 thru 114	
M4	Richards, Martha J. - guardian for 4 minors - 240,533,541, -J.A.,Hollie,Bedford, & Iddie Richards.	
R15	Richards, Samuel - Estate - 564,66	
R11A	Richardson, Alexander - 658,659	
M9	Richardson, N. P. - Decd. Estate - 436	
R10	Richardson, N. P. - 4,9	
M10	Richardson, R. O. - Decd. Estate - 82	

R16	Richardson, R. O. - Decd. - 496,98	
R11A	Riddle, Simeon - 633,637	
R27	Riffert, Beatrice W. - 27 - 436,479	
W3	Riffert, Beatrice W. - Will - 283,288	
M8	Riggs, J. W. - Declaration adopting & changing name of Mary Trannie Gray - 198	
R13	Riley, Robert Lee - Incompetent, Estate - 17 thru 21	
R13	Roan, Maude Smyly - to change name - 64	
R18	Roberts, Bobby Gaines - Minor - 18 - 143,146	
M8	Roberts, Daisey Lee & Stella May, adopted & name changed to Daisey Lee Nichols & Stella May Nichols - 412	
M7	Roberts, George - adoption & change of name - 80	
M9	Roberts, G. W. - guardian - W. Felix & Cora Lee Sims - 3	
R9	Roberts, G. W. - guardian - 106	
R11	Roberts, H. J. - Deceased Bond (Admr) - 589	
M10	Roberts, Humphrey P. - Decd. Estate of - 266 thru 269	
R11	Roberts, Humphrey P. - Decd. Estate - 491,492	
R13	Roberts, Humphrey P. - Estate of - 459 thru 462	
W2	Roberts, Humphrey P. - 8	
W1A	Roberts, Jas. M. - 181	
R21	Roberts, James Valford - Decd. Est. of - 21 - 954,959	
W2	Roberts, James Valford - 429	
M1(2)	Roberts, John T. - Decd. Estate - 278,279	
R12A	Roberts, John T. - Decd. Estate - 752 to 793,794	
M2	Roberts, J. W. - Estate - 215	
R24	Roberts, Margie Butler - Decd. - 24 - 143,158	
W2	Roberts, Margie Butler - Will - 521	
R15	Roberts, Norma Ruth - Minor - 44,46	
M1	Roberts, R. M. - 36,37	
M10	Roberts, W. A. - Decd. Estate - 248	
R11	Roberts, W. A. - Decd. Estate - 463,464,487,488	
M2	Roberts, W. A. D. - guardian for Ardonia & R. C. Willingham - 291 to -	

M8   Roberts, W. E. - Declaration adopting Verie Nelle Jones & changing name to
                                                 Verrie Nell Roberts - 457

R21   Roberts, William Edward - Decd. Est. of - 21 - 968,972

R15   Roberts, William H. - Decd. - 54,55

M9   Roberts, W. I. - guardian - 527

M10   Roberts, W. I. - Decd. Estate - Letters of administration - 342,421 thru 425

R11   Roberts, W. I. - Deceased Admr. - Petition - 590

R9   Roberts, W. J. - guardian - 142

R10   Roberts, W. L. - guardian - 512,529

R27   Roberts, Woodrow W. - Decd. - 27 - 228,240

W3   Roberts, Wodrow W. - 246,249

M6   Robertson, of Accounts - 304 thru 309

M5   Robertson, Caroline M. - Decd. Estate - 314,319

W1   Robertson, Caroline M. - 30

M10   Robertson, D. G. - Decd. Estate - 372

R14   Robertson, Miss Elizabeth - Decd. - 465 thru 473

W2   Robertson, Elizabeth - 121,122,123

M9   Robertson, Mrs. Fannie - Decd. Estate - 341,376

R10   Robertson, Mrs. Fannie - Decd. Estate - 144,145,146,210,211

M9   Robertson, Felix M. - Decd. Estate - 306,307,346

R10   Robertson, Felix M. - Decd. Estate - 74,75,152

W1   Robertson, Felix M. - 250

R13   Robertson, Harold - Decd. apointing Gdn., etc. - 390,391

R23   Robertson, James Dexter - Minor - 23 - 870,874

R23   Robertson, James R. - Decd. - 23 - 595,598

R10   Robertson, John Banks, Jr. & Eliz. Richards - 20 - 378,384

M2   Robertson, John C. - 733,743,754,767

M3   Robertson, J. C. - Estate - P. 75,670

R2   Robertson, John C. - Estate - 427 to 463, 293 to 304

R19   Robertson, John C. - Et.al. - ·spondent - 19 - 530 532

R15   Robertson, Joseph R. - Decd. ' ,261

W2	Robertson, Joseph R. - 181	
M6	Robertson, Lou - Admrx. Bond of - 290	
R13	Robertson, Mrs. Lucy Bell - Contest of Will of ___ - 297, thru 310,397 thru 401	
R14	Robertson, Mrs. Lucy Belle - Decd. Estate - 458 thru 464	
W2	Robertson, Lucy Bell - 72 thru 75	
M4	Robertson, Margarett - Decd. Estate - 368	
R4	Robertson, Margaret - Estate - 506,507	
M8	Robertson, Mrs. Mary F. - Decd. Estate 100,118	
M10	Robertson, Mary Fletcher - Minor, Estate of - 150,151	
R1A	Robertson, Mary - Estate - 24	
R8	Robertson, Mary F. - Decd. Estate - 54	
R11	Robertson, Mary Fletcher - Minor Estate - 342	
W1	Robertson, Mrs. Mary F. - 128,130	
R11A	Robertson, Reubin D. - 657,658	
R5	Robertson, Robert - Estate - 3,4,5,6,7	
M4	Robertson, Robertson - Decd. Estate - of - 351,361,362,364	
M10	Robertson, T. H. - Decd. Estate - 317,318,319	
R11	Robertson, T. H. - Decd. Estate - 565,566	
W2	Robertson, T. H. - 16,17	
R16	Robertson, Thomas H., Jr. - Decd. - 205,210,482	
W2	Robertson, Thomas H., Jr. - 266,267	
R6B	Robertson, Walter S. - Decd. Estate - 266,267	
M1(1)	Robison, Johnathan - Estate of - 123,128,129,135,451	
M4	Rogers, Elizabeth D. - Insane report of - 347	
R15	Rogers, Mrs. Etta - 137,145	
W2	Rogers, Mrs. Etta - 169,170	
M4	Rogers, J. W. - et.al. petition to petition - 179,203,208	
R4	Rogers, J. W. - Estate - 256 to 262	
M9	Rogers, Sarah - guardian - 506	
R13	Rose Hill Cemetery - Making boundaries, etc. - 115 thru 117	
R24	Rowland, Byrd - Inc. - 24 - 468,480	

R27   Rowland, Byrd - 27 - 703,782,835

R28   Rowland, Byrd - 28 - 56,69, (Vol. 28) 901,911

R11A Rowland, Hiram M. - 653,782,783

R28   Rowland, Lizzie - 28 - 225

R24   Rowland, Melvin E. - Decd. - 24 - 199,203

R28   Rowland, Zeb - 28 - 28,38

W3   Rowland, Zeb - 330

M10   Roycroff, D. J. - Decd. Estate - 99,100,101

R11   Roycroft, D. J. - Decd. Estate - 205, thru 211

M10   Roycroft, J. N. - Decd. Estate - 479, thru 482

R29   Rozell, Ellis Frank - 29 - 122,127

R28   Rozell, Luke - 28 - 721,724

M1(1) Russell, Mark, vs. Lunacy Caspard N. Rod - TWL J. - 194,195

R13   Russell, Odessa Rea Rasberyy - Petition of - 222

M8   Sanders, G. F. - etal. joint owner, salr of land for division - 204,215,222,234, 245,246

R8   Sanders, G. F. - etal. joint owners - sale for division - 204

M2   Sanders, H. M. - 86,699,700

R3   Sanders, James. - Estate - 351

M1(1) Sanders. J. J. - Appointed Guardian - 297

R3   Sanders, J. J. - Estate - 159 to 161

R4   Sanders, J. J. - Estate, H.M.Sanders, guardian - 42

R14   Sanders, James W. - Estate of - 209 thru 215

M8   Sanders, J. W. - guardian of Estate - Jewell Porter, Minor Heirs of R.G.Walker, Decd. - 484

R8   Sanders, J. W. - guardian - 576

R14   Sanders, J. W. - Estate - 334,335

W2   Sanders, James W. - 107

M1(2) Sanders, Joel, - Estate H.M.Sanders, guardian - 671

R3   Sanders, Joel - Estate - 270,271

W1A   Sanders, Joel - H.M.Sanders, guardian - 25,27

R13   Sanders, Nolin Dean - Minor Estate - 66,67

R16   Sampson, S. J. - Deceased - 343,44,385,86

R16   Sanders, Z. N. - Decd. - 523,25

W2   Sanders, Z. N. - 280

R25   Sanford, C. O. - Decd. - 25 - 1,19

R27   Sanford, Earline - 27 - 54,61,161,490,496

M2   Sanford, J. B. - appointed gdn. Admr. - 251

R23   Sanford, John R. - Decd. - 23 - 397,408

W2   Sanford, John R. - Will & Proof - 473

R27   Sanford, Lucinda - 27 - 648,651

M3   Saunders, James - Estate - H.M.Sanders, gdn. = P.186,319,695,711

M8   Savage, Effie - guardian for Charlie Savage, Minor - 526

R9   Savage, Effie - guardian - 40

M5   Savage, John - Estate - 90,96,97,98

M4   Savage, John - Estate - 329

R4   Savage, John - Decd. - Estate - 502

M8   Savage, Sula - etal. joint owners for sale 6f property for division - 458,474,
                                                                              485,492

M9   Savage, Mrs. Sula - etal. joint owners - 46

R9   Savage, Mrs. Sula - etal. joint owners - 166

R28   Savage, Vada - 28 - 663,688

W3   Savage, Vada - 441,443

R25   Savage, Vater - Inc. - 25 - 19,25

M7   Savage, Zack - Decd. Estate - 412,413

M8   Savage, Zack - Decd. Estate - 40,410,46,47,54,55

R7   Savage, Zack - Decd. Estate, Victor Savage, Admr. - 265,568, thru 571

M8   Sawyers, John T. - Decd. Estate, no Admr. - 265, thru 268

M9   Sawyer, John H. - Decd. Estate - 204

R25   Sawyer, Kermit - Inc. - 25 - 375,381

R28   Sayers, Elma - 28 - 151

W3   Sayers, Elma - Original filed in Jefferson Co., Case 15842 - 354,357

R16   Schwartz, Dora McKinney - Decd. - 86,94,132,138

W2   Schwartz, Dora McKinney - 232,233

M7   Scrivner, B. F. - etal. petition for Partition - 224,226,227,258,259

R7   Scrivner, B. F. - etal. joint owner sale of land for partition & Div. - 60 to 66

M1   September Term - 578

M1   September Term - 187   (1882)

M1   September Term, 1885 - 287

M1   September Term, a886 - 316

M7   Sexton, Julius - adoption of Lela Gaddis Sexton - 386

M8   Sexton, W. J. - father of Motie Ware - Emma May Sexton & Lester Sexton - 58,59

M7   Sexton, Y. O. - Decd. Estate of - 458,459,460

R7   Sexton, Y. O. - Decd. Estate - 328

M2   Shackleford, Elizabeth - guardian for Minor heirs of J.P.Taylor - 171

W1A   Shackleford, Elizabeth L. - Guardian for Heirs of J.P.Taylor - 110

M3   Sharp, D. J. - Petition for Pa tition - P.440,445,455

M9	Sheets, Frank - Estate - 52,53,58
R9	Sheets, Frank - Decd. Estate - 179,180,181,182
M1(2)	Shelton, Christen - Substitution of Deed - 150
M1(2)	Shelton, George A. - Decd. Estate - 311,322,343,347,348,349,397,398,416,419,421
	423,424,425
R12A	Shelton, George A. - 78 to 82
R1A	Shelton, George A. - Estate - 475,483,732
R12A	Shelton, G. A. - Decd. Estate - 748 to 749, 776 to 772
W1A	Shelton, George A. - 230 to 237, 302
R12A	Shelton, James D. - Estate of - 48 to 54
M(3)	Shelton, Jacob D. - Esatate of - 216 to 226,227,588,589,417 to 425
M1(2)	Shelton, Permelia - Decd. Estate - 157,181,189,262,608,614
R12A	Shelton, Permelia - Decd. Estate - 752 to 756
W1A	Shelton, Permelia - 337,338,668,669
R13	Shelton, Toliver W. - Estate - 490 thru 493
W2	Shelton, Toliver W. - 84
R12A	Shelton, Wesley A. - 82 to 86
M(3)	Shepherd, Elizabeth - Estate of - 313,312
R11A	Shepherd, Elizabeth - 20 to 24
R22	Shepherd, Emma F. - Decd. - 22 - 249,282
W2	Shepherd, Emma - Will & Proof - 436,437
M2	Shepherd, Jacob - 732,748,753,755
M3	Shepherd, Jacob - Estate - P. 153,202,210, to 211
M7	Shepherd, Jacob - Decd. Estate - 109,225,424,428
R2	Shepherd, Jacob - Estate - 277 to 291
R3	Shepherd, Jacob - Estate - 1 to 15, 178,179
R7	Shepherd, Jacob - Estate - 26 etc.
R14	Shepherd, J. C. - Estate of - 233,234,235
W2	Shepherd, J. C. & Clara Warren (agreement) 98
W2	Shepherd, J. C. - 110,111
R13	Shepherd, James W. - Estate - 214

W2   Shepherd, James Wilson - 51,52

R6B   Shepherd, John - Estate - 263,264,265

R22   Shepherd, Linnie - Decd. - 22, - 508,514

W2   Shepherd, Linnie - Will & Proof - 467,468

M6   Shepherd, Mariah - 546

M1(1)   Shepherd, Michael - Estate of - 10,27,50,70,137,160,161,162,427,472,473

M(3)   Shepherd, Michael - Estate of - 228, to 231,313,221,566

R1A   Shepherd, Michael - Estate - 611 to 614

R24   Shepherd, Pearl - Decd. - 24 - 870,878

W2   Shepherd, Pearl - Will & Proof - 560,561

R22   Shepherd, Phelan - Decd. - 22 - 427,433

W2   Shpeherd, Phelan - Will & Proof - 466,467

M(3)   Shepperd, R. M. - Estate of - 94 to 110

M7   Sherer, Ira E. - joint owners with John D. Sherer,Jr.- proceeding for sale for
                                                        division - 500,513
M8   Sherer, Ira E. & John Sherer,Jr. - joint owners Estate of - 4

R15   Sherer, J. E. - Decd. - 327,330

W2   Sherer, I. E. - 189,190

M7   Sherer, T. E. & John, Jr. - joint owners - 500

R7   Sherer, T. E. - Trustee joint owner - John W. Sherer, Jr. - 392

R13   Sherrill, W. R. - Estate - 392,393

M3   Shirley, Beverly - Estate - P, 21,85

R3   Shirley, B. V. - Estate - 135 to 137

R11   Shirley, DeWitt & Jess Willard - Minors - Naufleet, James Elwood Marshall, gdn -
                                                        193,194,195
M8   Shirley, Fenton - guardian of Estate of Maggie Shirley - Minor - 61,223

M1(2)   Shearly Gabirel - substitution of Deed of Trust -431,432,337

M1(1)   Shirley, Joshua - Estate of - 372,384,386,411,413,414,478,502,540,546,589 to 596

R7   Shirley, Maggie - Minor, Fenton Shirley, guardian -.582

M10   Shirley, Naufleet, James Elwood, Marshall - guardian - DeWitt & Jess Willard -
                                                        Minors - 95

- 154 -

M1(1)	Shirley, Robert - Estate of - 16,26,50,226,253,310,401,434,438 to 443,563
R11	Shirley, Sam Jones - uncound mind - 465,480,481,508
R6B	Shirley, W. B. - Decd. Estate - 419 to 425
W1	Shirley, William B. - 51,54
R6B	Shirley, Wm. B. - Decd. Estate - 256
R11	Shirley, William Marshall - Decd. Estate - 193,194,195
M7	Shirley, Y. J. - Decd. Estate of J.Marion Williamson, admr. - 524,525,537
R7	Shirley, Young J. - Decd. Estate - 530
M9	Sides, H. R. - Decd. Estate - 297,325
R10	Sides, H. R. - Decd. Estate - 59,60,189,190
R25	Simpson, Clifton Ormond - Decd. - 25 - 241,248
R15	Simpson, Mrs. Ella H. - Decd. - 331,343,344,345,346
W2	Simpson, Ella H. - 191
W2	Simpson, Geneva - Will & Proof - 470
W2	Simpson, S. H. - 287,288
R15	Simpson, Truman, Sharon & James Timothy - Minors - 132,133
R15	Simpson, Truman A. - Decd. -157,166
R22	Simpson, Truman Sheron & James Timothy - Minors - 22 - 223,248,601,608
M8	Simpson, William T. - Decd. Estate - Samuel H.& Thomas A. Simpson, Admr. - 282, 283,394
R8	Simpson, William T. - Decd. Estate - Samuel H. & Thomas A. Simpson, Adm. - 310
R23	Sims, Grace, Inc. - 23 - 621,627
R25	Sims, Jackie - Inc. - 25 - 830,836
M7	Sims, John - Decd. Estate - 234,293,296,302,306,328
R7	Sims - John - Decd. Estate - W.F.Roberts, Admr. - 90 thru 95
R21	Sims, John - Decd. Est. of - 21 - 941,953
R25	Sims, Ollie Frances - Decd. - 25 - 536,540
M1(1)	Sims, Richard - Estate of - 100,104,105,109,110,224,298,321,347
R14	Sims, R. M. - Decd. Estate of - 370,373,558,559
W2	Sims, R. M. - 127,128
M7	Sims, Travis - Decd. Estate - W. F. Roberts, Admr. - 427

R7   Sims, Travis - Decd. Estate - W.T.Roberts, Admr. - 324

M8   Sims, Troy - Name changed from Troy Dillard - 432

M10   Sisk, Searcy - Decd. Estate - 518,596

M1(1)   Sivenks, Katherine - Estate of - 265

M9   Sizemore, Mrs. A. J. - Mother of Minor - 400

M10   Sizemore, A. J. - Decd. Estate - 23

R10   Sizemore, A. J. - Decd. Estate - 589

R13   Sizemore, Carolyn & Husband - etal, vs. Fayette Co. - 507 thru 513

R14   Sizemore, John F. - Decd. Estate - 199 thru 202

R16   Sizemore, John F. - Decd. 127,128

W2   Sizemore, John F. - 106

M7   Sizemore, J. H. - Decd. Estate - 233,242,243,246

R7   Sizemore, J. H. - Estate - 80,81,82

W1   Sizemore, J. H. - 108

M7   Skelton, J. R. - Declaration adopting Claude McGuff - 502

M9   Skelton, Tom? - etal. joint owners sale of property to W. P. Davis - Decd.) -
                                                                                261

M7   Skoggs, Wm. H. - Trustee petition for sale for partition & Devices of Lewis
                              Frank & Howard Fulmer land -521,527,537

R27   Sloan, Tierce Sara - 27 - 693,694

M4   Smallwood, - Expertise for bail - 255

M7   Smith, A. L. - Decd. Estate - R.S.Smith, admr. - 388,390,394,395,405,492,474

M7   Smith, A. L. - Decd. Estate of - 388,390,391,405492,474

M7   Smith, A. L. - Decd. Estate of - 388,390,391,405,474,487,492,493

R7   Smith, Alxx L. - Decd. Estate, R.S.Smtih, Admr. - 250

M1(2)   Smith, Ann - Decd. Estate - 82,142,143,203,204,782,312

M1(2)   Smith, Ann - Estate - & 792

M9   Smith, Annie - guardian - 60 thru 63,69,70

R9   Smith, Annie - guardian - 193 thru 199,206 thru 211

R12A   Smith, Ann - Decd. Estate - 434 to 442

R10   Smith, Mrs. Annie - guardian - 45 ,

W1A   Smith, Ann - 262

R8   Smith, Ben D. - guardian - 376

M8   Smith, Ben D. - guardian for Estate of Ruth & Bessie Smith, Minors - 344

R12±   Smith, Braxton - 92 to 98

M8   Smith. B. S. - etal joint owner - 450,467,498

M8   Smith. B. S. - etal, joint owner - 584

M1(2)   Smith, B. W. - Decd. Estate - 144,145,177,178

R12A   Smith, B. W. - Decd. Estate - 799,500

M10   Smith, C. C. - Estate of - 17,59,60,114,11

R11   Smith, C. C. - Decd. Estate - 105 thru 109,234

W1   Smith, C. C. - 328

R10   Smith, C. C. - Decd. Estate - 566,567,568,569

R14   Smith, Carrie E. - Decd. Administration of Estate - 244 thru 261,309

                           - Sale of Personal Property - 262 thru 265

                           - Sale of Personal Property - 260 thru 281

R15   Smith, Carie C. - Decd. Estate - 564,66

R23   Smith, Carrie E. - Decd. - 23 - 239,244

R20   Smith, Clarence L. - Est. of - 20 - 37,44

W2   Smith, Clarence L. - Will & Proof - 390,91

R12A   Smith, Edmond - 107,108

M9#(3)   Smith, Edward - Estate of - 261,262,528,529,530

M3   Smith, Edward - Estate - P. 214

R3   Smith, Edward - Estate - 265

R11A   Smith, Edward - 77,79

W2   Smith, Edward Earl - Cert. Copy of Will - 469

R17   Smith, Elizabeth Jane - Name Change - 470

M9   Smith, G. L. - admr. of Estate of Mitchell Beard, decd. - 11

R10   Smith, G. L. - guardian for Arzella Johnson (col) - 192

R28   Smith, G. L. - 28 - 655,662

W3   Smith, G. L. - 437,440

M9   Smith, G. T. - guardian for Arzella Johnson - 368

R24   Smith, Hartford - Declaration of Legitimation - 24 - 230,231

M9   Smith, James etal. joint owners - 172, thru 176

M4   Smith, James A. - Decd. Estate - 426,627,635, 468

M5   Smithe, James A. - Estate - 36,50, thru 54

R5   Smith, James A. - Decd. - Sarepta Smith, Admr. - 118 to 127

R5   Smith, James A. - 466 to 472

W3   Smith, James Brewer? - 512 - Original on file Harris Co., Texas.

M9   Smith, J. C. - Decd. Estate - 232

R9   Smith, J. C. - Decd. Estate - 479,480

R20   Smith, J. C.- Decd. Esta. of - 20 - 347,372

W2   Smith, J. C. - Will & Proof - 379,380

M8   Smith, J. G.- guardian for Jesse Curry Smith - Minor - 196

M8   Smith, Dr. J. G. - Decd. Estate - 438,442

M9   Smith, J. G. - Decd. - 48,49

R8   Smith, J. G. - guardian for Jesse Curry Smith - 190

R8   Smith, J. G. - Decd. Estate - 510

R9   Smith, J. G. - Decd. Estate - 169,174,175,176

W1   Smith, J. G. - 138,139

R9   Smith, J. M. - Decd. Estate - 434, thru 438

M9   Smith, J. N. - Decd. Estate - 212,213

M8   Smith, Jeffie T. - Decd. Estate - J.Hamp Dodson, Admr. 178,280,286,360,369,372

R8   Smith, Jeffie F. - Decd. Esatate - 290,449

R23   Smith, Jennie - Unsound Mind - 23 - 717,720

R15   Smith, Jesse C. - Decd. - 487,490

W2   Smith, Jesse C. - 208,209

R27   Smith, Jimmy H. - 27 - 663,668

M9   Smith, John - guardian order granting letters - 492

M10   Smith, John - Guardian for J.D.Oakley,Jr., Ruth Gibbs & Dewey Hancock - 22

R10   Smith, John - guardian - 445,585,586 thru 588

R9   Smith, John A. - Decd. Estate - 3 6, thru 373

R15	Smith, John Alexander - Decd. 353,354,355	
M1	Smith, L. R. - order for removal to Tuscaloosa Co., - 418	
M9	Smith, Mrs. M. J. - guardian - 277 to 279	
M9	Smith, Martha J. - Decd. Estate - 327	
R10	Smith, Mrs. M. J. - guardian - 24 to 27	
R10	Smith, Martha J. - Decd. Estate - 114,115	
R19	Smith, Martha Jane - Decd. - 19 - 619,621,787,792	
R23	Smith, Martha Jane - Inc. - 23 - 229,232	
W1	Smith, Martha J. - 257,258	
M9	Smith, Mittie D. - Estate - 466,467	
R13	Smith, Mrs. Minnie N. - Estate - 118 thru 125	
R24x	Smith, Milton T. - Decd. - 24 - 355,361	
W2	Smith, Milton T. - Will & Proof - 538,540	
R28	Smith, Ned Allen - 28 - 625,639	
R15	Smith, Preston Brooks - Decd. - 254,258	
W2	Smith, Preston Brooks - 179,180	
M9	Smith, R. S. - Decd. Estate - 513,514,515	
R8	Smith, R. G. - etal joint owners - 334,445,46,447,448,415,416,417,421	
R20	Smith, R. S. - 510,511	
W1	Smith, R. S. - 319,320,321	
M8	Smith, Roxie - a Minor funds paid to Nann Smith, the mother - 556	
M9	Smith, Roxie Callie - decree ordering of disabilities non age - 84	
M4	Smith, Rutherford S. - guardian for Wealthy Smith - 317	
R4	Smith, Rutherford - guardian - 484,485	
R26	Smith, Sarah 9 Deceased) - 26 - 593,604 - Vol. 3, P.212,213	
W3	Smith, Sarah - Will - 212,213	
M9	Smith, Mrs. S. E. - etal, point owners - 298,299	
R10	Smith, Mrs. S. E. - etal. joint owners - 60,62,63	
M8	Smith, T. A. declaration of adoption of James K. Vardaman Hall & changing name	

70

R25   Smith, Thomas C., Sr. - 25 - 980,987

W3   Smith, Thomas C., Sr. - 74,76

M9   Smith, T. H. - Estate - 86

R9   Smith, T. H. - Decd. Estate - 241,242,243

R19   Smith, Theron - Estate of - 19 - 95,98

M9   Smith, Virginia V. - guardian - 296

R10   Smith, Virginia V. - guardian - 58

R14   Smith, William David - A minor - 417 thru 420

R18   Smith, William Eric - Est. of - 18 - 147,150

R10   Smith, W. F. - guardian - 396

R14   Smith, William H. - Incompetent - 206,207,208

W1   Smith, William R. - 55,58

M7   Smothers, B. H. - guardian of two children of M.C.Smothers - Decd. 154

M8   Smothers, B. H. - guardian of W.J.B. & Corine (Corine) Smothers - 85,92

R6B   Smothers, B. H. - guardian - 511 - etal.

R19   Smothers, Rickey, Jean & Martha, - Minors - 19 - 379,384,879,894

R8   Smothers, W.J.B. & Carinell - Minor heirs M.C.Smothers - Decd. - 20

M2   Sommers, Moses - Estate - 36,39

M10   South, Beatrice - Estate - 161 (Marked through)

R11   South, Beatrice & Braxton - Minor Estate - 118,119,350,362,363

M10   South, Braxton & Beatrice - Minors, Estate - 63,154,161

R28   South, Chloe - 28 - 453,460

W3   South, Chloe - 395

M10   South, C. M. - Decd. Estate - 53,thru 57,67 thru 70

R11   South, C. W. - Decd. Estate - 90 thru 97, 129 thru 136

M3   South, Dilonaes, - Deceased Estate - P. 631

M4   South, Dilersen - Decd. Estate - 110,122,126,127

R3   South, Dilonson - Estate - 575 to 578

R4   South, Dilausen - Estate - 340 to 349

R5   South, Delansen - 134

M5   South, E. A. - Decd. Estate - 237,238,257,271,272,273,402

R6B   South, E. A. - Decd. Estate - 22,23,30,186

M10   South, J. Fenton - Decd. Estate - 581,582

R12A   South, James M. - 86 to 92

M(3)   South, James R. - Estate of 357,356,355,354,353,352,351,350,357 to 367,450 to
                                                                                      461
R11A   South, James R. -(74-77), 685,690

M5   South, Josiah - Estate - 138,143,152,154

R5   South, Josiah - Decd. Estate - 543 to 547

W1   South, Josiah - 17,18

W1   South, Martha A. - (143) or 43

M9   South, Pearl - Decd. Estate - 200

R9   South, Pearl - Decd. Estate - 415,416

M3   South, Tilmon H. - Estate - P.477,486,496,497,565

R3   South, Tilmon H. - Estate - 538 to 542, 700 to 705

R17   Spann, Harvey B. - Decd. Estate - 156,57, 344,34

M8   Spann, J. B. - Decd. Estate - 76,77,78,81

R8   Spann, J. B. - Decd. Estate - 14

W1   Spann, J. B. - 199

R29   Sparks, Barry - 29 - 241,252

R13   Sparks, Calvert Coleman - Declaration of fatherhood - 527

R14   Sparks, Calvert Coleman - Declaration of Legitimizing child - 123

M(3)   Sparks, J. M. - Estate of - 296 thru 299

M1(2)   Sparks, John - Decd. Estate - 23,51,52,145

R12A   Sparks, John - Decd. Estate - 386 to 393

R29   Sparks, Rickey - 29 - 240,246

M9   Sparks, R. M. - adoption of James David Owens - 408

R12A   Sparks, R. M. - 114,115

R26   Sparks, Robert W. -26 - 162,167, (Vol. 27) 265,268

M1(1)   Sparks, Russell M. - Estate of - 68,73,74,77,309,329,415,448,482,507,508,556,575
                                                                            603,602,610

M(3)	Sparks, Russel M.- Estate of - 333,332	
M8	Sparks, W. Carroll - declaration adopting Freelin Logan - 421	
R1A	Sparks, Russell M. - Estate - 666 to 667	
R11A	Sparks, Russell M. - 691,693	
M9	Sparks, W. C. - Decd. Estate - 89,90,91	
R9	Sparks, W. C. - Decd. Estate - 251,252,253	
W1	Sparks, W. C. - 225,226	
M9	Sparks, W. S. - Will - 107	
R9	Sparks, W. S. - Will Decd. - 275,276	
W1	Sparks, W. S. - 227,228,229	
M6	Sparks, William - Estate - 1,2	
R6B	Sparks, William - Decd. Estate - 133	
W1	Sparks, William - 34	
M9	Spaulding, N. W. - etal, joint owners notice for oral testimony - 318	
M9	Spaulding N. W. - order to hear application of joint owners for sale - 369,373	
R10	Spaulding, N. W. - land sale of joint owners - 193	
M9	Speical Judge of Probate - W. L. Harris - 494	
R24	Spiller, Addie Little - Decd. - 24 - 35,88	
W2	Spiller, Addie - Will & Proof - 519,520	
R16	Spiller, G. T. - deceased - 408,09	
M10	Spiller, Tom - etal. (Condemnation of proceedings) vs. Fayette Co., Ala. - 360, thru 365	
R23	Sprinkle, James Kenneth - Decd. - 23 - 385,388	
M9	St. Louis - San Francisco R.R. vs. Gallaway Coal Co. & B.F.Herren - 181,182,183	
R9	St. Louis - San Francisco Cp. applicant vs. Gallaway Coal Co. & B.F.Herron, - dependent - 387,393	
M10	Stacks, Mrs. H. B. - etal. (Condemnation of lands) - 500 thru 507	
M1(1)	Stacener, Henry - Estate of - 552,568,569,607,608	
M(3)	Stracener, Henry - Estate of - 562	
R1A	Strasener, Henry - Estate - 72 to 73, 720	
M1(1)	Stacy, Elizabeth - Estate of - 69,83,89,109,124,143,153,274,293,320	
M9	Stallwooth, W. W. - Decd. Estat - 531	
R10	Stallworth, W. W. - decd. Estate - 534	

R15	Stamps, Christopher Columbus - 291,294	
W2	Stamps, Christopher Columbus - 185,186	
R13	Stamps, James T. - Estate - 439,440,441	
W2	Stamps, James. T. - 81,82	
M4	Stamps, John - Decd. Estate - 391,399,400	
R5	Stamps, John - Decd. - 60,61,62,63	
R22	Stanford, Kelly - Inc. - 22 - 613,617 (Vol. 24) 461,464,652,70	
R29	Stanford, Kelly - Inc. - 29 - __ 45	
M8	Stanley - Ada B. - Decd. Estate of F.M.Stanley, admr. - 250,314,317	
R8	Stanley, Ada B. - F.M.Stanley, Admr. 270	
R6B	Stanley, Jesse M. & Chappell James - Decd. Estate - 125	
M6	Stanley, Louis - Estate of Hiram Hyde - guardian for LUdie & Luther Stanley - 7:	
M10	Stanley, Sam Jones - Unsound Mind - 249,258,275,6,7	
R13	Stanley, Sam J. - Assumption Certificate to Gdn. Bond - B.O.Stanley - 370	
R13	Staanely, Sam, Jr. - Non Compes Mentes - 369,370	
M1	State vs. James H. Hide - 15	
M1	State vs. Jasper N. Smith - 9	
R29	State of Alabama vs. H.H.West - 29 - 89,121, vs. H.H.West - etal	
R1A	Stephenson, John - Estate - 97 to 98	
M9	Sterling, Savanah - Estate - 423	
R23	Sterman, Nettie N. - Decd. - 23 - 614,620	
W2	Sterman, Nettie M. - Will & Proof - 485	
M5	Stewart, B. L. - Mentes - 284	
M1(2)	Stewart, C. C. - Justice Bond substitution - 21	
M3	Stewart, C. C. - Estate - P.143,144,158,549,555 to 557,558,559,581,566,567,664	
M4	Stewart, C. C. - Decd. Estate - 356 (or 386) 394,453,471	
R3	Stewart, C. C. - Estate of 87 to 91	
R14	Stewart, Daisy & Bill - etal. vs. City of Fayette - 86 thru 98	
M4	Stewart, Fentibia D. - Decd. R.C.Stewart, Admr. - 345,350,428,437,453,471	
R14	Stewart, G.E. - Decd. Estate - 320,324	

R14   Stewart, G. E. - Decd. Estate of - 340,342

W2   Stewart, G. E. - 115 thru 117

M9   Stewart, J. F. - 524

M6   Steward, J. J. - Estate - 112

W1   Stewart, J. J. - 46,47

M1(1)   Stewart, Joseph K. - Estate of - 437,496

M(3)   Stewart, J. K. - Estate of - 331,330,526,527,528

R1A   Stewart, Josehp K. - Estate - 630

M6   Stewart, J. M. - 292,293,212,376,393

R6B   Stewart, J. M. - 344 to 348

R1A   Stewart, Joseph R. - Estate - 186,187,409,410

M5   Stewart, Lantalie D. - Estate - 4,70,76

M1(2)   Larkin P. - Decd. Estate - 99,100,100,112,123,663

M3   Stewart, Larkin P. - Estate - P.391,428 to 432,647 - Children __ C.J.;H.J.;John;
                                   Joe W.:James M.;M.A.;Marcellus;Matha,Scina;Abie H.

R12A   Stewart, Larkin - Decd. Estate - 429 to 434

R3   Stewart, Larkin P. - Estate - 465 to 473

R3   Stewart, L. P. - Estate - 172 to 174

R7   Stewart, Lee L - Decd. Estate - 430

M7   Stewart, Lee T. - Decd. Estate of Cordelia Stewart - 536

R13   Stewart, Louis Lee, Hollie & Mavis - Minors - 481 thru 486

R5   Stewart, Loutitia D. - Decd. - Reuben C.Stewart, Admr. - 1.259 to 267

R16   Stewart, Murray V. - Decd. - 318,322

W2   Stewart, Murray - 270

M1(1)   Stewart, Reubin - Estate of - 187,382

M6   Stewart, Reubin C. - 383,384,394,434

M7   Stewart, Reubin C. - Decd. Estate - 113

M7   Stewart, Reuben C. - Decd. Estate - 104,113,114

R6B-Stewart, Reubin C. - Decd. Estate - 393 etal. 410,411

R2   Stewart, Robert Wayne - Decd. Estate - 21 - 988,991

M(3)   Stewart, Samuel - Estate of 262,263,121 to 127,591

R16   Stewart, Sol - Decd. - 36,38,493,94

R8   Stewart, W. G. - Decd. Estate - certified copy ____ in Florida - 588

M1(18) Stewart, William M. - Estate of - 32,46,339

R22   Stewart, Winfield, - Inc. - 22 - 295,298

M5   Stillman, B. M. - Estate - 247,263

R6B   Stillman, B. M. - Estate - 50

W1   Stillman, B. M. - 28

M8   Stillman, J. B. - Decd. Estate - J.F.Freeman, Admr. - 576

M9   Stillman, J. B. - Becd. Estate - 73,77

R9   Stillman, J. B. - Decd. Estate - 54,124

W2   Stocks, Babe - 138,139

R14   Stocks, Jessica Robin - guardianship of - 121,122

R10   Stocks, Mrs. Lizzie - guardian to sell land - 166,167,168x,169

R14   Stocks, Robert - Decd. 138 thru 144

M9   Stocks, Willis - Decd. Estate of - Lizzie Stocks (guardian) - 356,357

R14   Stocks, (Stacks) - Decd. - 583,586

R17   Stoker, Earl - Etal. - vs. Fayette County - 217,220

R15   Stoker, W. S. - Decd. 270,271

W2   Stoker, W. S. - 182

M9   Stokes, Fred - guardian - 290,302

R10   Stokes, Fred - guardian - 47 to 49, 66

M9   Stokes, Mrs. Mary - Decd. Estate - 295,364

R10   Stokes, Mrs. Mary - Decd. Estate - 55,56,186,188,189

M1(1)   Stone, Nathan - Estate of - 58,82

M(3)   Stone, Susannah - Estate of - 338,337,586,587

R1A   Stone, Susannah - Estate - 121,122,410 to 412,736

R1A   Stone, Susannah, - Estate - 631 to 632

M10   Stough, J. H. - etals. (Condemnation of lands) 500 thru 507

R14   Stough, J. M. - Sale of lands - 343,348

M10	Stough, Lewis E. - Estate of - 4
R10	Stough, Lewis E. - Decd. Estate - 569,570
R28	Stovall, Andrew Jackson - 28 - 47,55
W3	Stovall, Andrew Jackson - 337,343
R13	Stovall, Fay Sabrina - Legetimation of Estate - 65
R22	Stovall, Harold - Decd. - 22 - 609,612 (Vol. 26) 717,723
W1	Stovall, John from Marvin & M. A. - 31
W1	Stovall, Marvin & M. A. to John Stovall - 31
M2	Stovall, W. P. - Estate - 425 to 429
M5	Straud, William B. - Estate - 162,170,172,192,203,226,297,317
M8	Strand, W. B. - Decd. Estate - T. R. Moore - 564
R5	Stroud, Wm. - 459 to 469
M1(2)	Stratton, H. H. - Decd. Estate - 10,11
M1(2)	Startton, H. H. - Decd. Estate - 310,325,326,355,356
R12A	Stratton, H. H. - Decd. Estate - 489 to 502,692 to 699
R1A	Strawbridge, Joseph - Estate - 360 to 367,712 to 716
R27	Strickland, Charles Sidney - Deceased - 27 - 241,251
W3	Strickland, Charles Sidney - 250,251
R24	Strickland, Cora - Inc. - 24 - 967,973
M1(1)	Strickland, Isaac - Estate of - 118,126,146,345,368,369,370
M5	Strickland, J. Calvin - Estate - 141
R5	Strickland, J. Calvin - Decd. Estate - 554, to 556
R1A	Strickland, John - Estate - 117,406,407
W2	Strickland, Mary Elizabeth - 283
M8	Strickland, Pleasant Thurman - Decd. Estate - 7,10,11
W1	Strickland, Pleasant Thurman - 127
M1(2)	Strickland, Wm. 0. - Decd. Estate - 344,349,350
M(3)	Strickland, Wm. 0. - Estate of - 536, thru 540
R11A	Strickland, William 0. - 673,681
R12A	Strickland, W. 0. - Decd. Esta⁴ - 577

M3	Strickling, J. C. - Deceased minor Heirs J.M.Amerson, Gdn. - P 509	
M9	Striegel, Ethel - guardian - 495,496	
R21	Stripling, Dennis Edward - Minor - 21 - 937,940	
R17	Stripling, Derwood - Incompetent - 138	
R15	Stripling, Durwood - Incompetent - 536,539	
R16	Stripling, Dorwood - Incompetent - 202,356,517	
R18	Stripling, Dorwood, - Inc. - 18 - 664,709	
R19	Stripling, Dorwood - Inc. - 19 - 339,342,443,456,895,912	
R21	Stripling, Dorwood - Decd. Est. of - 21 - 913,936	
R22	Stripling, Phillip Dean - Minor - 22 - 200,213 (Vol. 26) P. 625,644	
R29	Stripling, Phillip Dean - 29 - P. 26	
M(1)	Strong, John - Estate - 110,111	
R1A	Strong, Johnson - Estate - 313 to 315	
M4	Strong, William E. - Insane proceeding - 222	
M1(1)	Strong, William M. - Estate of - 28,29,30,31	
M1(2)	Stuart, C. A. - Estate - 728,744	
W1A	Stuart, C. A. - 66,67,90	
M2	Stuart, Larkin P. - Estate - 114	
M2	Stuart, Larkin - L. M. Wimberley, guardian - 140,500 to 502,514	
M2	Stuart, Larkin P. - Estate,L.M.Winberley, Adm. - 143,353 to 355,755,769,114 to117	
W1A	Stuart, L. P. - 25-112 to 116	
M1(2)	Stuart, Wm. - Estate - 728,776	
R26	Studdard, Hollie M. - 26 - 314,318	
R15	Studdard, James Jackson - Decd. - 239,242	
W2	Studdard, James J. - 18 178	
M9	Studdard, Samuel J. - Decd. Estate - 73,78	
M9	Studdard, Samuel J. - Decd. Estate - 92,93	
R9	Studdard, Samuel J. - Decd. Estate, sale five joint owners - 212,254	
M9	Studdard, W. T. - Decd. Estate - 383	
R10	Studdard, W. T. - Decd. Estate - 222,223	

R22   Strudivant, Onnie - Unsound Mind - 22 - 504,507

R23   Sturdivant, Onnie - 23 - 663,669

M4   Sudduth, Alexander - colored, declaration to lefitimate child - 493

M5   Sudduth, Alexander - Declaration to adopt & change name of Tollie Walters - 216

M5   Sudduth, Holland - 386,389,390,-397

R6B   Sudduth, Holland - Decd. Estate - 135

R6B   Sudduth, Holland - Estate - 135 to 142

M7   Sudduth, Holland Be.. - decree ___, disabilities of ___ age? - 466

M7   Sudduth, Holly - Dec. W.H.Brown - guardian - 55 to 60

R27   Sudduth, Philler Ward - 27 - 320,338

W3   Sudduth, Philler Ward - 252,255

M9   Suggs, Joel H. - Decd. Estate - 405

M9   Suggs, Joel H. - Decd. Estate - 424

R10   Suggs, Joel H. - Decd. Estate - 257,266,267

W1   Suggs, Joel H. - 275,280

R13   Suggs, John Lanthus - Estate - 159 thru 165

M10   Suggs, Mrs. Lester Espy - Decd. Estate - 483,486,487,488,489

W2   Suggs, Mrs. Lester Espy - 33

R7   Suggs, William H. - trustee joint owner with LEwis Frink & Howard Fulmer - 409,
                                                                                  410
M10   Sullivan, Annie Lee, Garland, Redas, Mary Edith & Hollis C. - guardianship - 188

M10   Sullivan, Annie Lee - Garland, Redas, Mary Edith & Hollis C. - Minors, Estate -
              Audrey Sullivan, - Guardian to sell lands - 189,190,191,192
R11   Sullivan, Annie Lee, Garland, Redas, Edith & Hollis C. - Gdn. of - 398

R11   Sullivan, Annie Lee, Garland, Redas, Mary Edith & Hollie - Minor Estate - 399,400
              Audrey Sullivan, gdn. sale of lands.
R18   Sullivan, Max Dodson - Minor - 18 - 239,243

R19   Sullivan, Max Dodson, - Minor - 19 - 746,762

R11A   Summers, Daniel P. M. - 662,667

M1(1) Summers, Moses - Estate of - 9,44,57,132,149,150,179,267,282,302,306,327,328,375,
              428,471,509,545,562,573,577,578,606
M1(2) Summers, Moses - Estate - 684,685,700,713

R1A   Summers, Moses - Estate - 686 t 691

R11A   Summers, Moses - 667,673

R3   Summers, Moses - Estate - 289,290

W1A   Summers, W. - 740 to 742,748,749, 750,753

W2   Swann, Glenn Walter - 400

M10   Swindle, Mrs. E. Annie - Decd. Estate - 350

R11   Swindle, Mrs. E. Annie - Decd. Estate - 604

R25   Swindle, Lewis - Inc. - 24 - 655,660

M8	Tacker, Frank - disabled from manual labor - 214
M1(2)	Eli - 304,308,389,390,414,432
R12A	Tanzy, E. G. - 557 to 561
R1A	Tanzey, Eli - Estate - 235,236
M1(2)	Tapley, James - Estate - 146,147,152,153,190
W1A	Tapley, James - 244,245,247
R14	Tarwater, Eddie - Minor - 242,243,563,566
R23	Tarwater, Eddie - Minor - 23 - 297,298
M9	Tarwater, J. B. - Decd. Estate - 442,443,444
R10	Tarwater, J. B. - 356
M1	Tarwater, J. V. - 358
R13	Tarwater, J. V. & Ida - et al, vs. Fayette Co. - 513 thru 526
R14	Tarwater, William H. - Deceased - 229 thru 232
W2	Tarwater, Wm. H. - 108,109
M3	Taxes, Delinquent - 1877 - P. 64 to 74 - order of Sale - 114 to 118
M10	Taylor, A. J. - Decd. Estate - 270,271,272,273,283,284,446,447
R11	Taylor, A. J. - Decd. Estate - 493 to 502,520,521
M9	Taylor, Alson M. - guardianship of Daniel Taylor & Minnie Taylor - 115
R9	Taylor, Alson - guardian - 285,287,288
R9	Taylor, Alson - etal. guardian Bond - 286
M9	Taylor, C. E. - et al. joint owners notice to non resident oral examination -290
M9	Taylor, C. E. - Et al. joint owners - 323 to 326
R10	Taylor, C. E. - et al. joint owners to sell land - 108 to 113
M10	Taylor, Mrs. Cora - guardian - 286,287
R11	Taylor, Mrs. Cora - Gdn. - 524
M10	Taylor, Curtis - Decd. Estate - 155,165,166,298,299
R11	Taylor, Curtis - Decd. Estate - 351,352,368,369,540, thru 543
R9	Taylor, Daniel & Mamie - nomination of guardian - 286
R17	Taylor, David Lee & Judy Ann - Minor - 88,95
M1	Taylor, Davis - 8,9

R27   Taylor, Dora Lee Smith - 27 - 875,878

R28   Raylor, Dora Lee Smith - 28 - 397 (Nolen, Enslen, Atty.)

R16   Taylor, Emmett - Estate of Incompetent - 413,19

R22   Taylor, Fannie E. - Decd. - 22 - 320,326

W2   Taylor, Fannie E. - 442,443

M1(1)   Taylor, Green B. - Estate of - 6,7,34,35,52,168,177,189,190,264,327,332,333 to 336
                                                                                                                      336

M10   Taylor, H.G. & C.Y. - et. al. (Condemnation proceedings) vs. Fayette Co., Ala. -
                                                    360,thru 365

R12A   Tapley, James - Decd. Estate - 602 to 606

M8   Taylor, J. D. - guardian, Frank & Bessie Olive, Minor - 334

R7   Taylor, J. D. - guardian for Frank & Bessie Olive - 472,508

M2   Taylor, J. P. - Estate - 601,608,640

R2   Taylor, J. P. - 309,310

M10   Taylor, John - Decd. Estate - 311, 312

R11   Taylor, John - Decd. Estate - 559

W2   Taylor, John - 14

M10   Taylor, Limmie - Incompetent - 460

MR1A   Taylor, Martha - Estate - 617

M(3)   Taylor, Martha - Estate of - 292 to 295

R15   Taylor, Murray Lee - Incompetent - 295,296

M8   Taylor, O. L. - guardian for Estate - Graden Lee Duck, Minor - 60

R7   Taylor, O. L. - guardian for Graden Lee Duck - Minor - 580

R15   Taylor, Robert - Decd. Estate - Homestead Exemption for widow - 120,126

M1(1)   Taylor, Sarah - Estate of - 262,265,271,289,574,600,601

M1(2)   Taylor, Thomas - Decd. Estate - 170

R12A   Taylor, Thomas - Decd. Estate - 647 to 649,794,795

M1   Taylor, T. M. - 18,19

R17   Taylor, Verdia - Decd. 45

W2   Taylor, Verdie - 278, - 27

M7   Taylor, Virgil A. - Decd. Estate - R.M.Weeks, Admr. - 539

M8   Taylor, Virgil A. - Decd. Estate - R.M.Weeks, Admr. - 8,320,326,327

R7   Taylor, Virgil A. - Decd. Estate - 472

R16   Taylor, Vodine - Decd. - 543,47

R25   Taylor, W. E. - Deceased - 25 - 653,667

W3   Taylor, W. E. - Deceased - Will & Proof - 35,38

R14   Taylor, W.Moody, et.al. Vs. City of Fayette - 86 thru 98

M3   Telephone Company - P. 660

R25   Terrell, Houston W. - Decd. - 25 - 965,968

M6   Terry, Martha A. - Estate - 386 to 390

W1   Terry, Martha H. - 90,91

R16   Terrell, Mithhell - Decd. - 499,503

W2   Terrell, Mitchell - 275

R13   Thomas, George Ann - Estate - 198,200

R15   Thomas, George Ann - Decd. 30,35

W3   Thomas, Luther Frank - 418

R23   Thomason, E. E. - Decd. - 23 - 783,790

W2   Thomason, E. E. - Will & Proof - 502,503

R10   Thomason, E. E. - guardian - 537

M8   Thomason, E. E. - guardian for Thelma Prewitt, a Minor - 563

M9   Thomason, E. E. - guardian for Thelma Prewitt Sparks - 358

R9   Thomason, E. E. - guardian Estate - Thelma Prewitt - 74

R10   Thomason, E. E. - guardian - Thelma Pruitt Sparks - 170,171,172

M8   Thomason, E. E. - guardian for Henry Franklin Walker, Minor heirs of Willa Jean
                                                            Walker - Decd. - 370
M9   Thomason, E. E. - guardian for Henry Franklin Walker - 237,310

R8   Thomason, E. E. - guardian for Henry Franklin Walker - Minor - 414

R9   Thomason, E. E. - guardian for Henry Franklin Walker - 488 to 499, - Bond - 470

R10   Thomason, E. E. - guardian Henry Franklin Walker - 81,82,562

M9   Thomason, E. E. - guardian for Curtis & Raymond Weeks - 362

R10   Thomason, E. E. - guardian for Curtis & Raymond Weeks - 178,179

R16   Thompson, Alma Swann - Decd - 445,48

W2   Thompson, Alma Swann - 274

M7   Thompson, Catherine A. - Decd. Estate of - 499

W1   Thompson, Catherine A. - 192,198

M8   Thompson, Franklin A. - Decd. Estate - Mary J. Thompson, Admr. - 304

M9   Thompson, Franklin A. - Decd. Estate - 427

R10   Thompson, Franklin D. - Decd. Estate - 271,272

R8   Thompson, Thrnklin N. - Decd. Estate - Mary J. Thompson, Admrx. - 332

M10   Thompson, George A. - Decd. Estate - 387

R15   Thompson, George Lee, Sr. - Estate - 214,215,511,514

R16   Thompson, George Lee - Decd. 96A, 96B

R25   Thompson, George Lee, Jr. - Decd. - 25 - 956,959

M7   Thompson, Jacob - Decd. Estate of - 498

W1   Thompson, Jacob - 186,191

M1(1)   Thompson, John - Estate of - 176,185,194,227,252,311,449,528,529,530

M3   Thompson, John M. - P.168,169,172,173,186

R3   Thompson, John M. - Estate - 146 to 149, 275,276

M9(3)   Thompson, Lemuel J. - Estate of - 205 to 213,204,511 thru 517

R9   Thompson, Lola - et al. joint owners - 284

R9   Thompson, Lola - et al. joint owners - 295,296

M9   Thompson, Lula - et al. joint owners - 124

M8   Thompson, Mary J. - guardian of Estate, Mary Lou Thompson, Minor - 320 (300)

M9   Thompson, Mary Jane - Decd. Estate - 421

R8   Thompson, Mary J. - guardian - Estate of Mary Lee Thompson, Minor - 320

R10   Thompson, Mary Jane - Decd. Estate - 269,270

R1A   Thompson, Samuel J. - Estate - 471 to 474,737 to 738

R11A   Thompson, Thomas - 738,752

R26   Thompson, Victor S. & Robert D. - 26 - 307,311

M1(1)   Thompson, William - Estate of - 63,66,84,147,163,173,472,501

M(3)   Thompson, William - Estate of = 563,564

R25   Thomson, Kathleen C. - Decd. - 25 - 486,502

R17   Thornton, Benjamin Eli - Decd. Estate - 166,183

R18   Thornton, B. E. - Decd. Estate - 18 - 19,27

W2   Thornton, Benjamin Eli - Will of - 299,300

M1(2)   Thornton, David - Estate - 415,432,433,434,459,470,574,588,622,650,643

R12   Thornton, David - Estate - P.W.Thonnton, Admr. - 593,599,770

M3   Thornton, David - Estate - P. 339

M5   Thornton, David - Decd. Estate, P.W.Thornton, Admr. - 114

R2   Thornton, David - Estate - 373 to 382

R3   Thornton, David - Estate - 427,432

W1A   Thornton, David - 388 to 390,248 to 252,615,616,639,176,275,276,307 to 317

M9   Thornton, Hollis G. - Decd. Estate - 229,241,249,316,317

R9   Thornton, Hollie G. - Decd. Estate - 471,472,514,515

R10   Thornton, Hollie G. - Decd. Estate - 91,92

M9   Thornton, H. H. - guardian for Belva Thornton - 280,358

R10   Thornton, H. H. - guardian for Belva Thornton - 28,29,169

M2   Thornotn, H. M. - Estate - 469 to 470, 471

M3   Thornton, H. M. - Estate - P.244,299

R3   Thornton, H. M. - Estate - 127 to 129,298 to 300

R10   Thornton, I. A. - et al. joint owner - 18 to 24

M9   Thornton, J. H. - Decd. Estate - 230,250,252,294

R9   Thornton, J. H. - Decd. Estate - 473,474,531, thru 535

R10   Thornton, J. H. - Estate - 53,54

M6   Thornton, Martha - Estate - 531,532

M7   Thornton, Martha - Decd. Estate - 213 to 216

R6B   Thornton, Martha - Estate - 450,451

R7   Thornton, Martha - Estate - 36,37,38

M9   Thornton, S. A. - et al. joint owners - 274 to 276

M9   Thornton, Samuel A. - guardian - 231

R9   Thornton, Samuel A. - guardian - 474,475

R13   Thornton, Ulysses - Estate - 547

M5   Threet, Turner - Decd. Estate - 44,45,133,408

R5   Threat, Turner - Decd. Estate - 448

R6B   Threat, Turner - Decd. Estate - 221,223,224

W1   Threet, Turner - 3,4,5

R16   Tidwell, Calvin C. - Decd. - 390,92

R13   Tidwell, Charley - Petition to Probate Will, etc. - 333 thru 356

R15   Tidwell, Charley - Decd. - 90,92

W2   Tidwell, Charley - 76

R16   Tidwell, George A. - Decd. 220,21,401,03

R15   Tidwell, Mary Jane - Decd. 64,65

M2   Tidwell, P. S. - guardian for J. Lawrence - 11

R17   Tidwell, Rayford - Incompetent - 98

R28   Tidwell, Rayford - Inc. - 28 - 745

R25   Tierce, Angue - Decd. - 25 - 227,240,368,374, (Vol. 27.) 585,587

M10   Tilley, C. A. - Decd. Estate - 185,186,254

R11   Tilly, C. A. - Decd. Estate - 391,392,393,475

W2   Tilley, C. A. - 3

M10   Tilley, James A. - Decd. Estate - 179,244

R11   Tilly, James A. - Decd. Estate - 388,393,394,426,459,460

M9   Tirey, Dee Boyd - Decd. Estate - 330,390

R10   Tirey, Dee Boyd - Decd. Estate - 116,117,236,238,239

R24   Tiylor?, Melvin Ernest - Decd. - 24 - 235,240

R13   Toback, Frank - Gdn. - 447

R20   Todd, Ada Farris - Inc. - 20 2x3 - 447,459

M1(1)   Todd, Mary - Estate - 216,220,238,261,281,314,498,547,573,576,597 to 599

R25   Town of Belk, Inc. - 25 - 108,170

M7 Town of Fayette extension Corporate Limits - 401

M7   Townley, J. N. - declaration adopting & changing name of Felix Webb - 436

M1(2)   Towns, John W. - 691,692,702

M2   Towns, John W. - Estate - 185

M4   Towns, John W. - Estate of Gustavus Legg, admr. - 462

W1A   Towns, John W. - 40,45 to 47, 167

R23   Trammell, Charles - Inc. - 23 - 886,892

M1(1)   Trawekk, Daniel W. - Estate of - 42,43,51,53,56,96,111,117,137,152,178,158,159,
                                166,167,169,170,178,290,304,305

M(3)   Traweek, D. W. - Estate of - 89 to 93, 256

R1A   Traweek, Daniel W. - Estate - 212,213,519 & to 522,733

R11A   Traweek, Daniel - 704,713

M1(2)   Traweek, George - Decd. Estate - 1,38, thru 43,48,49,106,107,108,163,189,262,263
                                264,265,267 thru 272,407,417,418,445,457,462,463

R11A   Traweek, George - 713,720

R12A   Traweek, Decd. Estate - 128 to 148,339 to 344,547 to 556,727,728

W1A   Traweek, George - 284 to 288,368,422,423

R13   Traweek, Mrs. Martha J. - Te set apart Exemption - 140

M7   Treadaway, A. J. - Bankrupt certificate - 205

M1(2)   Treadaway, Henry G. - Justice Bond substitution - 60

M5   Trentham, David W. - Decd. Last Will & Testament - 208,215

R5   Trenthall, David W. - Decd. Estate - 521 to 524

W1   Trentham, David W. - 24,25

R25   Trimm, Brenda - Inc. - 25 - 464,468

W2   Trimm, Cebran Burton - Will & Proof - 332,333

R14   Trimm, Donald Ray - Estate of - 579,582

R22   Trimm, Eual - Decd. - 22 - 311, 314

R22   Trimm, James Clyde - Decd. - 22 - 346,349

M6   Trimm, J. H. - Decd. Estate - 560 thru 565

R6B   Trim, J. H. - Decd. Estate - H.M.Trimm, Admr. - 433 to 437

M8   Trim, J. M. - et al. by joint owners - 475,482,487,494 - (Estate?)

M3   Trim, Mary A. - Estate, E.M.Jones, Admr. - P.147,148,149,167,168,190,191,634

R3   Trim, Mary Ann - Estate - 120 to 127,273,274,722

R16   Trimm, Murphy - Decd. - 404,06

R8   Trim, Mrs. N. M. - et al. - Estate - 526

M1(2) Trull, John A. - Decd. Estate - 139,140,158,159,229 thru 233,417,418,385,386, 40
                                        402,567,582,583,596,597

R12A   Trull, John A. - Decd. Estate - 354 to 363,659 to 664

W1A   Trull, John A. - 597,598,633,634 to 637,660

M10   Trull, Kittie - Decd. Estate - 33

R11   Trull, L. - Guardian Estate of - Harold & Sally Trull - 27,28

M10   Trull, L. - guardian, Estate of Harold & Sally Trull - 33

R23   Tucker, Betty Ann - Inc. - 23 - 633,639

R24   Tucker, Betty Ann, - Inc. - 24 - 388,396

R23   Tucker, Burcey Shelton - 23 - 765,768

R20   Tucker, Charlie Steve & Paul Michael - Minors - 20 - 423,441

R24   Tucker, Hollie B. - Inc. - 24 - 381,387

M7   Tucker, I. J. - Decd. Estate - 284,285

R7   Tucker, I. J. - Estate - 174

W1   Tucker, I. J. - 112,113

M(3)   Tucker, James A. - Estate of - 239 to 242,367 to 378

R1A   Tucker, James A. - Estate - 485 to 491

R11A   Tucker, James A. - 720,737

M(3)   Tucker, James A. - Estate of - 61 to 69

M9   Tucker, Rhoda - Unsound Mind - 453,483,416, (403)

R10   Tucker, Rhoda - Unsound Mind - 338, thru 343

R11   Tucker, Rhoda - Incompetent & Estate - 60, 61

M9   Tucker, W. A. - guardian - 415

M3   Tucker, William - Estate - P.1,2,25,252,472,478

M2   Tucker, William - Estate - 793,794,795

R3   Tucker, William - Estate - 76 to 86,351,352

M8   Turner, Dan - name changed & adopted Leather Brewer - 464

M1(2) Turner, E. T. - Decd. Estate - 223,222,244,246 thru 250,313 thru 318,446,458

M2   Turner, Elias - Estate - 626

R12A   Turner, Elias T. - Decd. Estate - 522 to 532,635 to 639,694,695

W1A   Turner, Elias T. - 367

M1(1) Turner, John - Estate of - 210,240,241,246,247,252,278,495,546

R1A   Turner, John - Estate - 90 to 97,569 to 571

M9   Tuscaloosa Cooperage C. settlement with O. Cl. Lawrence Cooperation Law - 4

M9   Tuscaloosa Cooperage Co. Agreement with O. C. Lawrence Under ___ __,124,125,126

M2   Tyson, J. R. - Application for apprenticeship - 525

R2   Tyner, G. R. - Apprenticeship - 24,25

M1(1) Vail, Joshua - Estate of - 164,165,171,172,247,346,347,385,399,404,423,424

M(3) Vail, Joshua - Estate of - 216,215,214,213

R1A   Vail, Joshua - Estate - 40 to 51,497

R16   Van Diver, Edward R. - Decd. - 27,30

W2   Van Diver, Edward R. - 223,224

R11A Van Diver, Manny - 776,779

R1A   Vanhoose, James - Estate - 207 to 210,610

M1(1) Van Hoose, Valentine - Estate of - 12

W2   Vaughn, Caleb F. - 39

M1(2) Vaughan, Henry - 113,114,126,135,136,399

W1A   Vaughn, Henry - 253

W1A   Vaughn, Hep - 229,230,253,470,471,524,527,531,532,669,670

R22   Vaughn, Horace W. - Decd. - 22 - 283 - 295

W2   Vaughn, Horace W. - Will & Proof - 420,424

M1(2) Vaughn, H.J. - Decd. Estate - 108,126,169,170,173 to 176,254 to 261,324,373,415,
                                    484,498,49 - 615,503,516,519,520,676,61

R12A Vaughn, Howard J. - Decd. Estate - 296 to 299,502 to 511,540 to 546,574 to 577.

M1(2) Vaughn, Thomas - Isham Cooper - guardian - 602

R20   Veazey, J. Thomas - Decd. Estate of = 20 - 405,413

W2   Veazey, J. Thomas - Will & Proof - 363,364

W2   Vernon, Frances Honora - 86

W2   Vernon, Frederick Henry - 85

R12A Vick, Abram - 54 to 56

R15   Vick, Charles H. - Incompetent - 480,86

R17, Vick, Charles H. - Incompetent - 49,65

W3   Vick, C. P. - 3 - 539

R27   Vick, C. T. - 29 - 71,88

R15   Vick, Mrs. J. P. (Jenie) Decd. - 481,83

W2   Vick, Mrs. J. P. (Janie) - 284

M10   Vick, Roy P. - Estate of 6

R10   Vick, Ray P. - Dedd. Estate - 545

R26   Vick, Tim - 26 - 516,524

W3   Vick, Tim - Deceased - 3 - 165,167

R13   Vinson, Will F. - Gdn. for Franklin Vinson - Minor - 201,202

R1A   Waddle, Jesse - Apprentice Fond to Mr. Kemp - 728

R28   Wade, Carl - Decd. - 28 - 728,744,782,783

       Wade, Carl - Vol. 3 - 458,463

M8   Wade, Clyde H. - guardian - 483

R10   Wade, James M. - Decd. - 362,363,366

W1   Wade, James M. - 291,292

M9   Wade, John C. - Decd. Estate - 510

M10   Wade, John C. - Decd. Estate - 43

W1   Wade, John C. - 308

R10   Wade, John E. - Decd. Estate - 538,537,504

M6   Wade, John H. - Decd. Wstate - 55,56

R6B   Wade, John H. - Decd. Estate - 168

W1   Wade, John H. - 36

M9   Wade, James M. - Decd. Estate - 457,458

M9   Wade, Mrs. L. C. - Decd. Estate - 457

M9   Wade, Mrs. L. C. - Decd. Estate - 533, 534

R10   Wade, Mrs. L. C. - Decd. - 364,365,551,552,553,550

M8   Wakefield, George D. - Funds belonging to his children - 401,402

M3   Wakefield, George W. - Deceased Estate - P.533,534,575,576,582

M5   Wakefield, George W. - Decd. Estate - J.M.Wakefield, Admr. with Will co___ - 230
                                                        249,250,368,353

R3   Wakefield, George W. - Estate - 631,765 to 769

R9   Wakefield, Marion & Marvin - 121,122,450,451

R17   Wakefield, Maya - Minor - 209,209

M6   Walden - Estate of - 131 to 149

M3   Waldon, Jonathan - Estate - P.218 to 220,225,226,595,603,604

R3   Walden, Jonathan - Estate - 207 to 216,672 to 677

M1(1) Walden, Reuben - Estate of - 355,375,384,402

R1A   Walden, Reuben - Estate - 88,89

R25	Waldrop, Miles - Decd. - 25 - 593,596
	to/
M8	Walker, Annie Belle - changed Annie Belle Brock by Della Brock - 332
R12A	Walker, A. F. (S.F.) - 112, to 114
	Walker, Arthur Ulysses - 523
M1	Walker, Bruly - 389,390
W2	Walker, Carless Tilton - 118
M10	Walker, E. F. & J.U. - Condemnation of Lands - 508 thru 517
M8	Walker, Henry Franklin - Minor, E.E.Thomason, guardian - 370
M9	Walker, Henry Frank - Minor - Estate - 482
M10	Walker, Henry Frank - Guardianship of - 18,37,38,81,94,116,274
R8	Walker, Henry Franklin - Minor - 414
R11	Walker, Henry Frank - Minor Estate - 39,40,41,163,164,165,191,197,247,248,503,
	Thru 507
M6	Walker, Josephine - Estate of - 372,373,413
R6B	Walker, Josephine - Decd. Estate - 430,431,432
M9	Wall, Lewis - change of name - 108,109
R24	Walker, Norman Mid. - Decd. - 24 - 963,966
M8	Walker, P. M. - Decd. Estate of U.E.Walker, admr. - 359
R8	Walker, P. M. - Decd. Estate - U.E.Walker, admr. - 386
M8	Walker, R. G. - Decd. Estate - A.L. Walker, admr. 469,472,388,451,462,464,546
R8	Walker, R. G. - Decd. Estate - 432,518
R11A	Walker, Robert - 694
M8	Walker, Thomas - changed to Thomas Brewer by Leathie Brewer - 332
R15	Walker, Ulysses - Decd. 347,348,349
M4	Walker, William F. - Decd. Estate - 536,537,546,562
M5	Walker, Wm. F. - Decd. Estate - 331,335,339,356
R5	Walker, William F. - Decd. Estate - 284,285,286,287
R18	Wallace, Beatrice, Carol, Clifton, Jo, Betty Ann, Jerry & Robert Michiel - Minors
	450,454

R20   Wallace, Beatrice, Earl Clifton, Jo, Betty Ann, Jerry & Robert Michael - 20 -

                                                                          707,763

R25   Wallace, Betty Ann, Jerry & Robert Michael - Minors - 25 - #749,776

R26   Wallace, Lula - Decd. - Vol. 26 - 168,203 - Will & Proof - 129,130,131

W3   Wallace, Lula - Will & Proof - 129,131

R17   Wallace, William G. - Decd. Estate - 164,165

M7   Walters, Billy V. - guardian - 510

M9   Walters, E. W. - guardian Georgia Mae Livingston - 494 (492)

M8   Walters, Henry A. - Decd. Estate - 465,466

R8   Walters, Henry A. - 521,522,523,571

M1(2) Walters, J. L., Esq. (Esc.) Adaline M. Peters - 756,757 *Wm pri kals hill*

M1(2) Walters, Moses - apprenticing - child - 69

R12A   Walters, Moses - ~~Decd. Estate~~ - 789,790 apprenticing child

M10   Walton, John D. - Decd. Estate - 393,394,395,396

W2   Walton, John D. - 24,25

M4   War, Willis - Decd. Estate - 4,5,6,281, to 286

R13   Ward, James W. - Decd. Estate - 337,338,420, to 423

R13   Ward, John Albert - et al. Vs. Fayette County - 507 thru 513

M4   Ward, Martha L. J. - Decd. Estate - James N. Ward, for Minors - 140

R12A   Ward, W. H. - Estate - 762 to 772

M1(2) Ward, William M., - Decd. Estate - 116,412,453,603

M1(2) Ward, William M. - Decd. Estate - 168,252,253,273,295,296,412,453,468,613

R11A   Ward, William M. - 108,121

R9   Ward, W. M. - Estate - Letters testamentary - 531

W1A   Ward, William - 286,394 to 408

M3   Ward, Willis - Deceased EState - P.708,709,710

R4   Ward, Willis - Decd. Estate - 214 to 222,225,465

M4   Warmack, George S. = Guardian - 347

M5   Wammack, G. S. - guardian - 81,108

M9   Wammack, M. J. - Estate - 398,399

R10   Wammack, M. J. - Estate - 248,249,250,251

W1   Wammack, M. J. - 273,274

W2   Warren, Clara & J. C. Shepherd (agreement) 98

R24   Watkins, Authie - Inc. - 24 - 710,716

R17   Wtakins, Belton - Decd. Estate - 127,132

W2   Watkins, Belton - Deceased - Will & Proof - 294

R23   Wtakins, Clennie L. - Decd. - 23 - 582,586

M9   Watkins, G. M. - Estate - 507,508

W1   Watkins, G. M. - 304

M9   Watkins, H. A. - et al. joint owners - 331,332,333,334

R10   Watkins, H. A. & G. W. et. al. joint owners - 120,122,123,125

M9   Watkins, J. T. - Paid 64.65 belong to 5 Minor children - 291

W1   Watkins, Lizzie (c.c. from Deed recd. Vol. 381,350)

W1   Watkins, Lizzie - 350,357

M9   Watkins, Luke H. O Decd. Estate - 335,347,348

R10   Watkins, Luke H. - Decd. - 126,127,128,129,155

R10   Watkins, S. M. - Decd. Estate - 490,493 - Probate Will - 494

R23   Watkins, Wayne - Decd. - 23 - 552,555

M8   Watkins, William L. - Decd. Estate - W.A.Watkins, admr. - 208

R8   Watkins, William Lester - Decd. Estate - W.A.Watkins, adm. - 220

M8   Watson, John - et al. joint owners - 80 A. Tract - 88,111,112,140,147,107

M8   Watson, John = et. al. joint owner - 40 A. Teact - 93,94,108,121,123,141,152

R8   Watson, John - et. al. joint owners - 86,401,110,80 & _____

M8   Weathers, Arlie - adopted & name changed to Arlie Berry by Henry T.Berry - 354

M8   Weathers, Elza - Decd. Estate J.E.Bell, Admr. - 176

M8   Weathers, Elza - Decd. Estate - Hiram Cockran, Admr. - 252,262,279,280

R8   Weathers, Eliza - Decd. Estate - J.E.Bell, Adm. - 176

M8   Weathers, Joseph Thurman - Decd. Estate - 308,310,31 ,349,361,378

R8   Weathers, Joseph Thurman - Decd. Estate - Thomas Charlton Smith, Exetr. - 344

W1   Weathers, Joseph Thurman - 134

M8   Weathers, Kate V. - guardian for Estel Thurman, Lomax Weathers - Minor - 319

R8   Weatehrs, Mrs. Kate V. - guardian of Estate of Thurman Lomax Weathers - 350

R17   Weàthers, Thurman L. - Decd. - 445,452

W2   Weathers, Thnrman L. - Will & Proof - 312, 313

M(3)   Weaver,   - Estate of 343

R24   Webb, Etta - Decd. - 24 - 371,380

W2   Webb, Etta - Will & Proof - 541,542

R28   Webster, Eunice Mithhell - 28 - 765,773

        Webster, Eunice Mitchell - 482,486

M7   Webb, Felix - adoption & change of name of H.N.Townley - 456

M3   Webb, Jonas - Deceased Estate - P.483,504,516,518,519,524

R3   Webb, Jonas - Estate - 617, to 619, 678 to 689

M10   Webb, Lottie - Decd. Estate - 378

R13   Webb, Lottie - Estate - 220,221

R18   Webb, Marcus - Estate of - 249,257

W2   Webb, Marcus - Will & Proof - 331

R15   Webster, T. A. - Decd. - 417,419

R15   Webster, Thomas Morten - Decd. 364,365

R15   Webster, Tolbert & Frances Annette - Minor - 362,363

M9   Weeks, Curtis - Minor, Estate of - 483

M8   Weeks, Etta - guardian - 431

R8   Weeks, Etta - guardian - 488

R28   Weeks, Euline - 28 - 418,430

        Weeks, Euline - Vol. 3 - 388,391

R14   Weeks, E. W. - Decd. Estate of - 99 thru 102

R23   Weeks, Jessie J. - Decd. - 23 - 684,690

W2   Weeks, Jessie J. - Will & Proof - 495-96

M10   Weeks, Malinda C. & John M. Couch - joint owners - 386

R14   Weeks, Malinda - Decd. Estate of 396,398

W2   Weeks, Malinda - 129

M10   Weeks, Raymond - Minor Estate of - 43

R11   Weeks, Raymond - Minor Estate - 57,58

M10   Weeks, R. M. (Andrew) Decd. Estate - 145

R11   Weeks, R. M. - Admr. - Decd. Estate - 331,332

R28   Weems, William Lennard - 28 - 204,210

       Weems, William Leonard - Vol. 3 - 360A - 370

M8   Weeks, Wm. H. - et al. joint owner - 407,413,422,423,426,430

R8   Weeks, Wm. H. - et al. joint owners - 484

M9   Welburn, Mrs. Fannie - guardian for Will Welburn - 343

M9   Welburn, Fannie - guardian - 441

M10   Welburn, Fannie - guardian - 320

R10   Welburn, Mrs. Fannie - guardian for Will Welburn - 148,149

R11   Welburn, Fannie - gdn. for Will Welburn - 567,568

R27   Welburn, Fannie & G. J. - 27 - 315,319

R26   Welburn, Grace W. - 26 - 341,350 - Will 3 - 151,154

M10   Welburn, Sam (Condemnation of Lands) 508, thru 517

W3   Welburn, Sam - Will & Proof - 151,154

M9   Welburn, W. J. - Minor Joint owners to sell land - 406

R10   Welburn, W. J. - Minor Joint Owners to sell land - 259,260

M7   Welburn, W. P. - Decd. - J.G.Smith - 51 to -

M10   Welch, Bura J. - Decd. Estate - 325,366,367

R11   Welch, Bura J. - Decd. Estate - 571,572

M(3) Welch, Jane - Estate of - 341

R1A   Welch, Jane - Estate - 198 to 206, 501,618 to 622

M4   Welch, John A. - guardian for A.J.Hallmark - 264

R16   Welch, Lela Ruby - Decd. 283-285,357,358

W2   Welch, Lela Ruby - 269

M1(2) Welch, Robert - Decd. Estate - 313,365,663,670

R11A Welch, Robert - 83,84,87,89,695,800

R12A Welch, Robert - 115 to 118, 49 to 655

W1A	Welch, Robins - 721 to 725
R1A	Welch, Sudie & Elizabeth - Apprentice - 244,502
R20	Williford, Mary - Decd. Estate of - 20 - 443,446
R22	West, Emma Jean - Minor - 22 - 327,330
R22	West, Elma Louise - Decd. - 22 - 338,345
W2	West, Elma Louise - Will & PRoof - 456,459
R22	West, Hosea - Estate of - 22 - 192,199
R29	West, H. H. et.al - 29 - 99,121 - Vs. State of Alabama.
R1A	West, John C. - Estate - 430 to 433,742 to 744
R25	West, James Lester - Decd. - 25 - 525,528
R11A	West, Stephen B. - 696,702
R6B	Wharton, Thomas C. - Decd. Estate - 121
R1A	Wheeler, B. P. - Apprentice Bond - 645
M6	Wheeler, C. A. - Estate of - 92,93
M7	Wheeler, C. A. - Decd. Estate of - 437,440,444
R7	Wheeler, C. A. - Decd. Estate - 296 to 303,310
W1	Wheeler, Dr. C. A. - 44,48
M8	Wheeler, C. K. - Minor Heir of C. A. Wheeler, Decd. M.B.McCollum - guardian - 69, 178
R6B	Wheeler, C. K. - guardian Bond - 268,269
R8	Wheeler, C. K. - M.B.McCollum - Guardian - 170
M6	Wheeler, C. Y. - Minor - Guradian Bond - 125
M1	Wheeler, D. A. - 556
M1(1)	Wheeler, Estate of - 37,38,52
R25	Wheeler, Mintie - Decd. - 25 - 860,872
W3	Wheeler, Mintie - 56,57
M1(2)	Wheeler, Peter C. - Decd. Estate - 46,47,183, thru 187, 473,486
R12A	Wheeler, Peter C. - Decd. Estate - 229 to 236
W1A	Wheeler, Peter C. - 444 to 447
M7	Whitehead, Boss - Decd. Estate - Admr. - 283,284
M7	Whitehead, Bess - Estate - 283,284
R7	Whitehead, Bess - Decd. Estate - 170

R26   Whitehead, Orville - 26 - 67,73

R15   Whitehead, Paul J. - Decd. - 356,361

W2   Whitehead, Paul J. (Prob.Ct.Rec.Vol. 15, pg. 357)

M10   Whitehead, Roscoe - Decd. Estate 2 - 121

R11   Whithehad, Roscoe - Decd. Estate - 263,264

R24   Whitehead, William Randy - Inc. - 24 - 348,354

M10   White, Andrew F. - Decd. Estate - 166,167,215

R11   White, A. F. - Decd. Estate - 115,116,369,370

R13   White, A. F. - Application for sale of Minors interest, etc. - 385 thru 388

M3   White, Andrew W. - Deceased Estate - P. 532,652,682,683

M4   White, Andrew W. - Decd. Estate - 104,183,202,221,231, to 234

M6   White, A. W. - Decd. Estate - 59 thru 65

M9   White, A. W. - guardian, Estate, Marion & Marvin Wakefield, Minors - 12,221

R9   White, A. W. = Guardian - Marion & Marvin Wakefield - 121,122

R18   White, Barbara Ann & Jerry Frank - Minors - 263,267

R19   White, Barbara Ann & Jerry Frank - Minors - 19 - 51,61

R13   White, Catherine & Betty - Minor - Estate - 1,2,3,4,442,443

R16   White, Duncan E. - Decd. - 63 to 73

W2   White, Duncan C. - 229,230

M7   White, D. O. - Declaration adopting Rudolph Hobson Otts - 77

M8   White, Eloise - Grand dau. of W.J.Nelson - Decd. - 531

M10   White, Frankie Lee, Myre, Loyd, Herry Colvin, Juanita, Rudolph - Minors - 63,216

R11   White, Frankie Lee - Estate, Minor - 115,116

M8   White, G. H. - Decd. Estate - 543

M9   White, G. H. - Decd. - 136,137

R9   White, G. H. - Decd. Estate - 42

R9   White, G. J. - Decd. - 316,317

M8   White, H. C. - Declaration recognizing adopt? & changing name from Troy Dillard
                                                                        to Troy Sims - 432

M1(1)   White, Jeptha - Estate of - 353,378,379,387

M10   White, Mrs. Jessie - Guardian - 329,330,331

R11   White, Mrs. Jessie - gdn. Iris White - et.al. - 577,578,579,580

M9   White, O. A. - Decd. Estate - 165

M10   White, O. A. - Decd. Estate - 405

R9   White, O. A. - Decd. Estate - 381,384

M1   White, P. H. - 32,33,34

M9   White, R. Lottie - Decd. Estate - 368,379,388,389,393,434,438

R10   White, R. Lottie - Estate - 206,209,213,214,215,231,232,292,293

M9   White, R. R. - Decd. Estate - 309

R10   White, R. R. - Decd. Estate - 79,80

M1(1)   White, Samuel - Estate of - 374,388,391,392

R1A   White, Samuel - Estate - 263, to 267

W2   White, Troy Andrew - 148

R17   White, T. E. - Estate - 322,25

R19   White, Mrs. T. E. - Estae of - 19 - 79, 93

R23   White, Travis Wade - Decd. - 23 - 495,498

M5   Whitley, Jasper - Estate - 233,248

R6B   Whitley, Jasper, Decd. Estate - 24,25,26

W1   Whitley, Jasper, - 25

M3   Whitley, Jonas - Deceased Estate - W. H. Whitley, Admr. - P. 723

M4   Whitley, Jonas - Decd. Estate - 98,117,153,262,431,433,434,460

R3   Whitley, Jonas - Decd. Estate - W.H.Whitley, admr. - 779 to 789

R4   Whitley, Jonas - Decd. Estate - R.A.Crawley, admr. - 529

R13   Whitley, Loyd & Charles - Minors - 497 thru 502

W3   Whitley, Robert Zell - 168,171

M9   Whitley, Sarah M. - Decd. Estate - 342,347

R10   Whitley, Sarah M. - Decd. Estate - 147,148,154,155

W1   Whitley, Sarah - 259,260

R13   Whitney, O. H. - Estate - 209 thru 213,238 thry 245

R24   Whitson, Betty Loy - Inc. - 24 - 597,612

R22   Whitson, Erania - Minor - 22 - 536,560

R25   Whitson, Gilbert Lee - Change of Name - 25 - 873,874

M7   Whitson, Raburn - Mrs. J.E.Copeland, guardian - 542

M3   Whitson, William D. - Substitution of Deceased - P. 510

M5   Whitson, William G. - Estate - 279,281,300,316,321,340,327,341,370

R6B   Whitson, Wm. G. - Decd. Estate - 55, 100

R6B   Whitson, William B. - Decd. Estate - 114,116

M4   Whittle, Thomas R. - Minor apprentice - 360

R23   Wiggins, Duffiee L. - Decd. - 23 - 538,544

W2   Wiggins, Duffie L. - Will & Proof - 486,487

M9   Wiggins, E. W. - Decd. Estate - 242 to 245

R9   Wiggins, E. W. - Decd. Estate - 515,516,517

M10   Wiggins, J. W. - Decd. Estate - 143,243,4

R11   Wiggins, J. W. - Decd. Estate - 325,326,449,450,457,458

R14   Wiggins, Mrs. Mamie - Decd. - 425 thru 428

W2   Wiggins, Mrs. Mamie - 133,134

M4   Wiggins, Norah - Insane - 244

M1(2)   Wiley, James K. - Estate - 405,421,422,423,429,536,550

W1A   Wiley, James K. - 639,279,280,303 to 305,638

M8   Wilks, Irene - guardian for Ernest Welks - Minor - 539,567

R9   Wilks, Irene - guardian Earnest Wilks - 32

M8   Wilks, Mordecai D. - Decd. Estate - 516,585

M9   Wilks, Mordecai D. - Decd. Estate - 18,19,20,22,23,31,33

R9   Wilks, Mordecai D. - Decd. Estate - 1,149,150

M1(2)   Willbanks, A. - 686,688,696,704,706,715,716,717

M2   Willbank, A. - Estate - 60

W1A   Willbanks, A. - 36,37,39,40,52,104

R13   Willcutt, Bee? - Decd. Estate - 375, thru 380

M7   Willcutt, E. W. - Declaration adopting Marion Wallace - 162

R11A Williams, Abraham - 24,25

M9   Williams, B. D. - Estate - 493,494

R10   Williams, B. D. - 455,457

W1   Williams, B. D. - 303,304

R1A   Williams, Benjamin F. - Apprentice - 210

M5   Williams, D. B. - Decd. Estate - Minor Heirs ___ Williams 2nd. - 142

M5   Williams, D. B. - Decd. Estate of - Thomas E. Goodwin, Admr. - 212,213,217,218

R5   Williams, Doc B. Ω - Decd. Estate - 524 to 530

W3   William, Esther - Estate of - 314,315,324,349,381,445

M10   William, G. W. - Guardian for Cora Patterson - Minor - 65

M1(1) Williams, & Harton - Writ of Adquardennum - 455,487

M7   Williams, Jobe - Decd. Estate - B.H.Williams, Admr. - 380,382,392,483,485

M9   William, Jobe - Decd. Estate - 460,461,462

R7   Williams, Jobe - Decd. Estate - B.D.Williams - Admr. - 240

R22   Williams, John- Decd. - 22 - 214,222

W2   Williams, John - 418,419

M1(1) William, John H. - Bastardy Bond - 400

M4   Williams, John H. - Decd. Estate - 265,430,434,455,456, 547

R4   Williams, John H. - Decd. Estate - 488,630

M5   Williams, John T. - guardian for N.H. & T.E.Lindsey - 224

R16   Williams - J. T. - Decd. - 181 to 182

M9   Williams, Julia - Decd. Estate - 482

M9   Williams - Paul Clifton - Minor disabilities of non age - 490

R24   Williams, Phillip - Decd. - 24 - 866,869

R12A Williams, Rachel - 98 to 100

R26   Williams, Rachel Elizabeth - 26 - 319,324

W3   Williams, Rachel Elizabeth - 143,147

R27   Williams, Simon - 27 - 953,956

R13   Williams, W. C. - et.al. Vs. Fayette County - 513 thru 526

R18   Williams, William Clinton - Estae of - 244,248

M3   Williams, William D. - Estate - P.43,44,82,83,211,246

R2   Williams, W. D. - Estate - 533 to 539

R3   Williams, Wm. D. - Estate - 174,175,365,366

R20   Williams, W. D. - Decd. Estate of - 20 - 385,391

W2   Williams, W. D. - Will & Proof - 409,410

W3   Williamson, Delma W. - 201,207

R26   Williamson, Delma W. - Decd. - 26 - 509,510,537,542,645,50

R27   Williamson, Delma - Will, etc. - 3 - 201,207

R13   Williamson, Cecil, Betty, Fay & Elwin Davis - Estate - 13,14,135,136,137,138,139

M10   Williamson, Geo. F. - Decd. Estate - 66

M9   Williamson, G. W. - guardian, Rena & Frank (or Dora) Patterson - 403

M9   Williamson, G. W. - guardian Miriam Patterson - 489

R10   Williamson, G. W. - guardian - Dora & Frank Patterson - 256,424

R11   Williamson, G. W. - gdn. for Cora Patterson, Minor - 124,125

R11   Williamson, George W. - Decd. Estate - 126,127,128,129

M(3) Williamson, Rachael - 267 to 270,582,583

R1A   Williamson, Rachel - Estate - 392 to 394,424,725, to 726

R24   Williamson, Sylvester - Decd. - 24 - 836,853

W2   Williamson, Sylvester - Will & Proof - 566,567

M10   Williamson, William Marion - 119,120

R11   Williamson, William Marion - Decd. Estate - 260,261,262,263

M10   Williamson, W. P. - Gdn. for Thomas Loyd Williamson - 292

R11   Williamson, W. P. - gdn. for Thomas Loyd Williamson - 531

R16   Williamson, William P. - Decd. - 153 to 155

W2   Williamson, Wm. P. - 257,258

R1A   Willingham, Beverly - Estate - 232,234

M5   Willingham, Elihu - Decd. Estate - W.A.Willingham, Admr - 28

M7   Willingham, Elihu - Dec. Estate of - 191,192, 93,199,208,217

M7	Willingham, Elihu - Estate - 191,192,199,208,218 to 221
R6B	Willingham, Elihu - Estate - 12
R7	Willingham, Elihu - Decd. Estate - 14 thru 23
R27	Willingham, Gladys S. - 27 - 695,702
W3	Willingham, Gladys Smith - Vol. 3 - 310,317
M(3)	Willingham, Isaac - Estate of - 110 to 118,378 to 386
R11A	Willingham, Isaac - 32 to 41
R12A	Willingham, Isaac - 118
R8	Willingham, James T. - et.al. joint owners, partition of property - 362,364,365, 400
M7	Willingham, Joanna - Decd. Estate - 434,460,462
R7	Willingham, Joana A. - Decd. Estate - 304,378
M7	Willingham, Joana A. - Decd. Estate of Monroe W.Willingham, Admr. - 434,460,462
M8	Willingham, James T. - et.al. joint owner for partition - 322,330,350,363,364,365
M10	Willingham, James T. - Decd. Estate - 466,467
W2	Willingham, James T. - 31
R20	Willingham, Jimmy S. - Minor - 20 - 373,377
M7	Willingham, John T. - Decd. Estate - 354
R7	Willingham, J. T. - Decd. Estate - 216
M8	Willingham, Lela - guardian for Lillian Willingham - Minor - 368,546
R8	Willingham, Lela - Guardian - Lillian Willingham, Minor - 410
M7	Willingham, Lonnie - Decd. Estate of Jackey Willingham, admr. - 423
M7	Willingham, Lonnie - Decd. Estate of - 423
R7	Willingham, Lonnie - Decd. Estate - 206
M5	Willingham, Martha Ann - adoption & change of name - 111
R16	Willingham, Mrs. Martelia - Decd. - 337,338 (338)
M6	Willingham, Mr.M. R. - 176,177,178,297,298
M2	Willingham, R. C. - Estate - 273 to ___, 551,583,595,731,745,759
M3	Willingham, R. C. - Estate - P.59,60,344
M3	Willingham, R. C. - P-242,257,344,365,366,370
R4	Willingham, R. C. - Decd. Estate - 290 to 294

R43   Willingham, R. C. - Estate - 264,265,419 to 426,436 to 439

M4   Willingham, Ruebin C. - Estate - 145,171,186, to 188

R2   Willingham, Reuben C. - Estate - 150 to 152,226 to 237

R17   Willingham, R. W. - Decd. Estate - 241,244

W2   Willingham, R. W. - Will & Proof - 303

R15   Willingham, Samuel B. - Decd. - 457-60

W2   Willingham, Samuel E. - 204

M5   Willingham, Thomas L. - Estate of - 333,366,367,368,369,371

R6B   Willingham, Thomas L. - Decd. Estate - 105

R6B   Willingham, Thomas L. - Decd. Estate - 148

M4   Willingham, W. R. - Decd. Estate of - 486

M1(1)   Willis, William - Estate of - 548,571,572,599

R1A   Willis, William - Estate - 107,108,528 to 532

R22   Wilson, Adele Clements - Decd. - 22 - 188,191

W2   Wilson, Adele Clements - 407,408,409

R25   Wilson, Archie D. - Inc. - 25 - 548,559

R25   Wilson, Archie - Inc. - 25 - 606,609

R27   Wilson, Archie D. - Inc. - 27 - 886,942, (Vol. 28) page 181

M1(2)   Wilson, B. W. - Justice Peace Bond Substitution - 53

M9   Wilson, Bryce & wife, Bessie - adopting 2 children of Gurly & Eva Wilson, Decd. 409

M10   Wilson, Mrs. Eula Logan - Condemnation of lands - 508 thru 517

R15   Wilson, Harold Owen - Minor - 52,53

M1(2)   Wilson, Harvey - Decd. Estate - 171,172,182,328,329,365

M2   Wilson, Harvey - Estate - 80

M3   Wilson, Harvey - Estate, Mary Wilson, Gdn. - P.338,339,360 to 362

R3   Wilson, Harvey - Estate - 407 to 413

R12A   Wilson, Harvy - Decd. Estate - 692 to 712

W1A   Wilson, Harvey - 105,260,261,451,717,720

M1(1)   Wilson, Jacob - Estate of - 201,215

R22   Wilson, J. Bradley - Decd. - 22 - 134,167

W2   Wilson, J. Bradley 0 Will & Proof - 399

M1(1)   Wilson, James - Estate of - 196,209

M1(2)   Wilson, James - Decd. Estate - 134,420,429,480,489,649,668

M3   Wilson, James - Estate - P.27,26,58,279, to 284,599,600,615,621

M4   Wilson, James G. J. Collins - Admr. - 147,158

R3   Wilson, James - Estate - 92 to 94,254,255,288,690 to 700

R4   Wilson, James - Decd. Estate - 249 to 255

R11A   Wilson, James - 752,765

R27   Wilson, James H. - 27 - 401,404

M1(1)   Wilson, James C. - Estate of - 54

M1(2)   Wilson, James M. - Justice Bone Substitution - 104

M10   Wilson, J. M. - Decd. Estate - 130,131

R11   Wilson, J. M. - Decd. Estate - 293,294 thru 297

W1   Wilson, J. M. - 351

M10   Wilson, James R. (Rube) - Decd. Estate - 132

R11   Wilson, James R. (Rube) - Decd. hstate - 298,299

R12A   Wilson, James W. - Decd. Estate - 790,791

R14   Wilson, Joan Crawford - Minor - 41 thru 47

M8   Wilson, Joel - Decd. Estate of - 504,510,531

R8   Wilson, Joel - Decd. Estate - 382

W1   Wilson, Joel - 213

M2   Wilson, John - Estate - 167

W1A   Wilson, John - 125 to 137 to 140

R9   Wilson, L. A. - Decd. Estate - 508,509

W2   Wilson, Lester - Will & Proof - 484

M9   Wilson, Lucy - guardian - 307

R10   Wilson, Lucy - guardian - 75,76,77

R23   Wilson, Margaret - Decd. - 23 - 499,520

R23   Wilson, Margaret - Decd. - 23 - 568,581

W2   Wilson, Margaret - Will & Proof - 512

M2   Wilson, Mary E. - guardian for Minor Heirs of Harvey Wilson - 100

M4   Wilson, Mrs. Mary E. - guardian for S. M. & R. A.Wilson - 321,324

R4   Wilson, Mary E. - guardian for Sarah M. & R.A.Wilson - 520

W1A   Wilson, Mary E. - guardian for minor heirs Harvey Wilson - 120

R27   Wilson, M. D. - 27 - 637,640

M9   Wilson, Minnie Lee Cockran - C. Minor Insurance Collective - 367

M8   Wilson, Mattie - Declaration adopting Walker Loftis - 468

M8   Wilson, Melton M. - Decd. Estate - 555

R9   Wilson, Melton M. - Estate - 50

M10   Wilson, Melton M. - Estate - 139,198,199,200

R11   Wilson, Melton M. - Decd. Estate - 314,315,316,410

R28   Wilson, Sidney Barnard - 28 - 395

M9   Wilson, Turner A. - Decd. Estate - 239 to 240

W1   Wilson, Turner A. - 247

R27   Wilson, Ulysses - 27 - 396,399

M7   Wimberley, J. R. - guardian for Minor Heirs of Burt Corbett, Decd. - 209

R7   Wimberley, J. R. - guardian for Melissa, Clemmie & Minnie Corbett, Minors - 30

M2   Windham, E. W. - adoption of child - 714, 1X 715

M5   Windham, Thomas R. - Decd. Estate - Saletta G. McGuire, Admx. - 221,222

R5   Windham, Thomas R. - Decd. Estate - 519 to 521

M(3)   Winstead, Missouri Ann - Estate of -

M(3)   Winstead, Missouri Ann - Estate of - 259,260,543,544,545,38,541

R1A   Winstead, Missouri Ann - Estate - 237,240,522 to 523

R11A   Winstead, Missouri A. - 702,703

R12A   Winstead, Missouri Ann - 108 to 110

M1(1)   Winsted, Susannah - Vs. John H. Williams for Bastardy - 138,152

R22   Wolfe, Agnes - Inc. - 22 - 369,372

W2   Woodward, Harvey G. - (c.c. from Je   rson Co.) - 151,163

M7	Woodard, J. E. - guardian for Azzie & Lewis McDuff - 372,450,454	
R7	Woodard, J. E. - guardian for Aggie & Lewis McDuff, Minors - 230	
R13	Woodard, Stephen Russell - Gdn. for Gladys, Stephen, Arthur & Bessie Jane Woodard	
		183 thru 189
R26	Wood, Ada M. - Vol. 26 - 96,100	
R18	Wood, Charles Donald - Minor - 86,91	
M8	Woods, Dan - Decd. Estate - 589	
R9	Woods, Dan - Decd. Estate - 92	
M8	Wood, E. A. - Declaration adopting Lula Wilson, Mary Mandy Barnett - 72	
R19	Woods, James F. - 19 - 389,390	
W2	Woods, James F. - Will - see Roberts Court Rec. Vol. 19 - 389,390	
M1(1)	Woods, James M. - Estate of - 130, 131,133,134,151,477,500	
M1(2)	Wood, Joel T. - Decd. Estate - 70,100 to 104,237 thru 242,362,363,364.504,505,	
		509,510,525
M1(2)	Woods, Joel T. - 524,546,547,548,550,626,632,633	
R12A	Woods, Joel T. - Decd. Estate - 206 to 212,736 to 744	
W1A	Wood, Joel T. - 485 to 490,494,495,515,541,543,578	
M6	Woods, J. W. - Estate - 322 to 331,330,377,379,378,380	
M7	Woods, J. W. - Decd. Estate of 163,167	
R6B	Woods, J. W. - Estate of - Ida Woods, Adm. - 560 to 564	
M7	Woods, Mrs. L. T. - Mother of Mary Etta & Eula Brown - 361	
R11A	Woods, Robert - 785,793	
M1(2)	Wood, Robert K. - Decd. Estate - 105,213,244	
M1(2)	Wood, R. K. - 439,464,465,478,479	
R12A	Woods, Robert K - 56 to 61,344 to 353	
W1A	Wood, R. K. - 385,429 to 442	
R18	Wood, Shirley Fay - Minor - 80,85	
M5	Woods, T. B. - guardian - Jannnie Black - 364	
M8(3)	Wood, T. M., Mort - 564 to 565	
M5	Wooley, Calis A. - Minor - A. B. Batson, guardian - 64,71,79,80,92,374	

R5   Wooley, Celia - Minor - A.B.Batson, guardian - 476,477,478

M9   Wright, A. J. - Decd. Estate - 224,225,226,227,402

R9   Wright, A. J. - Decd. Estate - 460,461,462,464,465,466 - Homestead

R10   Wright, A. J. - Decd. Estate - 253,254

R3   Wright, Alcy A. - Estate - 137,138

M10   Wright, B. - Decd. Estate - 327,404

R11   Wright, B. - Decd. Estate - 574,576

R14   Wright, David H. - Decd. Estate of - 188,189,190

W2   Wright, David H. - 100,101

M9   Wright, Delbert - Decd. Estate of Dizzie Wright - Admrx. - 236,237

M9   Wright, Mrs. Dezzie - guardian - 164

M9   Wright, Mrs. Dezzie - guardian - 508

R9   Wright, Mrs. Dezzie - guardian - 348,349

M9   Wright, Ellen - guardian - 132,134,135

M9   Wright, Ellen - guardian - 321,322

R9   Wright, Ellen - guardian - 305,310,312,314,315

R10   Wright, Ellen - guardian - 105,106,107

M9   Wright, Frances Marion - Decd. Estate - 83,103,104,106,140,144,145

R9   Wright, Frances Marion - Decd. Estate - 236,262,273,274,321,326

M1(2)   Wright, Henry - Estate - 627,629,630,632,633

W1A   Wright, Henry - 10,11,14,15,18,19

R11A   Wright, James - 41 to 47

R12A   Wright, James - 61,76 to 78, 92 to 94

M3   Wright, James Madison - Deceased Estate - P. 520,522,702,729,730

M4   Wright, James M. - Estate - 14,15,16,37,38,102,139,387,388,395

R5   Wright, James M. - Decd. Estate - 268

M1(2)   Wright, John - Decd. Estate - 124,125,137,138

M8   Wright, John - Declaration adopting Bud Johnson & changing name to Bud Wright -
                                                                                      340
R12A   Wright, John - Decd. - 284 to 297

W1A   Wright, John - 216,247,248

R9   Wright, Lester - Admr. 326

R9	Wright, Lester - Admr. 326	
M1(1)	Wright, Michael - Estate of - 362,370,374,404	
R1A	Wright, Michael - Estate - 52 to 64,349 to 351,726 to 727	
M9	Wright, Murry - Decd. Estate - 176,177	
R9	Wright, Murray - Decd. Estate - 375,376	
R27	Wright, Ricky - Minor - 27 - 210,314	
R9	Wright, Sarah E. - guardian - 96,122,123	
M8	Wright, Savannah E.- Guardian - 592	
M9	Wright, Savannah E. - guardian - 2,14	
M9	Wright, Savannah E. - guardian to sell lands joint owners - 354,355,354,355	
R10	Wright, Mrs. Savannah E. - guardian to sell lands - 163,164,165,166,224,225,226	
R15	Wright, Simon T. - Decd. - 148,151	
W2	Wright, Simeon - 171,175	
M8	Wright, T. J. - Decd. Estate - 446,452	
R8	Wright, T. J. - 523	
W1	Wright, T. J. - 204,205	
R22	Wright, Thomas J. - Decd. - 22 - 331,337	
W2	Wright, Thomas J. - Will & Proof - 455,456	
M10	Wright, Mr. & Mrs. T. F. - adoption of Marjorie Benton Murphy - 316	
M7	Wright, T. R. & P.T. - application for sale of lands for partition & div. - 308, 318	
M7	Wright, T.R. & P.T. - application to sell real estate for partition & Div. - 308, 318,319,338,339	
R7	Wright, T.R. & P.T. - application for owner of sales lands partition & Div. - 18?	
M2	Wright, William H. - Estate - 460 to 468,512 to 513,540,546,712,719,725,734	
M9	Wright, William M. - Decd. Estate - 459,460	
R3	Wright, William M. - Estate - 271,285,286	
W1	Wright, William M. - 287,290	
R14	Wycoff, S. W. (L.W.) - Decd. Estate of - 194,195,196	
W2	Wycoff, S. W. - 104,105	

M8   Wyers, J. A. - Decd. Estate - J. R. Wyers, Admr. - 249,256,257,314,316

R8   Wyers, Jno. A. - Decd. Estate - J.R.Wyers, Admr. - 256

M8   Wyers, J. R. & Tiller Wade - et.al. joint owners proceeding for sale of for
                                                   division - 358,366,371,
                                                          373

R8   Wyers, J. R. - Toller Wade, - et.al. joint owners in property - 390

M2	Yarbrough, Ambrose - Estate - 440 to 444
M6	Yarbrough, Hiram - Estate - 16
R12A	Yarbrough, Mary E. - 111,112
M4	Yarbrough, Stacy - Edward Bobo, guardian - 40
R3	Yarbrough, Stacy - Edward Bobo, guardian - 738 to 741
M2	Yarbrough, Sarah - guardian for Sarah F. Yarbrough - 266
M2	Yarbrough, Stephen - Estate - 88,487 to 492,634,642,646,647,648,656,657,667,668, 669,701,702,743
M3	Yarbrough, Stephen - Estate - P. 17, to 20,197,380,404,405,406,407
R2	Yarbrough, Stephen - Estate - 206 to 216
R3	Yarbrough, Steven - Estate - 176 to 178,444 to 453
M1(2)	Yarbrough, Willis - Decd. Estate - 4, 5, 34, 35, 36, 37, 319, 320, 321, 322, 323, 368, 369, 370 371, 485, 495, 496
M2	Yarbrough, Willis - Estate final settlement - 258,534 to 535,555,556,624,625,635, 650
M2	Yarbrough, Willis - Decd. Estate, Edward Bobo, guardian of Stacy Yarbrough - 348,349,418,419,386,350 to 352
M2	Yarbrough, Willis - Estate - 635,650,789
M3	Yarbrough, Willis - Estate - P. 18,19,20,57,120,265
R12A	Yarbrough, Willis - Decd. Estate - 264 to 271,679 to 684
R2	Yarbrough, Willis - Estate - 39 to 42,48,186 to 192
R3	Yarbrough, Willis - Estate - 53 to 57,352,353
W1A	Yarbrough, Willis - 459, to 465
R11A	Yardle, William B. - 774,775
	Yates, Charlie M. & (Charles M) - 464, Original on file state of Michigan, Wayne Co.
R12A	Yerby, Amon - 119,120
M4	Yerby, F. M. - Estate - 442
M6	Yerby Hogan - Decd. Estate - 337
R6B	Yerby, James - Decd. Estate - 157
M1(2)	Yerby, John T. - Justice Bond Substitution - 53
M6	Yerby, Mary - Estate of G.W.Horne - guardian - 34,35,36,38
R6B	Yerby, S. E. - et. al. Bond to M.W.Terley - 418

M9   Yerby, T. B. - Decd. Estate - 432,438

R10   Yerby, T. B. - 281,282

R20   Young, Effie Humber - Decd. Estate of - 20 - 415,422

W2   Young, Effie Humber - Will & Proof - 365,366,367

M5   Young, George W. - Decd. Estate - 149,156,157

R6B   Young, George W. - Estate - 1

W1   Young, Geo. W. - 19,20

M7   Young, Hugh - Minor heir of G.H.Young, Dec. - R.J.Smith, guardian - 256

R7   Young, Hugh - Minor R.J.Smith, guardian - 114

R26   Young, James Dorsey - 26 - 325,340 (Will - 3) 148,150

        Young, James Dorsey - Will & Proof - 148,150

W2   Young, James D. - 216,218

M8   Young, John A. - Decd. Ustate - J.D.Young, Admr. - 419

R8   Young, John A. - Decd. Estate - J.D.Young - 480

R15   Young, Dr. J.D. - Estate - 567,71

M10   Young, Maury - Decd. Estate - 380

R20   Youngblood, Billie Roger - Inc. - 20 - 393,404

R29   Youngblood, Choiley Hollis - 29 - 226,   239

        Youngblood, Charley Hollis - Will & Proof - 544,550

R12A   Younghance, Edward L. - 112,113

R14   Yucklye, Ruby Wilson - Decd. Estate of - 147, thru 153

R15   Yuckly, Ruby Milam - Decd. - 521,-30

R17   Yuckley, Ruby Milam - Decd. - 229,-32

W2   Yuckley, Ruby Milam - 97,98

www.ingramcontent.com/pod-product-compliance
Lightning Source LLC
Chambersburg PA
CBHW080622030426
42336CB00018B/3044